This Happened in My Presence

This Happened in My Presence

Moriscos, Old Christians, and
the Spanish Inquisition in the Town of Deza,
1569–1611

EDITED AND TRANSLATED BY PATRICK J. O'BANION

UNIVERSITY OF TORONTO PRESS

Library and Archives Canada Cataloguing in Publication

This happened in my presence : Moriscos, Old Christians, and the Spanish Inquisition in
    the town of Deza, 1569–1611 / edited and translated by Patrick J. O'Banion.

Includes bibliographical references and index.
Issued in print and electronic formats.

ISBN 978-1-4426-3514-2 (hardback).—ISBN 978-1-4426-3513-5 (paperback).—
ISBN 978-1-4426-3515-9 (html).—ISBN 978-1-4426-3516-6 (pdf).

    1. Inquisition—Spain—Soria (Province)—Sources. 2. Trials (Heresy)—Spain—Soria
(Spain : Province)—Sources. 3. Soria (Spain : Province)—History—16th century. 4. Soria
(Spain : Province)—History—17th century. 5. Moriscos—Spain—Soria (Province)—
History—16th century. 6. Moriscos—Spain—Soria (Province)—History—17th century.
7. Christians—Spain—Soria (Province)—History—16th century. 8. Christians—Spain—
Soria (Province)—History—17th century. I. O'Banion, Patrick J., 1975-, editor, translator

BX1735.T45 2017   272'.20946355   c2016-903400-3
                                                       c2016-903401-1

We welcome comments and suggestions regarding any aspect of our publications—please feel free to
contact us at news@utphighereducation.com or visit our Internet site at www.utppublishing.com.

North America
5201 Dufferin Street
North York, Ontario, Canada, M3H 5T8

2250 Military Road
Tonawanda, New York, USA, 14150

ORDERS PHONE: 1-800-565-9523
ORDERS FAX: 1-800-221-9985
ORDERS E-MAIL: utpbooks@utpress.utoronto.ca

UK, Ireland, and continental Europe
NBN International
Estover Road, Plymouth, PL6 7PY, UK
ORDERS PHONE: 44 (0) 1752 202301
ORDERS FAX: 44 (0) 1752 202333
ORDERS E-MAIL: enquiries@nbninternational.com

Every effort has been made to contact copyright holders; in the event of an error or omission,
please notify the publisher.

The University of Toronto Press acknowledges the financial support for its publishing activities of
the Government of Canada through the Canada Book Fund.

Printed in Canada.

For Joshua

Contents

Illustrations

Acknowledgments

Many people contributed to the completion of this volume, and I am grateful to all of them. I first encountered the Moriscos of Deza in the spring of 2006, while conducting dissertation research. That serendipitous encounter was made possible by the graces of Marcelino Angulo García, the director of the Archivo Diocesano de Cuenca. Gonzalo Díaz Migoyo, whose work on Román Ramírez the younger has influenced my thinking about that remarkable and complex man, showed tremendous generosity in sharing with me a flash drive brimming with digitized archival materials. The twenty-first-century *vecinos* of Deza warmly welcomed my family in the days surrounding the Festival of San Roque in 2013. Their courtesy and hospitality, especially that of Julio Ramiro Vicioso González and María del Carmen Elgarrista Iso, left us with fond memories and the hope of future visits. My friend Vicente Alejandre Alcalde, who some years ago rescued Deza's rich municipal archive from the trash heap and subsequently became the town's archivist and historian, granted me full access to those papers and has patiently fielded my questions about local geography and the more obscure corners of Deza's past.

The idea for this collection coalesced during a fruitful time of research afforded by a James K. Cameron Faculty Fellowship from the Reformation Studies Institute at the University of St. Andrews. The encouragement of the faculty there—Andrew Pettegree, Bridget Heal, Emily Michelson, Chris Given-Wilson, and others—as well as many fruitful interactions with postgraduate students stimulated this project. At home, the faculty of Lindenwood University's History and Geography Department picked up the administrative slack while I was abroad. Hal Parker, as always, has been a great encourager and faithful friend. My colleague Maite Núñez-Betelu offered translation advice on some particularly tricky passages. I appreciate the feedback I received on this project from the brain trust of the Pre-Modern Spanish Historical Association of the Midwest, as well as from a variety of students, chief among them Kami Ahrens, Kimberly Elfrink, Sarah Hinds, and Michelle Setzer.

My wife, Rachel, has not so much endured my interest in the people of early modern Deza as joined me in it. Many of the project's most rewarding moments have come when we've shared the discoveries. This book is dedicated to my son, Joshua, who visited the town when he was very, very little.

Notes to the Reader

ON NAMES, NAMING, AND TITLES

The naming practices of early modern Spaniards are likely to be unfamiliar to most readers. Wives, for example, typically did not take the last names of their husbands, nor vice versa (except rarely, as in the case of the Aragonese Juan de Ropiñón, who became Juan de Hortubia, after his wife, probably because the members of her family were citizens of Deza). Children normally took their father's name, but the name was sometimes (though not always) given in a gendered ending—thus, Juan Montero but Juana Montera. Spelling was not standardized, and names appear in a remarkable variety of ways. For the sake of clarity and ease of reading, all names have been standardized for spelling in this volume.

It was very common to recycle names over the generations and for parents to name a son after the child's father and/or grandfather. This quickly becomes confusing. (It was not uncommon for daughters to be named after mothers or grandmothers, but this causes less confusion since the last names of women changed over the generations.) The problem was frequently solved by adding a suffix to the name, as we do when we affix "Jr." or "Sr." to a person's name. In the Deza documents the suffixes "the younger [*el menor*]" and "the elder [*el viejo*]" are the most common, but occasionally "the lad [*el mozo*]" or "the youngest [*el más mozo*]" are used as well. In this book, suffixes, which sometimes were dropped or added as generations died or were born, have been standardized. If potentially confusing, footnotes have been added to indicate to whom the name refers, thereby allowing the reader to trace individuals back to the Cast of Characters more easily.

Some Dezanos went by nicknames. Lope de Deza, for example, was variously known as Lope del Sol (without explanation) and Pascual de la Pituerta (because his father was named Pascual and his wife was club-footed—*pies tuertos*). Likewise, Íñigo de Hortubia was known as "the

Soldier" (because he had been one), and his son, Juan, seems to have inherited the nickname.

Titles were another important element of naming practices. Members of Spain's lower nobility (*hidalgos*) were granted the titles "don" or "doña." Other titles indicated professional status or education. Thus, a *bachiller* had earned a university degree, while a licentiate had an advanced degree (which usually required additional years to complete). The title of licentiate might also indicate that a person had been licensed to practice in a profession, such as the physician Licentiate Antonio Páez. Finally, the title *mosén* was an honorific used mostly in the Kingdom of Aragon. It could be roughly translated as "master" but was very flexible and sometimes was applied to *hidalgos*, members of the clergy, or even an authority on a specific subject, such as a physician.

ON MONEY

Translating the buying power of early modern currency to the present is notoriously difficult. The endeavor is made all the more treacherous because prices were not holding steady during the period. Instead, Spain experienced a bout of significant inflation (sometimes called the "Price Revolution") during the sixteenth and seventeenth centuries.

The basic exchange rates are, of course, simple: 1 *real* = 34 *maravedís*; 8 *reales* = 1 ducat = 1 *escudo* = 2 guilders.

Anything beyond this gets very complicated very quickly. Yet, without wading too deeply into treacherous waters, we can draw upon Earl Hamilton's *American Treasure and the Price Revolution in Spain, 1501–1650* to say the following about prices and wages in late-sixteenth-century Castile:

- A liter of wheat cost less than six *maravedís* in the early 1570s but was approaching nine by the end of the century.
- A liter of wine cost about eight *maravedís* in 1569 but jumped to over 20 *maravedís* in some years by the end of the century.
- A laborer earned, perhaps, two *reales* (or 68 *maravedís*) for a day's work in 1568, and wages, if they rose at all, tended to do so much more slowly than prices.

The intrepid and economically minded inquirer may pursue the question of the buying power of those currencies in, among other places, John H. Munro's article "Money, Prices, Wages, and 'Profit Inflation' in Spain, the Southern Netherlands, and England during the Price Revolution Era."

Timeline

711	North African Muslims cross into Iberia.
714	The area around Deza comes under the control of the Muslim Berber Banu Mada clan.
c. 800	Deza founded near the ruins of a Roman settlement.
c. 1120	Deza conquered by King Alfonso I of Aragon.
before 1136	Deza comes under the control of the kings of Castile.
1390s	Forced conversions of Jews in some areas of Spain.
1442	Deza comes under the control of the counts of Medinaceli.
1469	Isabella of Castile marries Ferdinand of Aragon.
1474–1504	Reign of Queen Isabella.
1479–1516	Reign of King Ferdinand.
1478	Pope Sixtus IV grants the Spanish monarchs permission to establish the Holy Office of the Inquisition.
1479	Isabel of Castile elevates the count of Medinaceli to the rank of duke.
1492	Conquest of the Kingdom of Granada and signing of the Treaty of Granada; expulsion of unbaptized Jews; and Columbus's first voyage to the Americas.
1499	The Mudéjares of Granada revolt.
1502	Treaty of Granada declared null and void. All Castilian Muslims are ordered to be baptized or leave the kingdom.
1515	Expulsion of unbaptized Muslims from the Kingdom of Navarre.

1516–56	Reign of King Charles I of Spain (aka Emperor Charles V).
1526	Expulsion of unbaptized Aragonese Muslims.
1533–34	Juanes de Altopica, Deza's vicar and inquisitorial representative, ousted from his offices after pursuing a case against a Judeoconversa member of a locally prominent family.
c. 1535	Antonio Páez moves to Deza from Atienza.
1540	Birth of Román Ramírez the younger in Deza.
1544–75	Don Juan de la Cerda is the Duke of Medinaceli.
1545–63	The Council of Trent meets.
1548–58	Construction of the main body of Deza's new parish church.
1550s–70s	Construction of the Duke's House and Garden in Deza.
1556–98	Reign of King Philip II of Spain.
1556	Miguel Benito becomes vicar and inquisitorial commissioner in Deza.
1560	Battle of Djerba. Don Gastón de la Cerda, son of the duke of Medinaceli, is captured.
mid-1560s	Some of Deza's Moriscos purportedly hire an Islamic instructor from Aragon to teach them "Moorish writing."
1568–71	The Moriscos of Granada rise in rebellion.
1569	Inquisitor Licentiate Alonso Jiménez de Reynoso conducts a regional visitation that includes a stop at Deza.
1570	Inquisitor Dr. Diego Gómez de la Madriz arrives in Deza offering the Moriscos an Edict of Grace.
1571	Moriscos Alexo Gorgoz, Román Ramírez the younger, Francisco de Miranda, and others negotiate with the king for a more lenient Edict of Grace. The new Edict is taken by 173 of Deza's Moriscos.
1575–94	Don Juan Luis de la Cerda is the Duke of Medinaceli.
1577	Death of Licentiate Antonio Páez in Deza.

1579	Construction is completed on the roof and ceiling of Deza's parish church.
1580	Licentiate Miguel Benito shares the vicarage of Deza with his uncle, Miguel Benito.
1581	Licentiate Reynoso proposes expelling all Moriscos from Spain to Philip II.
1581	Inquisitor Dr. Francisco de Arganda conducts a visitation that includes a stop at Deza.
1584	Bishop of Sigüenza decides to withhold communion from all but the most Christianized Moriscos in Deza.
1591	Deza's co-vicar and inquisitorial commissioner, Miguel Benito, dies. His nephew, Licentiate Miguel Benito, becomes the sole vicar of the town and commissioner in his own right.
c. 1594	Death of Angela de Miranda, the first wife of Román Ramírez the younger.
1595	Román Ramírez the younger is arrested in Soria but released and confined to Deza upon payment of a bond of 2,000 ducats.
1598–1621	Reign of King Philip III of Spain.
1599	Trial of Román Ramírez the younger recommences in Cuenca; Ramírez's health declines and he dies in December in the Hospital of St. James.
1599–1600	Martín del Rio publishes *Investigations into Magic*.
1599–1607	Series of denunciations against local Moriscos are made by some of Deza's Old Christians.
1600	King Philip III, Queen Margaret of Austria, and the Duke of Lerma attend the auto-da-fe in Toledo where Ramírez's bones are consigned to the flames.
1602	King Philip III and Queen Margaret of Austria visit Deza.
1605	Death of Licentiate Miguel Benito and the discovery of the hidden denunciations.
1607–11	Final inquisitorial assault on Deza's Morisco community. More than 50 Dezanos are eventually arrested and

transported to Cuenca's secret jails. Others flee to Aragon or elsewhere.

1609   Beginning of the expulsion of Spain's Moriscos.

1611   The Moriscos of Deza are expelled on 8 July. In November, Miguel Ramírez, Román el Romo, and Juan Mancebo are released from custody and ordered to comply with the Edict of Expulsion.

1612   Bell tower of Deza's parish church is finally complete, bringing an end to a building project that spanned more than six decades.

1614   King Philip III proclaims the successful completion of the Morisco expulsion.

Introduction

Few history books mention the small Spanish town of Deza, and few Dezanos could be considered famous, especially between the mid-sixteenth and early seventeenth centuries. In fact, the primary-source documents included in this volume tell us little about the lives of celebrated or influential people. Instead, the documents' chief value lies in what they reveal about individuals who lived relatively humble and obscure lives and who appear to be far less important than the powerbrokers that usually dominate our stories about the past.

That claim may initially sound counterintuitive. If it is true, why would we want to know about such people? Very few inhabitants of the early modern period (roughly 1500–1700) were kings or queens, nobles or courtiers, wealthy merchants or great warriors, religious leaders or influential intellectuals. Most were common folks: men and women who spent much of their time just getting by and dealing with the demands of daily life. Thus, the Dezanos who appear in this volume were in general far more representative of the early modern experience than were the lives of the high and mighty, and they help us understand how, precisely, such common people fit into the world in which they found themselves.

Yet studying their lives presents a challenge, for most common folks did not leave documentary records of the sort that historians typically use to study the past. Many early modern people lacked the ability (or need) to write, so they left fewer records of their thoughts and actions. And because most people in these societies viewed only elites as noteworthy, few of the people who could write made the effort to record information about anyone else.

Evidence of what common folks were up to is therefore elusive. For example, without the documents like the ones included in this book, we would know almost nothing about the people who lived in Deza. They would rarely be more than names on a page in the parish registry, where the town's baptisms, marriages, and burials were recorded. Fortunately, in the case of Deza other documents *have* survived the centuries. They rarely tell us all that we would like to know, but they provide rich glimpses into the life of a small town during a period that was complex and tumultuous— not just for Deza but also for Spain, Europe, and the entire world.

But why *these* documents about *these* people? Primarily because they bring into focus a critical issue in Spanish history during the late sixteenth and early seventeenth centuries: relations between Moriscos and Old Christians, two key groups within Spanish society. Moriscos were the descendants of Spanish Muslims who converted to Christianity under pressure early in the sixteenth century; Old Christians claimed that their families did not descend from Jews or Muslims. During this period, many Old Christians came to question whether Spain's Moriscos were trustworthy. Were they true Christians and loyal subjects of the king? Or were they secret Muslims working to ally with Spain's enemies? And if the Moriscos could not be trusted, then what should be done about them? Public opinion was often divided, both at the highest government levels and among the Old Christians and Moriscos who lived in the cities, towns, and villages of Spain.

The sources included in this volume allow English-language readers to explore relations between Old Christians and Moriscos in early modern Spain. This is a topic that is valuable in its own right, but it will also provide insights into larger issues at stake in the early modern world, such as the challenges of conversion, the role of social discipline, and the formation of identities. Readers are invited to enter into the conversation about these and other topics by examining primary sources and drawing conclusions based on the analysis of those sources—fundamental skills of the historian.

With respect to relations between Moriscos and Old Christians, although important research on the topic has been published over the decades, primary sources remain hidden away in archives. Few have been made widely accessible, and even fewer have been translated into English.[1] And while I might have focused on almost any community in Spain with a population of Old Christians and Moriscos and a good set of records, Deza's sources are particularly rich. When we read them with a historian's critical eye, we catch glimpses of people who once lived and breathed, loved and hated, laughed and mourned. So Deza it is.

More broadly, these documents also provide valuable insights into the way in which early modern people engaged powerful religious, political, and economic institutions. The most notable example here is the Spanish

---

[1] But see Francisco Núñez Muley, *A Memorandum for the President of the Royal Audiencia and Chancery Court of the City and Kingdom of Granada*, ed. and trans. Vincent Barletta (Chicago: University of Chicago Press, 2007), as well as portions of Jon Cowans, ed., *Early Modern Spain: A Documentary History* (Philadelphia: University of Pennsylvania Press, 2003); Lu Ann Homza, ed., *Spanish Inquisition, 1478–1614: An Anthology of Sources* (Indianapolis: Hackett, 2006); and Richard L. Kagan and Abigail Dyer, eds., *Inquisitorial Inquiries: Brief Lives of Secret Jews and Other Heretics* (Baltimore: Johns Hopkins University Press, 2004).

Inquisition (or as it was more properly known, the Holy Office of the Inquisition), which exercised legal disciplinary authority over a range of religious infractions committed by Christians. The Holy Office produced a vast number of records as it went about its business. Yet, again, very few of them are available to an English-language audience.[2] Most of the documents included in this collection were written by or for inquisitorial agents, but they vary dramatically in style, form, and function. While popular imagination associates inquisitors almost exclusively with the sadistic torture of those who challenged the status quo, these documents offer a better sense of the breadth of inquisitorial work, as officials in Madrid and Cuenca interacted (and disagreed) with one another and with the local representatives of the Holy Office in Deza.

Undeniably, the activities of Deza's Moriscos troubled the Inquisition, which feared that instead of becoming good Christians, they were reverting to Islam (or, as early modern Spaniards called it, the Law of Mohammed). From the 1550s, on the infrequent occasions that an inquisitor visited town, he focused on the religious behaviour of the Moriscos. The documents in this volume certainly reflect that inquisitorial interest, but they also provide rich details about how Deza's citizens interacted with one another (and with outsiders, like the inquisitors). As a result, readers can explore for themselves what life was like for early modern Spaniards as they sought to make sense of their world and their place in it.

THE TOWN OF DEZA

In the middle of the sixteenth century, Deza was a small but growing town nestled among the foothills of northeastern Castile near the Aragonese border.[3] The Henar River flowing west of town created a fertile valley, while a pair of springs north of town formed the Argadil, a stream that flowed through Deza, powering mills, providing drinking water, and removing sewage. Two royal roads running southwest to northeast framed the town—the northerly one connected Madrid to Pamplona (passing through Almazán and Ágreda) and then on to France, while the southerly route began in Toledo, passed through Sigüenza, and ended in Zaragoza.

---

[2] Among these are Kagan and Dyer, *Inquisitorial Inquiries*; Gustav Henningsen, ed., *The Salazar Documents: Inquisitor Alonso de Salazar Frías and Others on the Basque Witch Persecution* (Leiden: Brill, 2004); Francisca de los Apóstoles, *The Inquisition of Francisca: A Sixteenth-Century Visionary on Trial*, ed. and trans. Gillian Alghren (Chicago: University of Chicago Press, 2005); Homza, *Spanish Inquisition, 1478–1614*; and *Records of the Spanish Inquisition, Translated from the Original Manuscripts* (Boston: Samuel G. Goodrich, 1828).

[3] Deza's history is described in Vicente Alejandre Alcalde, *Deza: Entre Castilla y Aragón*, 2 vols. (Calatayud: Diputación Provincial de Soria, 2009).

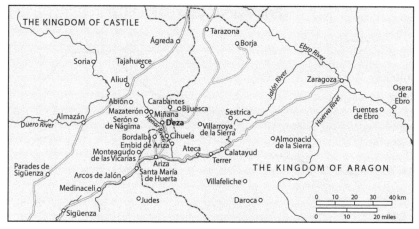

The Aragonese-Castilian Border near Deza

Two royal roads framed the town—the more northerly one from Madrid to Pamplona passed through Ágreda, and the southerly one from Toledo ended in Zaragoza. Other roads of more regional significance passed directly through Deza.

Several minor thoroughfares, trails, and passes tied Deza to nearby villages, towns, and cities.

Initially founded by Muslim settlers (whom Christians later pejoratively called Moors) from North Africa in the late eighth or early ninth century, Deza was conquered by Christians around 1120 as they fought a series of on-again, off-again wars, which historians call the Reconquest. These wars expanded Christian control of the Iberian Peninsula southward in fits and starts. Securely under Christian dominion by the fourteenth century, Deza then became an important fortification during the wars between the rival Christian kingdoms of Castile and Aragon. As borders solidified, Deza emerged as a town near the Aragonese border but directly controlled by the kings of Castile. By the fifteenth century, however, the Castilian monarch made Deza a seigniorial town—that is, he placed it under the authority of a noble. The powerful dukes of Medinaceli became Deza's lords, but their lands were vast and they had many responsibilities. Although they occasionally visited, they rarely spent long periods in the small town. Instead they appointed wardens (*alcaides*) to function as local representatives, occupy the fortress, and mind its arsenal.

When Isabella the future queen of Castile (r. 1474–1504) married Ferdinand the future king of Aragon (r. 1479–1516) in 1469, their union paved the way for peace between the kingdoms. In the wake of the marriage, however, Deza's military importance declined. Yet, because of its proximity to

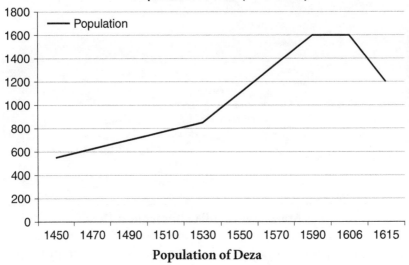

Population of Deza (1450–1612)

Population of Deza

the Aragonese border, it continued to function as a "dry port," an official border crossing between the two kingdoms where goods could be assessed and taxed by customs officials. Many Dezanos maintained close ties with Aragonese friends, relatives, and business associates. In fact, many of the town's Moriscos worked as muleteers, leading mule trains packed with goods over the border and across Spain.

Deza was growing during these years, swelling from about 900 inhabitants in the 1530s to over 1,600 by the 1590s, making it one of the region's larger towns.[4] (See Figure 0.2.) About three-quarters of the inhabitants identified themselves as Old Christians, claiming "purity of blood."[5] But New Christian minorities—which included both Judeoconversos (the baptized descendants of Spanish Jews who had converted under pressure in the

---

[4] This was a fairly standard pattern in Castile during these decades. The primary engine of growth was immigration from rural villages to towns and cities. After the mid-1590s, urban growth stalled and began declining in the seventeenth century. See Gonzalo Anes, "The Agrarian 'Depression' in Castile in the Seventeenth Century," in *The Castilian Crisis of the Seventeenth Century*, ed. I.A.A. Thompson and Bartolomé Yun Casalilla (Cambridge: Cambridge University Press, 1994), 61.

[5] "Purity of blood" (*limpieza de sangre*) became a powerful diagnostic for inclusion and exclusion in a society that believed that bad blood bred heresy and that heresy spread like a contagious disease. Important works on the topic include Ruth Pike, *Linajudos and Conversos in Seville: Greed and Prejudice in Sixteenth- and Seventeenth-Century Spain* (New York: Peter Lang, 2000); Gretchen Starr-Lebeau, *In the Shadow of the Virgin: Inquisitors, Friars, and Conversos in Guadalupe, Spain* (Princeton, NJ: Princeton University Press, 2003); and Max-Sebastián Hering Torres, María Elena Martínez, and David Nirenberg, eds., *Race and Blood in the Iberian World* (Munster: Lit Verlag, 2012).

later Middle Ages) and Moriscos—lived there too. Judeoconversos were a small group in Deza, and by the later sixteenth century, most (but not all) had become so integrated into Old Christian society that their neighbors rarely thought of them as Jews. Moriscos, by contrast, constituted about one-quarter of the population. Rather than assimilating like the Judeoconversos, many of Deza's Moriscos kept their Old Christian neighbors at a distance.

As population increased, Deza changed physically. A newer area of town, called the Upper Neighborhood, was built up to the northeast of the old medieval core and outside of the old walls; it was inhabited principally by Moriscos. The old parish church was demolished and slowly replaced by a beautiful and much larger one dedicated to the Virgin Mary. The duke

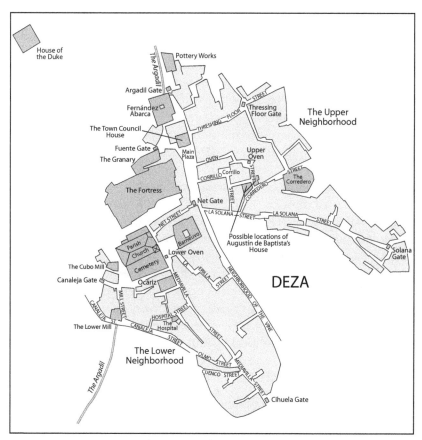

The Town of Deza, c.1600
The town's two main neighborhoods—the Upper and Lower—pivoted around the Main Plaza.

of Medinaceli built a large house with substantial gardens just to the north of town, outside of the walls. Indeed, in the second half of the sixteenth century, Deza was on the rise. Many of its citizens became wealthier and a small but active group of minor nobles (*hidalgos*) emerged.

Of course, most Dezanos were not nobles of any kind, but striking diversity existed even among the commoners. Some were quite wealthy, owned land and homes, and kept servants. Mateo Romero and his wife Ana Almoravi, for instance, were poor in the mid-1550s when they moved to Deza from Aragon; by the late 1560s they had become rich.[6] Others slipped into poverty, like Juan Corazón, a "poor day laborer who gets work where he can find it."[7] Life in a small town was semi-rural, and most Dezanos were involved in agricultural labor, even if they also performed other types of work. Some were craftsmen or merchants; millers, fullers, and muleteers; butchers and fishmongers; taverners and shopkeepers; weavers, tailors, and cobblers; bricklayers and carpenters; blacksmiths, potters, and tile makers; and so forth.

Parents often farmed out adolescent children, putting them to work in other households, where they learned domestic duties or specific skills. Adolescent boys might be apprenticed to a master craftsman to learn a trade. Servants (and apprentices) were expected to obey their masters and show humility, but they were not necessarily socially marginalized or oppressed. Miguel García Serrano (1563–1631), for instance, was an educated citizen with political clout. Yet his daughter María served with a local family at the beginning of the seventeenth century. By contrast, the few slaves who passed through Deza, like the Native American boy owned by Hernando de Torres, were on the bottom rung of the social ladder.[8]

Most of the people who lived in Deza were citizens (*vecinos* or *vecinas*). From a legal perspective, a citizen was a male head of household, but his wife and children were regarded as citizens based on his status. Citizenship, however, was a malleable concept, and unmarried or widowed women were often viewed as *vecinas* in their own right. Citizens had to pay taxes, but they also claimed membership in the commune, which was the town's foundational political institution, its republic. The commune, in turn, selected annual local office holders—the town's magistrates and aldermen—and submitted their names to the duke for approval.

---

[6] For Romero and Almoravi, see Docs. 10, 11, and 14 below.
[7] Archivo Diocesano de Cuenca, Sección Inquisición (ADC), legajo 377, expediente 5342 (inquisitorial trial against Juan Corazón, testimony of the accused, July 1, 1608).
[8] See Doc. 58 below.

Still, not everyone who lived in Deza was a citizen. In fact, some people lived there for years but were still regarded (by themselves and others) merely as "inhabitants." Despite living in town for nearly 15 years, the Aragonese couple Mateo Romero and Ana Almoravi never became citizens. Deza's size and its role as a dry port drew laborers, merchants, conveyors of goods, government officials, travelling priests and friars, companies of gypsies, and the itinerant poor. Even foreign dignitaries, like the Venetian ambassador Segismundo Cavalli, passed through on his way to Madrid in 1567. His party arrived and dined at Deza, "a place of 250 hearths, belonging to the Duke of Medinaceli, of unimpressive construction, where (since it was the point of entry into Castile) the horses were registered and a duty was paid on everything."[9]

Early modern people expected formal authority (whether political, religious, or familial) to be wielded by men, but women exercised a great deal of influence as well. According to Spanish moralists, women were subordinate to men—especially as daughters and wives. Their proper place was within the home. One popular writer suggested that women should follow the example of the tortoise, which never leaves its shell and has no voice, by "remaining at home and practicing silence," lest they fall prey to the temptations and dangers of the outside world.[10] Yet this sort of rhetoric expressed an ideal rather than the reality. The women of Deza (Dezanas) often showed submission to the men in their lives and tended to be tied more closely to the domestic sphere—rearing children, cooking, and cleaning—but they also held jobs outside of the home, worked in family trades, and traveled regionally. A few lived alone as widows, as *beatas* (lay holy women), or simply as single women on their own. If they could not sit on the town council or become priests, they nevertheless exercised power more informally. Dezanas were active participants in the town's religious, economic, and social life.

Members of the clergy represent another important group of Dezanos. While the pope claimed ultimate religious authority over the Church on earth, he delegated that authority to archbishops and bishops. They, in turn, appointed priests to minister among the Christians living in cities, towns, and villages throughout the Roman Catholic world. During these years, Deza had between six and eight priests attached to the parish church. They said mass, preached sermons, instructed laypeople in Christian doctrine, and sometimes taught them to read. They administered baptisms,

[9] Alcalde, *Deza*, 1:248.
[10] Luis de León, *La perfecta casada*, ed. Elizabeth Wallace (Chicago: University of Chicago Press, 1903), 94.

heard confessions, visited the sick, performed weddings, and buried the dead. They also kept records of baptisms, marriages, and burials in the town's parish register.

The chief minister in town was the vicar. From 1556, this was Miguel Benito, but after 1580 he shared the vicarage with his nephew, who, confusingly, shared his uncle's name. The younger man, however, was always distinguished by his title: licentiate. The "old vicar" and "young vicar" worked together until 1591, when the uncle died and the nephew gained the office in his own right. When Licentiate Benito died in early March 1605, Licentiate Mateo de Luna succeeded him and served as vicar for the next two decades.[11]

In addition to being vicar, the Benitos also successively held the office of commissioner (*comisario*), which made them the chief local representative of the Inquisition. The Inquisition did not have jurisdiction over every crime or sin, but it did exercise authority over a range of specific offences when committed by a member of the Christian Church. And from time to time Dezanos presented themselves before the commissioner to denounce people whom they had witnessed speaking scandalous, blasphemous, or heretical words or behaving in ways that suggested they had departed from Christianity.[12] Because Old Christians often questioned whether their Morisco neighbors were true Christians, the former might denounce the latter. The older Benito tended to be punctilious about informing his superiors (the inquisitors based in the Castilian city of Cuenca) about these denunciations. His nephew, however, proved more flexible. In fact, by 1599, Licentiate Benito began *hiding* denunciations against local Moriscos. They remained buried among his papers for years and came to light only after his death. The man who discovered them claimed that bribery had motivated Benito's silence.[13]

A number of other men served as priests besides the Benitos. Many of them grew up in Deza and knew the town and its inhabitants well. For example, Juanes de Altopica was born at the end of the fifteenth century and served as vicar and inquisitorial representative in the 1520s and 1530s. He remained an active priest in Deza until his death in 1573. Local clerics often worked as chaplains, presiding over a smaller side chapel within the parish church. They typically received a salary, called a benefice, from

---

[11] The title "licentiate," which suggests university training beyond the baccalaureate level, indicates that the "young vicar" and Luna, like many of Deza's priests, were well educated.

[12] It was less common, but not unheard of, for someone to confess his or her own sins to the commissioner.

[13] ADC leg. 361, 5131 (inquisitorial trial of Ana Guerera, testimony of Gabriel de León, July 27, 1606).

an endowment. In addition to clerical fixtures, who spent decades (if not their entire lives) in Deza, some of the priests who appear in the documents—like Fray Marcelo and Alonso de Yllana—were merely passing through. In fact, priests often visited the town on business, as missionary preachers, or to serve as extra confessors during the busy penitential season before Easter.

As the Benitos' different approaches toward inquisitorial denunciations suggest, the personalities and motivations of Deza's clerics differed from person to person. While we might be inclined to imagine church authorities (whether episcopal representatives, visiting inquisitors, missionary friars, or long-serving local clerics) as two-dimensional characters, they actually had many different responsibilities and competing agendas. They not only had to be faithful to their bishop and respectful to inquisitors; they also had to honor the duke, minister to their flock, and manage their own interests. And they did not always keep to the straight and narrow—as a younger man, for example, Juanes de Altopica had carried on an affair with a Morisca midwife and, as we've seen, Licentiate Benito may have accepted bribes.

OLD AND NEW CHRISTIANS

Most of the people who lived in Deza regarded themselves as Old Christians, and they saw this as a good thing. New Christians—either Judeoconversos or Moriscos—comprised the remainder of the population and could be viewed by their neighbors as religiously suspect and inferior on account of their impure blood.[14] While New Christians certainly could rise economically and socially, they generally had to distance themselves from their ancestry in order to be fully embraced by Old Christian society. Those who held onto the past risked a great deal. Yet the relationship between Old and New Christians was not always (or simply) antagonistic.

---

[14] The literature on New Christians—both Judeoconversos and Moriscos—is vast. A good place to start is James S. Amelang, *Parallel Histories: Muslims and Jews in Inquisitorial Spain* (Baton Rouge: Louisiana State University Press, 2013). For English-language overviews of the Morisco or Judeoconverso experience, see L.P. Harvey, *Muslims in Spain, 1500–1614* (Chicago: University of Chicago Press, 2005), and Yitzhak Baer, *A History of Jews in Christian Spain*, 2 vols. (Philadelphia: Jewish Publication Society, 1961–66). Another entry point is the essays collected by Kevin Ingram in the three volumes of *The Conversos and Moriscos in Late Medieval Spain and Beyond* (Leiden: Brill, 2009–15). For a discussion of female New Christians, see Renée Levine Melammed, "Judeo-Conversas and Moriscas in Sixteenth-Century Spain: A Study of Parallels," *Jewish History* 24 (2010): 155–68. An important discussion of the medieval development of conflict between minority and majority groups in Europe is David Nirenberg, *Communities of Violence: Persecution of Minorities in the Middle Ages* (Princeton, NJ: Princeton University Press, 1996).

Instead, suspicion and wariness combined with neighborliness and the need to work together in order to get by. And sometimes business deals, shared labour, marriages, sexual liaisons, and even friendships stretched across the divide.

In Deza as elsewhere, much of daily life was characterized by a rough coexistence (sometimes called *convivencia*) that saw Old Christians, Judeo-conversos, and Moriscos finding ways to live together. Jews, after all, had survived in Spain as a minority group since antiquity, and North African Muslims had conquered much of the Iberian Peninsula in the eighth century. So, during most of the Middle Ages, Iberia was a land of three religions, where Judaism, Christianity, and Islam coexisted even amidst military conflict. By the end of the fifteenth century, however, the Christian monarchs of Castile and Aragon, who by then controlled all but the very southern reaches of Spain, bent their wills toward consolidating power. Religious uniformity among their subjects was one consequence of pursuing that goal. A region of Europe that had been home to Jews, Christians, and Muslims living (sometimes uneasily) alongside one another was now to become the land of a single faith: Christianity.[15]

JUDEOCONVERSOS
From the late fourteenth century, Jews had been pressured, even compelled, to accept baptism in some parts of Iberia. Mass conversions followed, but many Old Christian observers became concerned. They wondered, not unreasonably, whether forced conversions produced true believers or (despite the sacramental efficacy of the baptismal waters) merely secret Jews. In 1478, Pope Sixtus IV granted permission to the Spanish monarchs to establish the Holy Office of the Inquisition in Castile and soon thereafter in Aragon as well. Initially, the Inquisition's primary purpose was to address the problem of Jews who, beginning in the 1390s, had been pressured to convert and were believed to be "Judaizing," that is, returning to Judaism after having been baptized into the Christian Church.[16]

---

[15] Helpful overviews of religion in Spain include Helen Rawlings, *Church, Religion and Society in Early Modern Spain* (Basingstoke, UK: Palgrave, 2002); William A. Christian, Jr., *Local Religion in Sixteenth-Century Spain* (Princeton, NJ: Princeton, 1981); John Edwards, *Religion and Society in Spain, c. 1492* (Aldershot, UK: Ashgate, 1996); and Stanley G. Payne, *Spanish Catholicism* (Madison: University of Wisconsin Press, 1981). Stuart Schwartz, *All Can Be Saved: Religious Tolerance and Salvation in the Early Modern Atlantic World* (New Haven, CT: Yale University Press, 2008) offers a provocative argument about the existence of religious toleration in inquisitorial Spain.

[16] For secondary works about Judeoconversos, see footnote 14.

The problem escalated after March 1492, when Ferdinand and Isabella declared that all Jews either had to convert or leave Spain. Those who accepted baptism and stayed faced inquisitorial scrutiny and the suspicion of their neighbors. Both secular and ecclesiastical authorities established restrictions limiting where Judeoconversos could live, what occupations they could hold, and how high they could rise socially. The Inquisition tried thousands of these New Christians for continuing to practice Judaism in the late fifteenth and early sixteenth centuries, and many Judaizers were "reconciled" to the Church, a formal process that required them to confess, abjure their errors, and publicly repent. This often included wearing (sometimes for the rest of their lives) a distinctive tunic called a *sanbenito*. By contrast, those who refused to repent or who relapsed after having been reconciled risked death by burning at the stake. In a process known as "relaxing," the Holy Office displayed the obstinate or relapsed heretics at large public spectacles known as autos-da-fe (acts of faith) and then handed them over to secular authorities, who did the dirty work of carrying out the execution.

Despite these challenges, over time many Judeoconverso families acclimated to Old Christian society and played important roles in the religious, political, and economic life of Spain. Like the family of St. Teresa of Avila (1515–82)—which went in the space of two generations from a relapsed Judaizing grandfather to a celebrated saintly granddaughter—many Spaniards of Jewish descent integrated into mainstream Old Christian culture. One historian has commented that "the history of the Jews in Spain is the history of assimilation, that is, the successful integration of thousands of *Conversos* and their families into the ranks of Spanish Society."[17]

Deza's Judeoconversos followed a similar course, integrating into the majority population during the sixteenth century and, as far as we can tell, losing their distinctly Jewish identity. In fact, many of the most important families in town were either of Jewish descent or related to Judeoconversos by marriage. The Judeoconversa María del Castillo, for example, married into the prominent Ocáriz family of Deza early in the sixteenth century.[18] A number of witnesses denounced her to the Inquisition in 1533 for Judaizing, including Juanes de Altopica, the town's vicar and an inquisitorial representative. When Altopica attempted to pursue the case, the Ocáriz family and its allies (among them Deza's most prominent families) rallied in support, drove Altopica from his offices, and

---

[17] Teofilo F. Ruiz, *Spanish Society: 1400–1600* (London: Routledge, 2014), 103.

[18] Around this time, the Inquisition tried several Ocárizes from Deza who, as it happens, were also of Jewish descent and may have been related to a branch of Teresa of Avila's family.

(briefly) exiled him from town.[19] The inquisitors at Cuenca dispatched a representative to assess the situation. He reported that many of the town's "most principal" inhabitants were Judeoconversos, "although they denied it."[20] The Holy Office let the matter drop, and Altopica never regained his position.

Beatriz Pérez de Luna also married into Deza's Ocáriz family.[21] Her father, Álvaro de Luna, had been executed as a relapsed Judaizer in 1549. Despite this lineage, his daughter wore fine clothes and jewelry and his grandsons rode horses like noblemen. Neighbors addressed them with the titles *don* or *doña*, which suggests that they were viewed as *hidalgos*, members of the lower nobility. Yet the descendants of a Judaizing heretic should not have been permitted such honors. Even visiting inquisitors seemed a bit uncertain about how to deal with the incongruity. When one witness testified against doña Beatriz, the inquisitorial scribe initially included her title, but he later struck it out. Ultimately, it was determined that the evidence against her was merely "hearsay" and therefore invalid. Once again, the Holy Office chose not to act.

Licentiate Antonio Páez (c. 1510–77) appears in several sources and, like doña Beatriz, helps us to understand how Deza's Judeoconversos interacted with their Old Christian neighbors.[22] Páez grew up in the Castilian town of Atienza, where his father was arrested and tried by the Holy Office. In about 1535, the son moved to Deza, where he worked as the physician for more than four decades. His Jewish background should have restricted him from being licensed as a physician, but Páez had a university education and, seemingly, an outgoing personality. Besides, small towns had a hard time attracting and keeping skilled medical personnel.[23] Some way was found to get around the impediments, and he became an important fixture in local society.

Although a number of Páez's neighbors remarked upon his sometimes unusual religious behavior, the inquisitors never investigated him, perhaps because their attention increasingly gravitated toward Deza's Moriscos. Páez married well and his daughter, who wed a local *hidalgo*, did even better.

---

[19] Although stripped of his offices, Altopica (c. 1495–1573) remained in Deza for the rest of his life. He continued to work in the church and kept a close eye on the town's Judeoconversos, as seen in his testimony in Doc. 5 below.

[20] ADC, leg. 759, exp. 712 (letter from Licentiate Góngara to the inquisitors in Cuenca, October 22, 1534).

[21] See below, Docs. 41 and 60.

[22] For Páez, see Docs. 3, 5, 7, 9, 12, 16, 25, 40, and 60.

[23] Michele L. Clouse, *Medicine, Government, and Public Health in Philip II's Spain* (Ashgate, UK: Aldershot, 2011), 148–49.

In 1559 his granddaughter was baptized as "doña Isabela," and when Páez died in August 1577, he was laid to rest in a place of honor in the parish church. So, despite the restrictions placed against them and the attention of the Inquisition, many of Deza's Judeoconversos were eventually fully integrated into the community, even entering the ranks of the gentry. Deza's Moriscos, however, had a very different experience.

MORISCOS

North African Muslim armies crossed into Spain in the early eighth century and quickly conquered much of the peninsula. During the Middle Ages, Christian kings in the far north drew upon religious ideology as well as more worldly motivations to mobilize men and arms. Advancing fitfully over centuries, they conquered the villages, towns, cities, and kingdoms under Muslim control.[24] This meant conquering the people—Christians, Jews, and Muslims—who lived in them. And while the Christians might view this as liberation, the Jews and Muslims saw it differently. Initially, the latter groups were allowed to continue practicing their religions, but they experienced increasing pressure to convert to Christianity in the later Middle Ages.

In 1492, after a long campaign, Queen Isabella of Castile and King Ferdinand of Aragon accepted the surrender of the last remaining Islamic state in Iberia: the Kingdom of Granada in the far south of the peninsula. The hundreds of thousands of practicing Muslims now living under Christian rule, known as *mudéjares*, continued to worship quietly, fund religious schools, and support Islamic instructors (known as *alfaquís*). Some *mudéjares*, especially those farther north, had lived under Christian rule for centuries, and, especially in inland Castile, the relatively few Muslims were widely dispersed among the many Christians. As a result, the tendency was for Castilian *mudéjares* to fall out of step with the greater Islamic world over time. Yet elsewhere in Iberia, especially along the Mediterranean coast and the recently conquered south, things were different.

It was in the south that tensions exploded. Within a few years of the conquest of Granada, despite a surrender treaty that allowed Islam to be practiced, the *mudéjares* there found themselves suffering increasingly rough treatment, especially from Cardinal Francisco Jiménez de Cisneros. In 1499, the *mudéjares* revolted but were quickly (and harshly) suppressed.

---

[24] See David Lomax, *The Reconquest of Spain* (London: Longman, 1978); Bernard Reilly, *The Contest of Christian and Muslim Spain, 1031–1157* (Cambridge: Blackwell, 1992); and Joseph O'Callaghan, *Reconquest and Crusade in Medieval Spain* (Philadelphia: University of Pennsylvania Press, 2003).

King Ferdinand now concluded that the uprising had violated the terms of the treaty signed at the surrender of Granada, which had granted Muslims religious toleration in exchange for peaceful submission. He nullified the treaty, and by 1502 all Castilian Muslims, from north to south, had to either depart or accept baptism. This program of coerced conversions spread to the Kingdom of Navarre in 1515 and to Valencia and then Aragon in the 1520s.

Hundreds of thousands of *mudéjares* were baptized and became known as *nuevos conversos de moros* (new Moorish converts) or Moriscos. Few of them received instruction in the Christian faith, and most continued to practice the traditions with which they had grown up. As Muslims, they had avoided pork and alcohol, learned Arabic prayers, circumcised their sons, fasted during the month of Ramadan, and performed ritual ablutions (*guadoc*) before reciting prayers (*azala*) throughout the day. Fridays, in particular, were set apart. While the Church expected the sacramental efficacy of baptism to transform the hearts of these new converts, many continued to engage in the same practices as always.

Church leaders recognized that the Moriscos needed to behave like Christians, but here arose a difficulty. Where was the line to be drawn between Islamic devotion and mere cultural tradition? If fasting during Ramadan was clearly in the first category, what about Moriscas who wore veils or dyed their skin with henna? What about men who refused to drink wine? Or bathed frequently? What about the distinctive marriage and burial ceremonies of Deza's Moriscos? Even with the perspective of centuries, modern historians have a difficult time distinguishing broadly cultural activities from specifically religious ones in such cases. So did contemporary observers, who increasingly viewed any distinctively Morisco activities as suspect and incompatible with Spanish Christianity. They feared that Moriscos were mere deceivers, pretending to be Christians but secretly remaining Muslims. One Old Christian woman married to a Morisco expressed this fear well: "They're just as much Moors now as they've always been!"[25]

Transforming Moriscos into sincere converts proved to be a thorny problem for Old Christian authorities in Spain, and all the more so because the character of Morisco communities varied by region. They were especially dense in the south, particularly around Granada, where Moriscos comprised half the population. Many of these Granadan Moriscos worked as artisans and independent farmers. They even boasted an elite upper

---

[25] See Doc. 7 below.

class, descended from families that had wielded power before the Christian conquest. Some of those elites opted for collaboration and adopted Old Christian cultural practices. While many others continued at least some Islamic practices and traditions, acculturation was occurring gradually at all levels of Morisco society.[26]

Moriscos were also dense in the eastern kingdoms of Valencia (at least 100,000 people or about one-third of the population) and Aragon (around 50,000 or one-fifth of the population). In Valencia, Moriscos maintained a strong Islamic identity. They tended to live together in settlements apart from Old Christians, and in remote areas they spoke nothing but Arabic. Aragonese Moriscos were more assimilated than those in Valencia and few knew Arabic, but here too entire villages were populated with Moriscos, who supported *alfaquís* and produced Islamic literature.[27] They also bore the brunt of the Inquisition's assault against Islamizing during the sixteenth century.[28]

North of Granada, Moriscos in the Kingdom of Castile tended to be rather dispersed. Populations were thinner and separated by greater distances. Although some sizeable communities existed, they often lived alongside Old Christians.[29] And, in general, for lack of religious leadership, Castilian Moriscos had a less firm grasp of how to be Muslim than their counterparts in Granada, Valencia, or Aragon. Some evidence suggests that during the sixteenth century many had begun to adopt Christianity and acclimate to Old Christian cultural practices.[30]

Deza did not altogether fit this typical Castilian model. Its Morisco community was probably never more than 500 people, but that amounted to one of the densest Morisco populations in the region. While some of the town's Moriscos seem to have embraced Christianity sincerely, many maintained a sense of Islamic identity. Yet others vacillated between the faiths or failed to distinguish clearly between them. Secret (or crypto-)

---

[26] Amalia García Pedraza, *Actitudes ante la muerte en la Granada del siglo XVI: Los Moriscos que quisieron salvarse* (Granada: Universidad de Granada), 339–443.

[27] Much of the literature was written in *Aljamiado*, which was phonetically Spanish but written in a stylized Arabic script.

[28] William Monter provides a survey of Aragonese and Valencian Moriscos' interactions with the Holy Office in *Frontiers of Heresy: The Spanish Inquisition from the Basque Lands to Sicily* (Cambridge: Cambridge University Press, 2003), 189–230.

[29] The city of Ávila, for example, had a significant Morisco population. Serafín de Tapia Sánchez, *La comunidad Morisca de Ávila* (Salamanca: Gráficas Varona, 1990).

[30] See James Tueller, *Good and Faithful Christians: Moriscos and Catholicism in Early Modern Spain* (New Orleans: University Press of the South, 2002) and Trevor Dadson, *Tolerance and Coexistence in Early Modern Spain: The Moriscos of the Campo de Calatrava* (Woodbridge, UK: Tamesis, 2014).

Muslims hid their religious convictions while participating in elements of Christian religious devotion. Under normal conditions, Muslims were expected (among other things) to perform ritual washings, fast during Ramadan, and go on pilgrimage to Mecca once in their lives. They were also forbidden from participating in Christian worship, which was seen as idolatrous. Nevertheless, the Muslim principle of *taqiyya* (often translated "dissimulation") granted Muslims whose lives or livelihoods were threatened the flexibility to conform to Christianity outwardly while inwardly guarding their true convictions.[31]

Dezanos who wanted to be good Muslims could learn how with relative ease because of the town's proximity to Aragon. Aragonese Moriscos formed a kind of religious lifeline for Deza's crypto-Muslims. In the mid-1560s, for instance, a group of Moriscos (including Román Ramírez the younger and Alexo Gorgoz) paid an *alfaquí* from Aragon to come to town and tutor them in "Moorish writing."[32] They learned to read Arabic letters, studied religious texts, and memorized prayers. Other Dezanos traveled to Aragon and spent time there. While young children were often kept in the dark about these practices, women played an important role, and once the young reached a certain level of maturity (often in their early teens), they were initiated into the world of crypto-Islam.[33] For Christian Spain, then, the Morisco problem was rooted in the family and was intergenerational. Church and governmental authorities feared that the town's Moriscos would be (or perhaps had already been) irreversibly corrupted by their Aragonese counterparts and that Islam would spread further into Castile.

Deza, however, was only one potential breeding ground for Islam, and its Moriscos attracted little attention during the first half of the sixteenth century. The situation changed in the 1560s when Spanish authorities decided to address concerns about ongoing Islamic activities in the Kingdom of Granada. They imposed strict new laws on Moriscos there, ordering them to abandon traditional practices—such as using Arabic, avoiding pork and wine, and wearing traditional garb—all of which linked them to

---

[31] On *taqiyya*, see Devin Stewart, "Dissimulation in Sunni Islam and Morisco *Taqiyya*," *Al-Qantara* 34 (2013): 439–90; Maria del Mar Rosa-Rodriguez, "Simulation and Dissimulation: Religious Hybridity in a *Morisco Fatwa*," *Medieval Encounters* 16 (2010): 143–82; and, on Deza in particular, Patrick J. O'Banion, "'They will know our hearts': Practicing the Art of Dissimulation on the Islamic Periphery," *Journal of Early Modern History* 20, no. 2 (2016): 193–217.

[32] ADC, leg. 249, exp. 3352, 48v-49r (inquisitorial trial of Ana de Almoravi, testimony of the accused, February 5, 1571).

[33] Mercedes García-Arenal, *Inquisición y Moriscos: Los procesos del Tribunal de Cuenca* (Madrid: Siglo XXI, 1978), 65–66.

an Islamic past.[34] The tense situation erupted into war between 1568 and 1571. Morisco guerillas entrenched themselves in the Sierra Nevada Mountains, where they fought a bloody war trying to hold out for reinforcements from Islamic North Africa and the Ottoman Empire.[35]

In 1569, with the war still raging, King Philip II (r. 1556–98) ordered the removal of Granada's Moriscos—whether they had supported the revolt or not. He transported them north and dispersed them in small groups among the population of Castile. He hoped that this decisive action would make Granada's Moriscos more docile, receptive to the instructions of the Church, and loyal to the Spanish state. But in some areas the experiment backfired, as new arrivals exerted an Islamizing influence on the old Castilian Moriscos alongside whom they now lived. None of the exiles were sent to Deza, perhaps because authorities already considered that town's Morisco community too dangerous. Yet these events still had serious consequences for the town because they convinced the inquisitorial tribunal at Cuenca to investigate the Moriscos under their jurisdiction by sending inquisitors on formal visits to towns and villages. For Deza, such visits occurred first in 1569 and again in 1581.

The situation remained unstable throughout the remainder of the sixteenth century. Religious and secular authorities pressured Moriscos to conform to Christianity and abandon Islam, but Old Christian fears and doubts made it difficult for Moriscos to integrate even if they wanted to do so. In Deza, for example, a local inquisitorial commissioner and lay deputies (known as *familiares*) monitored Morisco behavior. And from the mid-1580s the bishop of Sigüenza barred all but a handful of particularly Christianized Moriscos from taking the Eucharist at Easter, the central ritual of the Christian year. These efforts were meant to reform but instead tended to isolate and marginalize Moriscos. Some pious Spaniards invested time, energy, and money to reach Moriscos, and they became the focus of

---

[34] See David Coleman, *Creating Christian Granada: Society and Religious Culture in an Old World Frontier City, 1492–1600* (Ithaca, NY: Cornell University Press, 2003). For one Morisco's response to these pressures, see Núñez Muley, *A Memorandum*.

[35] Spanish fears about the threat of Mediterranean Islam were not unfounded and often drove government policy. Some of these elements are teased out, for example, in Andrew C. Hess, "The Moriscos: An Ottoman Fifth Column in Sixteenth-Century Spain," *American Historical Review* 74, no. 1 (1968): 1–55, and *The Forgotten Frontier: A History of the Sixteenth-Century Ibero-African Frontier* (Chicago: University of Chicago Press, 1978); Miguel Ángel de Bunes Ibarra, "The Expulsion of the Moriscos in the Context of Philip III's Mediterranean Policy," in *The Expulsion of the Moriscos from Spain: A Mediterranean Diaspora*, ed. Mercedes García-Arenal and Gerard Wiegers (Leiden: Brill, 2014), 37–59; and M.T. Green-Mercado, "The Mahdī in Valencia: Messianism, Apocalypticism and Morisco Rebellions in Late Sixteenth-Century Spain," *Medieval Encounters* 19, no. 1–2 (2013): 193–220.

ministry for some clerics. Yet many Old Christians seem to have doubted whether these New Christians would ever become faithful Catholics. In Valencia, for example, after years of labor devoted to winning the hearts of Moriscos under his care, Archbishop Juan de Ribera finally concluded that the task was impossible.[36]

Some, of course, regretted the failed opportunity represented by the Moriscos. Commentators noted how odd it was that Spain, which had successfully spread Roman Catholicism from the Americas to Asia, had done so little to convert those close to home.[37] Still, evidence was piling up that Spain's Moriscos were secret Muslims, in league with the enemies of the Catholic Church and its chief defender, the Spanish monarch—or at least that's how it seemed at the time. Courtiers and royal advisors became convinced that something dramatic had to be done about the Moriscos, even as some churchmen and many nobles counseled patience. As early as May 1581, the inquisitor Licentiate Alonso Jiménez de Reynoso (who had visited Deza in 1569 and tried several of its Moriscos) suggested that expelling all Moriscos from Spain would solve the problem, but Philip II rejected the idea.[38] In an unexpected twist of fate, Deza may have had something to do with convincing the next Spanish monarch to reverse course on this issue.

ROMÁN RAMÍREZ THE YOUNGER

The new king, Philip III (r. 1589–1621), attended an auto-da-fe in Toledo in early March 1600, where the bones of Román Ramírez the younger, one of Deza's Moriscos, were consigned to the flames. Ramírez (1540–99) is, perhaps, the most famous of all Dezanos, and several of the documents in this volume focus specifically on him. He was renowned in the region as a storyteller, healer, and leader in the Islamic community. He had traveled widely around Spain, working in his youth as an agricultural laborer and a guard at the dry port. He claimed to have recited chivalric tales "many times" before King Philip II at the royal palaces at Aranjuez and El Pardo, outside Madrid.[39] He had an encyclopedic memory and a short temper and

[36] See Benjamin Ehlers, *Between Christians and Moriscos: Juan de Ribera and Religious Reform in Valencia, 1568–1614* (Baltimore: Johns Hopkins University Press, 2006), 9–35 and 80–105.
[37] Pedro de Valencia, *Tratado acerca de los Moriscos de España*, ed. Joaquín Gil Sanjuán (Málaga: Editorial Algazara, 1997), 128.
[38] Stephen Haliczer, *Inquisition and Society in the Kingdom of Valencia* (Berkeley: University of California, 1990), 265.
[39] If Ramírez was telling the truth about this, it probably happened in the 1570s, before Philip III was born. The Morisco claimed to have been in Madrid in January of 1571 and for several months between October 1575 and April 1576. The performance at El Pardo might have occurred on either of those occasions.

was something of a scoundrel. As a younger man, he was arrested at least twice (for horse smuggling and quarreling with Deza's warden) and went on the lam once (after getting into a duel with Páez when they disagreed about a cure).

Despite these indiscretions, Ramírez frequently served on Deza's town council. This was not particularly unusual, for the town's lord granted Moriscos the privilege of *mitad de los oficios* (half the offices) on the council. Yet, at least two successive dukes of Medinaceli showed Ramírez special favor, even renting to him the "Duke's House and Garden," located just outside the town walls. (After Ramírez's death, his son, Miguel, continued to control the property.) In fact, the support shown to the town's Moriscos by their dukes—who guaranteed them a political voice, supported them in their interactions with the Inquisition, and provided jobs and financial opportunities—was a repeating theme in the sixteenth and early seventeenth centuries. The noblemen's purpose was probably to balance the growing power of the Old Christians (especially the *hidalgos*) by favoring the Moriscos, but if so they ultimately helped drive a further wedge between the New and Old Christian communities of Deza.

Yet, when it came, Ramírez's downfall was not a byproduct of town politics. Rather, in 1595, just after the death of his first wife, Angela de Miranda, the Morisco unexpectedly found himself drawn into a feud brewing in the city of Soria. Ramírez, who happened to be serving as one of Deza's co-magistrates that year, became collateral damage when he inadvertently offended one party in the dispute, which subsequently set in motion a process that ended with his being denounced to the Inquisition for having made a pact with the devil. (His accusers claimed that this explained his phenomenal memory!) Despite the accusations and his arrest, Ramírez returned to Deza and paid a hefty bond of 2,000 ducats to "have the town as his jail." He married a second time, had two additional children, and served once again on the town council.[40] There he stayed until the spring of 1599, when he was finally transferred to Cuenca's inquisitorial prison. Eventually, he confessed not only to having kept a devil named Liarde as his familiar spirit but also to being a secret Muslim.

By the fall, Ramírez's health had taken a turn. He was transferred to the Hospital of St. James in Cuenca but died in December 1599. His trial

---

On Ramírez as a performer, see L.P. Harvey, "Oral Composition and the Performance of Novels of Chivalry in Spain," in Joseph J. Duggan, ed., *Oral Literature: Seven Essays* (Edinburgh: Scottish Academic Press, 1975), 84–100.

[40] Archivo Histórico Municipal de Deza [AHMD], caja 282, doc. 6 (Libro de Cuentas de Propios, 1595–98).

continued and he was posthumously declared guilty. His bones were delivered to the city of Toledo where, in March 1600, they featured prominently in the auto-da-fe, the only one Philip III ever attended. The king was accompanied at the event by his young wife, Margaret of Austria (1584–1611), and his chief advisor, the Duke of Lerma (Francisco Gómez de Sandoval; 1553–1625). Here was public proof that Spain's Moriscos were not only crypto-Muslims who longed for the return of Islamic dominion to Iberia, but also the devil's own allies. Word of these crimes made a deep impression on contemporaries. The learned Jesuit Martín del Rio (1551–1608) included a famous description of the case in his *Investigations into Magic* (published in three volumes in 1599 and 1600).[41] Early in the seventeenth century, the playwright Juan Ruiz de Alarcón (1581–1639) wrote a (much fictionalized) comedy about Ramírez entitled *He Who Walks in an Evil Way, Ends in an Evil Way*.[42]

Did the condemnation of Ramírez and the revelation of his identity as a crypto-Muslim and demon-summoning wizard influence the king, queen, and Lerma? It may well have, for not long after the auto-da-fe, the royal couple (and perhaps Lerma as well) paid a visit to Deza. They passed through, it seems, in 1602.[43] The entourage did not stay long—the town was hardly prepared to host so august a company in the manner it deserved—but the guests were entertained and fed.

We do not know why they stopped at Deza, to whom they spoke, or what subjects were discussed. While the visit could have been mere coincidence, it seems more likely that Ramírez's notoriety (and the couple's presence at his condemnation) influenced their itinerary. In any case, after the royal visit, relations between Deza's Old Christians and Moriscos deteriorated quickly. Perhaps it triggered the lingering concerns of Old Christians about the inhabitants of the Upper Neighborhood. By late 1602 the tensions became violent; some Moriscos threatened the town's bailiff when he came to the Upper Neighborhood and attempted to enforce attendance

---

[41] For an (unfortunately abridged) English translation, see Martín del Rio, *Investigations into Magic*, ed. and trans. P.G. Maxwell-Stuart (Manchester: Manchester University Press, 2000), 105–7. The complicated relationship between witchcraft, superstition, and diabolism in Spain can be explored in Gunnar Knutsen, *Servants of Satan and Masters of Demons: The Spanish Inquisition's Trial for Superstition, Valencia and Barcelona, 1478–1700* (Turnhout: Brepols, 2009) and María Tausiet, *Urban Magic in Early Modern Spain: Abracadabra Omnipotens* (New York: Palgrave, 2013).

[42] O. Hegyi, "Literary Motifs and Historical Reality in Ruiz de Alarcón's *Quien mal anda en mal acaba*," *Renaissance and Reformation* 18 (1982): 249–63.

[43] Reference to the visit is made in a letter written by the Duke of Medinaceli to the town council. AHMD, leg. 16a, doc. 7 (August 8, 1602).

at Sunday mass.[44] Later, an armed mob of Old Christians gathered in the streets yelling, "Die! Die! You Moorish dogs!"[45]

A clique of Old Christians organized a lawsuit, intending to exclude Moriscos from holding civic office. Remarkably, the Moriscos counter-sued in the royal appellate court—and won. But soon the town's inquisitorial commissioner began receiving a new series of denunciations about the Moriscos' religious behavior.[46] By the autumn of 1607, the Holy Office had arrested more than a dozen Moriscos and was holding them in Cuenca's secret jails. Eventually, many of them testified against neighbors back home, and over the next few years more than 50 of the town's Moriscos were arrested. Others sold their goods and fled.

During these same years, King Philip III was trying to solve his Morisco problem. By the early seventeenth century, most of his councilors agreed that the Moriscos posed a political as well as a religious threat to Spain. Only in 1609 did Philip decide on expulsion.[47] He began with the Moriscos of Valencia, where the population was densest and the threat of an alliance with an Islamic power in the Mediterranean (or even with Protestants in France) was greatest. Over the next five years, the decree was implemented piece by piece throughout the rest of Spain. According to an inscription in Deza's baptismal register, "On the eighth day of July 1611 the Moriscos of this town of Deza departed; they were four hundred people on foot."[48]

In 1614, the expulsion was officially pronounced a success. Perhaps one in ten Moriscos avoided the decree. Some places fared better than others. In Villarubia de los Ojos, for example, thanks to the support of local Old Christians and the town's lord, the Morisco community remained substantially intact.[49] Some exiled Moriscos returned home after a time, like the character Ricote in Miguel de Cervantes's *Don Quixote* (1605–15). In Deza, a very few Moriscos—those who had fully embraced Christianity and Old Christian culture—avoided expulsion. We do not know for sure where the exiled Dezanos spent the rest of their lives, but they were

---

[44] ADC, leg. 820, exp. 7992, fols. 6r-7v (petition regarding the naming of officials to the council of Deza, testimony of Juan de Peñafiel the elder, January 12, 1604).

[45] Archivo de la Real Chancillería de Valladolid, Registro de Ejecutorias, leg. 1999, exp. 90, fol. 2r.

[46] These were the denunciations that Licentiate Benito hid among his papers. They were not discovered until his death in March 1605, when his executor forwarded them to the inquisitors in Cuenca.

[47] On the expulsion, see García-Arenal and Wiegers, eds., *The Expulsion of the Moriscos from Spain*.

[48] Archivo Diocesano de Osma-Soria, Libro Sacramental de la Villa de Deza, 1605–46.

[49] Dadson, *Tolerance and Coexistence*, 147–82.

probably marched to the coast, put on boats, and offloaded in Muslim North Africa.

THE HOLY OFFICE OF THE INQUISITION

Clearly, many different individuals and institutions played a role in the fate of Deza's Moriscos. The Holy Office of the Inquisition was only one of them, but it was an important one. In fact, all of the documents included in this book come from an inquisitorial archive. Most of them were written by, for, or to inquisitorial officials. So, to clarify its role in the documents that follow and in the lives of the Dezanos, a closer look at this curious institution is in order.[50]

The pope granted Ferdinand and Isabella the authority to establish an inquisition in Spain in 1478, and within two years its first components were operating. Its authority extended only to baptized Christians, and initially inquisitors focused on Judaizers. Later, however, they pursued other heretics, including secret Muslims. Various regional tribunals were established and overseen by the Council of the Supreme and General Inquisition (or *Suprema*). The *Suprema* was led by an inquisitor general and composed of six members, who met as a council of state and reported to the monarch. In theory, the *Suprema* had authority over the regional tribunals, but in practice the latter tended to operate independently much of the time according to general guidelines and did not always conform to the *Suprema*'s expectations.[51]

Deza came under the jurisdiction of the tribunal at Cuenca, which projected its authority into the town in various ways. For example, Cuenca appointed an inquisitorial commissioner to oversee local affairs and receive denunciations. He was often the vicar of the parish church. The commissioner was assisted by a handful of lay *familiares*, who functioned as eyes and ears, carried messages for the Holy Office, and performed other tasks.

---

[50] The classic study of the Spanish Inquisition is Henry C. Lea, *A History of the Inquisition in Spain*, 4 vols. (New York: MacMillan, 1906–07). It should be supplemented with Henry Kamen, *The Spanish Inquisition: A Historical Revision*, 4th ed. (New Haven, CT: Yale University Press, 2014); Helen Rawlings, *The Spanish Inquisition* (Malden, MA: Blackwell, 2006); and John Edwards, *The Spanish Inquisition* (Stroud: Tempus, 1999). For a broader perspective on the Inquisition, see Francisco Bethencourt, *The Inquisition: A Global History* (Cambridge: Cambridge University Press, 2009). For a series of essays that tackle how women interacted with the Holy Office, see Mary E. Giles, ed., *Women in the Inquisition: Spain and the New World* (Baltimore: Johns Hopkins University Press, 1998).

[51] Eduardo Galván Rodríguez, *El secreto en la Inquisición española* (Las Palmas de Gran Canaria: Universidad de las Palmas de la Gran Canaria, 2001), 35–37.

In addition to these local representatives, the tribunal of Cuenca sometimes became more directly involved in local affairs. In 1569 and 1581, for example, spooked by political threats of Morisco uprisings and betrayals elsewhere in Spain, inquisitors conducted visitations of the various towns under their jurisdiction, including Deza. The first of these was conducted by Licentiate Alonso Jiménez de Reynoso and the second by Dr. Francisco de Arganda. Visitations began with the reading of an official proclamation from the pulpit at the end of Sunday mass. This Edict of Faith, as it was called, exhorted townsfolk to scour their conscience to recall any offences that they should confess. And, in case listeners were confused about precisely what should be confessed to the inquisitor, the proclamation provided a list of pertinent offences. In Deza, the Edict of Faith focused on crypto-Islamic behaviors such as fasting during Ramadan, washing frequently, avoiding pork and wine, or slaughtering animals in accordance with Islamic dietary practice. Any witness who failed to denounce such behavior automatically became excommunicated.

A few days after the Edict had been read, the inquisitor and his entourage would arrive in town, establish an audience chamber, and invite the townsfolk to "unburden their consciences." Most of those who came forward in order to comply with the proclamation did so of their own volition, but occasionally an inquisitor summoned witnesses to corroborate or comment upon evidence. While some may have been tempted to use this as an opportunity to destroy a rival or enemy by making false accusations, the Holy Office took perjury seriously and dealt harshly with anyone who interfered with its proceedings.

Those who made denunciations during the visitations were not themselves on trial; the inquisitors merely used their testimonies to gather information for possible future trials. Furthermore, even when evidence was presented against an individual, the inquisitor had to determine whether or not the offense fell under his jurisdiction. And even if it did, the denunciation rarely led to an arrest or trial. In fact, none of the denunciations received during the inquisitorial visitations to Deza in 1569 or 1581 led to full-blown trials, except for the denunciations made against Moriscos. Clearly, the inquisitors' primary interest during these visitations was identifying and addressing those who engaged in Islamic practices.

If a visitation revealed evidence of widespread heresy—perhaps a large population of crypto-Muslims, as in Deza—the Inquisition might respond by offering an Edict of Grace. This was an opportunity for those who had turned away from the Church to repent by taking advantage of a special dispensation of grace. After Reynoso's 1569 visitation, the tribunal at Cuenca decided that the best way to reform the Moriscos in Deza (and elsewhere in the region) was to offer an Edict of Grace. In 1570, the inquisitor Dr. Diego Gómez de la Madriz arrived in Deza from Cuenca, Edict in hand. Moriscos who voluntarily confessed their sins would be reconciled to the Church. They would not undergo the rigors of an inquisitorial trial, but some or all of their property might be confiscated, and they would be barred from holding civil office.

Jealous of their property and privileges, few Dezanos took the Edict. Instead, several Moriscos, including Róman Ramírez the younger, Alexo Gorgoz, and Francisco de Miranda, worked behind the scenes with the support of the Duke of Medinaceli and negotiated a new Edict of Grace directly with the king.[52] In early 1571, a revised Edict—one that waived the confiscation of goods and allowed those who took it to continue holding office—arrived, and 173 Moriscos, most of the adult population, responded. Like Ramírez, whose confession and reconciliation is included in this volume (Doc. 34), the Moriscos confessed their heresy, abjured it, and received forgiveness, although they still had to pay a fine to cover the expenses of the Holy Office. Moreover, the Edict carried a threat: anyone who took it and then relapsed into heresy could expect no further mercy.

In addition to commissioners, visitations, and Edicts of Grace, the Inquisition also projected its authority into local communities via arrests and trials. Early in the sixteenth century, a handful of Deza's Judeoconversos had been tried, but by the 1550s the Holy Office was interested primarily in the town's Moriscos. Once inquisitors had sufficient evidence, the accused were arrested, transferred to the inquisitorial jails in Cuenca, and presumed guilty. Inquisitorial trials were not necessarily the horrific affairs imagined by popular culture. They were, in fact, more careful about following proper procedure than most other law courts in early modern Europe.[53] Yet trials frequently stretched on for years, and, when defendants were believed to be withholding the truth, torture might be used.

The Inquisition's goal was *not* to send sinners to the stake. In fact, turning a heretic over to secular authorities represented a *failure*, for the Holy Office sought to return sinners to full communion with the Church and God. In fact, by the mid-sixteenth century, the Holy Office rarely condemned defendants to death. More commonly, they were penanced (*penitenciado*) or reconciled (*reconciliado*). Both of these terms indicate that the

---

[52] See Julio Fernández Nieva, "Don Diego Gómez de Lamadrid, Inqisidor apostólico en Cuenca (1566–1578) y Obispo de Badajoz (1578–1601)," *Revista de estudios extremeños* 36 (1980), 68–107.

[53] See Monter's comments in *Frontiers of Heresy*, 74.

sinner had repented of his sins and been received back into fellowship with the Church, although being reconciled usually entailed more serious punishment than being penanced. By contrast, sometimes the accused offered a solid defense, and while the Holy Office rarely returned an acquittal, such trials might be "suspended," meaning that the defendant was released but remained under suspicion. The case could be reopened at any time in the future if new evidence came to light.

Over the years, Deza produced many defendants. Between 1524 and 1611 the tribunal at Cuenca pursued about 200 trials against the town's Moriscos. Some underwent multiple trials, like Luis de Cebea the younger, who appeared before inquisitors in 1570, 1581, and 1608–11. When the inquisitor Dr. Arganda carried out his visitation to Deza in 1581, he summoned all of the Moriscos who had taken the Edict of Grace in 1570–71 and formally (albeit briefly) reexamined each of them. Yet none of these checkups led to arrests or full-blown trials. Although early in the seventeenth century some Moriscos whom the Inquisition sought fled to avoid arrest, a substantial portion of the town's Morisco population underwent some level of inquisitorial scrutiny between the 1560s and 1610s. Everyone knew someone who had been tried; most families had members who had seen the inside of Cuenca's secret jails, wore the *sanbenito*, or had been handed over to the secular authorities for execution. Every Morisco and Morisca in Deza understood that they could end up suffering the same fate. The fear must have become intense after 1607, when, in response to a new wave of denunciations made by Deza's Old Christians, the Holy Office began a renewed assault, leading to the arrest of dozens of Deza's Moriscos over the next three years. Little did they know that the fatal blow to their community would not come from inquisitors but rather from the king.

POLITICS AND THE SPANISH STATE

Many historians regard 1492 as the pivotal year in Spanish history.[54] Granada fell, the Jews were baptized, and Christopher Columbus established contact with the Americas. Subsequent decades saw Spain go from strength to strength as it drew upon the wealth of the New World to dominate in Europe and establish an empire. From 1516, the Austrian Hapsburg family gained control of the crowns of Castile and Aragon when Ferdinand and Isabella's grandson inherited their titles and ruled as King Charles I

---

[54] Several good overviews of early modern Spanish history exist. The classic is J.H. Elliott, *Imperial Spain, 1469–1716* (New York: St Martin's Press, 1964). To this can be added Henry Kamen, *Spain, 1469–1714: A Society of Conflict* (London: Routledge, 2014); Ruiz, *Spanish Society*; and James Casey, *Early Modern Spain: A Social History* (London: Routledge, 1999).

(r. 1516–56) in Spain. Charles's inheritance included not only Spain but also much of Central Europe, the Low Countries, Franche-Comté, the Duchy of Milan, southern Italy, parts of North Africa, several Mediterranean islands, and the American holdings. In 1519, he was elected Holy Roman Emperor. In the next generation, Charles's son, Philip II, expanded into Asia and Africa. He claimed the Philippines for Spain and gobbled up Portugal and its empire in 1580, when the royal house of Aviz died out.

Yet all was not rosy for the Spanish monarchy. With increased territories came new responsibilities and challenges. The sheer bureaucratic weight of managing a global empire was staggering. Charles and his descendants, especially Philip II, wore themselves out trying to defuse one crisis after another across the globe. (To help manage the burden, later monarchs relied heavily upon royal favorites, like Philip III's Duke of Lerma.) Furthermore, empire was expensive. Despite the influx of American silver the Crown was unable to manage its expenses and fell into ever-increasing cycles of debt. Inevitably and repeatedly, kings declared bankruptcy. Although doing so gave the Crown breathing room, bankruptcies only further weakened its financial health.

A major cause of increasing expenses was the economic demand of war, for Charles and his descendants faced enemies at every turn. In the Mediterranean an expansive Ottoman Empire threatened Christendom and Barbary corsairs attacked shipping and coastal settlements.[55] From the late fifteenth century, the Hapsburgs clashed with the Valois kings of France over dominance in Italy, and although Spain emerged victorious in 1559, France would rise again in the next century.

In addition to economic problems and political rivalries, Spain also faced religious challenges. The Spanish monarchs presented themselves as the great defenders of Roman Catholicism (even when they occasionally found themselves at odds with the pope himself). Early in the century, an Augustinian friar named Martin Luther (1483–1546) touched off a movement for religious reform in the Saxon town of Wittenberg. It preached justification by faith alone and subordinated the authority of the pope and Church tradition to the authority of scripture. Saxony was part of the complex federation of Germanic states known as the Holy Roman Empire, which Charles ruled as emperor between 1519 and 1556. He did his best to eliminate what he viewed as dangerous heresies, like Luther's, but

---

[55] On this topic, see Ellen G. Friedman, *Spanish Captives in North Africa in the Early Modern Age* (Madison: University of Wisconsin Press, 1986).

ultimately failed. The various Protestant groups that were born from this Reformation spread across Europe and eventually the world.[56]

Initially, the hierarchy of the Roman Church attempted to address the Protestant movement in a piecemeal fashion, but this proved inadequate as the movement grew. Therefore, in 1545 the Council of Trent was convened and met in three sessions (with long breaks in between) until 1563. There, cardinals, bishops, and theologians addressed both the theological challenges of Protestantism and the corruption and abuse that existed within the Church. The Council's decrees helped reinvigorate Roman Catholicism, which became the world's first truly global religion.[57] At Trent, Luther's theology was thoroughly rejected and, henceforth, Christianity in Western and Central Europe was divided. Spanish King Philip II urged his bishops to quickly summon regional councils and synods to implement the reforms of Trent, and (as it did in Deza) the Inquisition provided additional support to discipline the unorthodox.

In Spain, as elsewhere in Europe, Christianity became increasingly politicized during this period as confessional groups gained support from (and provided support to) one ruler or another. Although Protestantism was stillborn in Spain (thanks to the combined efforts of Church and Crown), it spread to the Netherlands, ruled first by Charles and then by his descendants. There, religious convictions mixed with anti-Spanish sentiments and sparked a revolt that saw the Dutch United Provinces fight Spain to a standstill, force a truce in 1609, and gain their independence later in the century. (In fact, hoping to overshadow the bad news of the 1609 truce with the good news of the Morisco expulsion, Philip III publicized both on the same day.) Like the Netherlands, England had been a Spanish ally earlier in the century. England's Queen Mary I (r. 1553–58) had married the future Philip II, but the union was unhappy and produced no heirs. After Mary's death, her Protestant sister Elizabeth I (r. 1558–1603) became a thorn in Spain's side. From the 1560s English privateers harried Spanish shipping and the English Crown allied with Spain's enemies. Between 1585 and 1604, the two countries were at war.

All of this cost money, and Spanish kings had little to spare. Eventually, reliance upon imported American silver weakened the Spanish economy

---

[56] Among the helpful overviews of the Reformations—both Protestant and Roman Catholic— in early modern Europe are Diarmaid MacCulloch, *The Reformation* (New York: Viking, 2003); James D. Tracy, *Europe's Reformations, 1450–1650*, 2nd ed. (Lanham, MD: Rowman & Littlefield, 2006); and Carter Lindberg, *The European Reformations*, 2nd ed. (Oxford: Wiley-Blackwell, 2010).

[57] R. Po-Chia Hsia, *The World of Catholic Renewal, 1540–1770*, 2nd ed. (Cambridge: Cambridge University Press, 2005) is a useful guide to early modern Roman Catholicism.

and disoriented society.[58] Rather than promoting industry, Spanish wealth migrated into government bonds, and increased taxation, especially in Castile, proved crippling to economic growth at the local level. By the mid-seventeenth century, the mighty Spanish empire was coming apart at the seams; twin revolts erupted in Catalonia and Portugal in 1640. Spain was still enmeshed in fighting on several fronts outside of Iberia, none of which were going particularly well. Royal finances were in shambles, the American silver mines were playing out, and the internal economy of Spain was stunted.

Philip III's decision in 1609 to expel the Moriscos, by all accounts an industrious and hardworking portion of the population, certainly did not improve Spain's economic fortunes. It would be going too far to suggest that the expulsion pushed Spain over the edge into decline, but in Deza the effects were dramatic. A fifth to a quarter of the inhabitants disappeared. A large portion of the town was abandoned, and it was not until the nineteenth century that the population fully recovered. The local economy went into decline as well. It took decades before some industries, like the Morisco-run pottery works, were producing again. In 1617, offering the loss of the Moriscos as an excuse, the town announced they were unable to pay the full amount owed in taxes and requested a reduction; similar petitions were still being made almost 50 years later.[59]

SOURCES AND TRANSLATION

The documents in this book are drawn from manuscripts housed in the inquisitorial section of the Diocesan Archive at Cuenca. They were chosen because they cast light on life in early modern Spain, especially the nature of relations between Moriscos and Old Christians at the local level. They also provide a window onto early modern Spaniards' interactions with powerful institutions, here especially the Inquisition. To that end, seven groups of sources, dating to between 1569 and 1611, have been included:

1. Documents 1–33: The visitation of Licentiate Reynoso (1569), comprising 33 inquisitorial interviews.
2. Document 34: Román Ramírez the younger's confession for the Edict of Grace (1571).

---

[58] On the destabilizing effects of American bullion, see Elvira Vilches, *New World Gold: Cultural Anxiety and Monetary Disorder in Early Modern Spain* (Chicago: University of Chicago Press, 2010). The classic study of Spanish economic history is Jaime Vicens Vives, *An Economic History of Spain* (Princeton, NJ: Princeton University Press, 1969).

[59] Manuel Danvila y Collado, ed., *Actas de las Cortes de Castilla*, 61 vols. (Madrid, 1877–2004), 29:282 and 61:17.

3. Documents 35–72: The visitation of Dr. Arganda (1581), including 38
    inquisitorial interviews.
4. Documents 73–76: Dr. Arganda's examination of Román Ramírez the
    younger and his first wife, Angela de Miranda (1581).
5. Document 77: The final sentence of Román Ramírez the younger and
    a report of the auto-da-fe in Toledo where his bones were consigned
    to the flames (1600).
6. Documents 78–86: Nine letters written from Cuenca by a group
    of incarcerated Moriscos to their friends and family back home
    (1611).
7. Documents 87–92: A series of documents detailing the efforts of
    several of Deza's Moriscos to avoid serving on the royal galleys
    (1611).

These documents span a period of more than four decades and provide
the reader with not only a snapshot of early modern life but also a series of
images that change over time. Although all of the sources are tied to the
actions of the Inquisition in one way or another, multiple genres are represented: letters, notes of apology, reports, legal depositions, denunciations,
confessions, declarations of sentence, and so on.

While several of the letters were written by Deza's Moriscos, inquisitorial officials penned most of the documents. Yet much of what they set
down purports to be an accurate record of the words spoken by other
people: witnesses or defendants. Those witnesses and defendants, in turn,
often repeated statements they claimed to have heard from others, sometimes even third-hand. Even so, these records do not represent a verba-
tim account of what was said. Early modern scribes—while good at their
jobs—did not have audio recorders or stenotypes. They frequently sum-
marized statements and occasionally made mistakes. Ostensibly, they
intended to create accurate accounts of what they heard, but no doubt they
were sometimes influenced by their own assumptions or prejudices. These
biases may well have influenced the official record of the testimony.

Yet simply dismissing these sources on this account would be overly
hasty. Once recorded, statements were read back to witnesses or defendants, who acknowledged them to be a faithful record of the words they
had spoken. The testimony of witnesses had to be confirmed before a trial
could begin—sometimes years after the testimony was originally given—
in case a witness decided to make a retraction or emendation. Even confessions made under torture were not simply accepted. They had to be
confirmed by the defendant after he or she had recovered. Because of these
complex issues, scholars remain divided on how much trust to place in

inquisitorial documents as historical sources. Readers will need to judge for themselves in what ways they are useful for studying the past.[60]

Whenever practical, this volume provides translations of archival sources in their entirety. This is the case with the 1569 and 1581 visitations. Román Ramírez's 1571 confession and the 1581 examinations of Ramírez and Angela de Miranda are also complete. At over 260 folios, Ramírez's 1599 trial was too long to include a translation of the entire source, so only the final summary and sentencing are given here. This provides an overview of the Inquisition's perspective on Ramírez's case and was the document read before the king and queen at the 1600 auto-da-fe in Toledo. Likewise, of 35 extant letters written by the Moriscos of Deza from Cuenca's royal jails, only nine are included here.

All of the documents in this book have been translated into English from Spanish (with occasional Latin or Arabic phrases) from previously untranscribed archival manuscripts. The originals contain many archaic, repetitive, and clumsy speech patterns, making translation difficult. In preparing this collection for an English-language audience, I have aimed at readability rather than wooden literalism. This has meant breaking up long sentences, inserting punctuation, imposing paragraph breaks, clarifying pronominal referents, and smoothing out verb usage. In the documents, the information enclosed within parentheses *is original* although the parentheses themselves are not. Words or phrases in brackets are *not original* but have been added to clarify the meaning of the text. While, unfortunately, all of this tinkering disconnects readers from the flow and form of the original, any other approach would have made reading the documents truly daunting.

Occasionally, the author of a document made grammatical mistakes or lost his train of thought. In such cases, I have translated the passage

---

[60] Some important efforts to come to grips with this question are Carlo Ginzburg, "The Inquisitor as Anthropologist," in his *Clues, Myths, and the Historical Method* (Baltimore: Johns Hopkins University Press, 1989), 156–64; John H. Arnold, "The Historian as Inquisitor: The Ethics of Interrogating Subaltern Voices," *Rethinking History* 2, no. 3 (1998): 379–86; and the introduction to Andrea Del Col, ed., *Domenico Scandella Known as Mennochio: His Trial before the Inquisition (1583–1599)* (Binghamton, NY: MRTS, 1996). Examples of historians using inquisitorial documents as historical sources include Carlo Ginzburg, *The Cheese and the Worms: The Cosmos of a Sixteenth Century Miller* (Baltimore: Johns Hopkins University Press, 1980) and *Night Battles: Witchcraft and Agrarian Cults in the Sixteenth and Seventeenth Centuries* (New York: Penguin, 1983); Richard L. Kagan, *Lucrecia's Dreams: Politics and Prophecy in Sixteenth-Century Spain* (Berkeley: University of California Press, 1990); and Sarah T. Nalle, *God in La Mancha: Religious Reform and the People of Cuenca* (Berkeley: University of California Press, 1992) and *Mad for God: Bartolomé Sánchez, the Secret Messiah of Cardenete* (Charlottesville: University of Virginia Press, 2001).

according to its meaning (as I understand it) rather than preserving the error, unless it was possible to preserve both. In a very few instances, the meaning of a passage is deeply obscure, and these have been indicated in a footnote. Usually the obscurity is a result of grammatical errors in the original document, an illegible or missing word, or a ripped page. But occasionally the meaning of the passage, which presumably was understandable at that time and in that place, is simply lost here and now.

Sometimes early modern authors edited documents after their initial composition. They underlined words, crossed out errors, and inserted words or phrases. These have been preserved in the translated text. In the visitation records, inquisitorial scribes occasionally included notes in the margins or at the bottom of pages. These have been preserved as well and are indicated by typographic symbols (†, ††, §, ‡) that draw the reader's attention to the notes at the end of the pertinent section. Numbered footnotes, by contrast, represent my own efforts to clarify obscure references, provide context, and tie sources together. They are not original to the documents.

The Cast of Characters, which follows this introduction, provides short biographies for many of the individuals who appear in the book. Those about whom we know virtually nothing (besides what is in the translated documents) and those whose role is tangential to the drama have been omitted. The information for the entries has been cobbled together from a wide range of archival sources in order to provide as many details as possible. The names of those included in the Cast of Characters appear in bold at their first appearance in each of the primary source documents.

Cast of Characters

Following each entry is a list of numbers indicating in which of the primary source documents the individual appears.

ALEJOS, THE SON OF ANTÓN DE DEZA: *See Deza, Alejos de.*

ALIGER, ALONSO (c. 1541–bef. 1581): A Morisco healer and potter from Deza who married the Morisca Ana de Arévalo in about 1565. In 1570, he was arrested by the Holy Office for Islamic activities and reconciled to the Church but condemned to three years' rowing in the royal galleys. He does not seem to have survived his time at the oar and was certainly dead before 1581. He was **Luis de Cieli**'s father-in-law and the grandfather of **Lope** and **Juan de Cieli**. (Docs. 7, 9, 12.)

ALIGER, GABRIEL (DE) (c. 1531–c. 1600): A Morisco muleteer and farmer from Deza. He was the elder brother of **Alonso Aliger** and married three times. Gabriel took advantage of the Edict of Grace in 1571 and was reexamined by **Dr. Arganda** as part of his 1581 visitation. He served on Deza's town council in 1581 and 1591. (Docs. 7, 9, 12, 45, 48, 68.)

ALMANZORRE, ANA DE (1541–bef. 1581): A Morisca native of Deza who married **Mateo Romero the younger** in 1567. Her son, Juan, was born in 1568 and by the following summer she was again pregnant. She was tried in 1570 by the Holy Office based on information that came to light during **Licentiate Reynoso**'s 1569 visitation. In June of 1570, she was reconciled to the Church and sentenced to be incarcerated for three years. Her goods were confiscated and she was ordered to wear the *sanbenito*. Having demonstrated repentance, humility, and Christian devotion, Ana was released in 1573 and permitted to remove her penitential habit, but she survived her release by only a few years. At her trial, Ana gave her birth date as 1547 or 1548, which would have made her just older than her husband, but the parish records indicate that she was actually born in 1541. (Docs. 10, 11, 14.)

1

ALMORAVI, ANA (b. 1521): A Morisca who lived in Deza for about a dozen years. She was born to a Muslim family in Terrer (Aragon) and was baptized in 1526, when the Aragonese Mudéjares were converted. A first marriage produced three children but she had only stillbirths from her second marriage, in 1552, to **Mateo Romero the elder**. Ana and Mateo moved to Deza in 1558 and amassed some wealth. Ana traveled around the region selling goat cheese and milk. She and her family were in the process of returning to Aragon when **Licentiate Reynoso** arrived in Deza. In September of 1570, she was arrested in Sestrica (Aragon) for Islamic activities and placed in the custody of the Holy Office in Cuenca. In February of 1571 she was penitenced. Her punishment included perpetual incarceration in Cuenca and wearing a *sanbenito* for the rest of her life. (Docs. 10–11, 14, 34.)

ALTOPICA, JUANES DE (c. 1495–1573): Raised in Deza, he became both town vicar and the local inquisitorial representative around 1520. Altopica was forced out of the vicarage in 1534 by a group of his own parishioners who saw him as too aggressive in persecuting local Judeoconversos, especially those who belonged to the foremost families in town. His enemies charged him, among other things, with carrying a sword "day and night," failing to conduct masses for the souls of the dead (although he had been paid "a lot of money" to do so), and having an affair with a Morisca midwife. Despite losing the vicarage and, eventually, his inquisitorial appointment as well, Altopica remained active as a local cleric, confessing sinners and denouncing heretics almost to the very end of his life. (Docs. 5, 73, 75–76.)

ANA, THE WIFE OF LOPE DE DEZA: *See Arellano, Ana de.*

ARCOS, FRANCISCO DE (c. 1548–aft. 1611): A Morisco born near Ágreda who was sent to Deza when he was eight years old to learn to read from local cleric **Gonzalo de Santa Clara**. Like his father, Francisco was a blacksmith. In 1570, he was arrested by the Holy Office after being implicated in Islamic activities by **Lope de Obezar**, who was denounced during **Licentiate Reynoso**'s visitation. In December of that year, Francisco confessed his sins and was reconciled to the Church. As penance, he was sentenced to serve three years rowing in the galleys, but his goods were not confiscated thanks to the special Edict of Grace brokered by the Moriscos. When he returned to Deza, he married Juana López and fathered at least five children. By 1609, his family had moved to Mazaterón, apparently at the request of the Duke of Medinaceli, to work the forges. He was denounced again early in the seventeenth century but the record has been lost and he does not seem to have been arrested. Francisco was the older brother of Lope de Arcos, Deza's blacksmith and a leader in the Morisco community after the death of **Alexo Gorgóz**. (Doc. 78.)

ARELLANO, ANA DE (1549–1607): A Morisca from Deza who married **Lope de Deza** (aka Pascual de la Pituerta) in about 1567 in the town of Aguilar, near Ágreda. She and her husband raised five children. She took advantage of the Edict of Grace in the early 1570s and in 1581 was reexamined by **Dr. Arganda** during his visitation. She died in December of 1607, just as the final inquisitorial assault against Deza's Moriscos was heating up. (Docs. 28, 68.)

ARÉVALO, ANA DE (1542–aft. 1594): A Morisca from Deza who married **Alonso Aliger** around 1565. She bore three sons—Bartolomé, Gabriel, and Luis Aliger. The eldest two were unmarried and still living at home in 1594. She does not appear ever to have been investigated by the Holy Office. (Docs. 7, 9, 12.)

ARGANDA, DR. FRANCISCO DE (d. 1600): Served as the prosecuting attorney (*fiscal*) for the tribunal of the Holy Office at Seville before being named an inquisitor at Cuenca in the 1570s. Arganda was no moderate when it came to Moriscos. By 1583, he was arguing that more intense persecution—including capital punishment for first offenses—was the best course. By 1584, he was a canon of the cathedral at Alcalá de Henares and in 1592 he became a canon of the Cathedral of Toledo, although he continued to serve as an inquisitor until his death. His strength seems to have waned toward the end, as he was only intermittently involved in **Román Ramírez the younger**'s trial. (Docs. 35–75.)

BAPTISTA, AGUSTÍN DE (c. 1504–aft. 1581): A Morisco from Deza who was hard of hearing. He married **Isabel de Baptista** (sometimes known as Isabel de la Huerta) and lived on the *Corrillo*. Agustín knew how to sign his name but not how to read; he worked as a healer and specialized in poultices. The Holy Office tried him in 1570 for Islamizing, and in 1573 he was penitenced with a sentence of perpetual imprisonment in the secret jails. By that time, being "old, deaf, and disabled," he found it difficult even to make the journey out of his cell to attend religious services. (Docs. 27–29, 42, 53.)

BAPTISTA, FRANCISCA DE (1554–aft. 1611): The wife of **Luis de Cebea the younger**. She bore five sons, among them **Juan de Cebea**. She took the

Edict of Grace in 1571 and was reexamined in 1581 during **Dr. Arganda**'s visitation. In 1608, believing that she had relapsed into heresy, the Holy Office ordered her arrest. No information exists regarding her fate. (Docs. 7, 9, 12, 68, 80–81.)

BAPTISTA, FRANCISCO DE (THE YOUNGER) (c. 1551–bef. 1594): A Morisco farmer from Deza sometimes called Francisco de Gonzalo, after his father, Gonzalo de Baptista. He took the Edict of Grace offered to the town's Moriscos and was reexamined during **Dr. Arganda**'s 1581 visitation. Francisco married **Luisa Vizcaina**, who outlived him. (Docs. 24, 27–30, 67.)

BAPTISTA, ISABEL DE (c. 1505–bef. 1581): A Morisca originally from Ágreda and sometimes known as Isabel de la Huerta. She married **Agustín de Baptista** in around 1526, but the couple was childless. They lived in Deza on the *Corrillo*. (Docs. 28, 42, 53.)

BARBA [DE GUZMÁN], *MOSÉN* JERÓNIMO (1539–1612): One of Deza's clerics and a native of the town. He was active in the parish church (keeping records and frequently acting as a witness to baptismal ceremonies) as early as 1556, when he was identified as "Jerónimo Barba, student." His name begins to appear with the title *mosén* in the records from 1561. He probably began his studies in theology at the University of Valencia in 1565 and continued there until at least 1570. Although he died in Deza, no record of his ministry there exists between 1570 and his death. (Docs. 6–8.)

BENITO, MIGUEL (c. 1520–91): Held the office of vicar in Deza from 1556 until his death. From 1580, he shared the post with his nephew, **Licentiate Miguel Benito**. He was also the local commissioner of the Holy Office from the 1570s until his death, and he carried out his duty rigorously. (Docs. 7, 36, 40, 60, 62–66, 73, 75.)

BENITO, LICENTIATE MIGUEL (d. 1605): The nephew of **Miguel Benito** and one of Deza's priests. His title indicates university training beyond the bachelor's degree. He ministered in Deza from 1580, at which time he shared the post of vicar with his uncle. Upon the latter's death in 1591 Licentiate Benito became vicar in his own right. He also inherited the title of commissioner of the Holy Office but proved to be much less rigid than his predecessor. After his death, the local inquisitorial scribe discovered that Licentiate Benito had hidden several denunciations against local Moriscos rather than forwarding them to the tribunal at Cuenca. The scribe claimed that Licentiate Benito had been in the habit of accepting "presents" from the Moriscos. (Docs. 7, 40, 60, 62–63.)

BLASCO, MARTÍN (b. c. 1541): An Old Christian baker originally from Villaroya de la Sierra (Aragon). Martín lived in Deza for about five and a half years, during which time he worked the public oven located in the Upper Neighborhood. By 1581, he had moved back to Villaroya. (Docs. 57, 68.)

BORQUE, FRANCISCA (b. c. 1540): The widow of **Gonzalo Martínez the elder** and a citizen of Deza. (Docs. 45, 59.)

CASTILLO, GERÓNIMA DEL (c. 1530–1583): An Old Christian citizen of Deza. Married Juan Morales, a farmer, around 1550 and bore at least three children, the first in 1552. (Doc. 4.)

CASTRO, JUAN (c. 1520–c. 1572): The scribe of the town council in 1566. Married to María Morales. Although they were not technically members of the lower nobility, his wife was sometimes granted the honorific title of doña, which suggests the high esteem accorded to the family. Intriguingly, he seems to have interacted socially with Deza's Moriscos, not only attending their weddings but also standing as godfather for many of their children. (Doc. 9.)

CEBEA, JUAN DE (c. 1588–aft. 1611): A Morisco from Deza who worked as a farm laborer and a transporter of goods. A son of **Luis de Cebea the younger** and **Francisca de Baptista**, he was still unmarried in 1608. Juan was arrested by the Holy Office for Islamic activities not long after his older brothers, **Luis** and Francisco. He was reconciled to the Church in 1611 and sentenced to serve three years on the king's galleys. Despite his efforts to have his sentence commuted, he began his service later that year. His fate is unknown. (Docs. 81, 87–89.)

CEBEA, LUIS DE (THE ELDER) (c. 1524–1609): A Morisco from Deza. His father died when he was very young and his mother in about 1534. Luis was apprenticed to a cobbler named Lope López until he was 17 at which point he and **Gabriel de Saleros** spent three years as soldiers. When Luis returned to town around 1544, he married **María de Hortubia** and went into service with the **Commander Martín Fernández**. He worked on Fernández's estates for 29 years before retiring. He took the Edict of Grace offered to Deza's Moriscos and was examined during **Dr. Arganda's** 1581 visitation. Cebea was arrested by the Holy Office in 1607 on the basis of testimony offered by an informant within the secret jails and the confessions of other Moriscos. He was tried as a relapsed heretic. In March of 1609, he died from natural causes in the inquisitorial jails of Cuenca. His trial was concluded posthumously and, two years later, Luis's bones were exhumed and consigned to the flames. **Luis de Cebea the younger** is his son. (Docs. 7, 9, 12, 24, 68.)

CEBEA, LUIS DE (THE YOUNGER) (1547–1611): A literate Morisco from Deza and the son of **Luis de Cebea the elder**. He was tried as a heretic in 1570, just after becoming engaged to **Francisca de Baptista**. He was reconciled to the Church but given a penance of three years' rowing in the king's galleys. Thus, in 1571, he participated in the Battle of Lepanto but survived and eventually returned to Deza, where he married Francisca. He was reexamined by **Dr. Arganda** in 1581 during his visitation and arrested again in 1608 on the basis of testimony given by an inquisitorial informant and the confessions of other Moriscos. The Holy Office tried him as a relapsed heretic. He was examined, tortured, confirmed guilty, and relaxed to the secular arm in May of 1611. His public execution followed at an auto-da-fe held in Cuenca on Trinity Sunday of that year. According to one report, he had amassed a secret fortune of over 2,000 ducats by the time of his death. He is the father of **Luis (the youngest)**, Francisco, and **Juan de Cebea**, all of whom were arrested by the Holy Office in the early seventeenth century. (Docs. 7, 9, 12, 68, 80.)

CEBEA, LUIS DE (THE YOUNGEST) (c. 1580–aft. 1611): A Morisco from Deza and the eldest son of **Luis de Cebea the younger** and **Francisca de Baptista**. He married María de Hortubia (not to be confused with his grandmother of the same name), the daughter of **Juan de Hortubia** and **Isabel de Liñán**. In 1608, the Holy Office arrested him. Around the same time his wife gave birth to a daughter named María. He was eventually reconciled to the Church, sentenced to the galleys, and transferred to Cuenca's royal jail. His efforts to have his galley sentence commuted proved unsuccessful, and his fate is unknown. (Doc. 80–81, 85, 87–89.)

CERDA, DON GASTÓN DE LA (c. 1547–c. 1562): The second son of **Duke Juan de la Cerda**. Don Gastón was captured by the Turks at the Battle of Djerba off the Tunisian coast in May 1560 when a fleet under the command of his father was brought to grief by the Ottoman admiral Piali Pasha (c. 1515–78). Legend has it that don Gastón was taken prisoner, held in Constantinople, and died around 1562. (Doc. 13.)

CERDA, DON JUAN LUIS DE LA (1544–94): The eldest son of **Juan de la Cerda** and brother of **don Gastón de la Cerda**. He became the fourth marquis of Cogolludo in 1552 and, upon the death of his father, inherited the duchy of Medinaceli (r. 1575–94). He served the king of Spain as an ambassador to Portugal. In Deza, he finished building the House of the Duke, which his father had begun, and rented it and its gardens out to **Román Ramírez the younger**. (Doc. 41.)

CERDA, DON JUAN DE LA (c. 1515–75): The third marquis of Cogolludo (r. 1536–44) and fourth duke of Medinaceli (r. 1544–75). In the 1550s, he began construction of a large house and gardens in Deza, just north of the town center. He served as viceroy of Sicily from 1557 until 1564 or 1565. In that capacity, he commanded the Spanish vessels in a multinational crusading enterprise that attacked Tripoli. He was later defeated by the Ottoman admiral Piali Pasha (c. 1515–78) at the Battle of Djerba (1560), where his son, **don Gastón de la Cerda**, was captured. Later, he was made viceroy of Navarre and, in 1570, the head of the household of the Spanish Queen, Anne of Austria (1549–80). (Doc. 13.)

CIELI, JUAN DE (1539–1607): A Morisco bricklayer and carpenter from Deza. He was **Luis de Cieli**'s younger brother. Beginning at age 10 or 11, Juan spent two years as a soldier in Daroca (Aragon) with **Íñigo de Hortubia**. After returning to Deza, he spent four and a half years learning to work with "plaster and wood" from an otherwise unknown New Christian named Luis Frances. A journeyman period saw him working at jobs around the region, both in Castile and Aragon, before finally settling down in Deza. In May 1568, he married Catalina de Liñán (d. 1606), the daughter of **Luis de Liñán**. They had several children, three of whom reached adulthood. Following the accusations made against him during **Licentiate Reynoso**'s 1569 visitation, Juan was tried by the inquisitorial tribunal at Cuenca and reconciled to the Church in 1570. As penance for his sins, he was sent to row in the royal galleys for a period of three years. He may well have participated in the Battle of Lepanto in 1571. He survived, returned to Deza, and was examined by the Holy Office a second time during **Dr. Arganda**'s 1581 visitation. (Docs. 26, 79.)

CIELI, LOPE DE (THE YOUNGER) (1557–aft. 1610): A literate Morisco from Deza who made sandals and wove canvas but who also had acquired a good deal of local land and luxury goods. He was the son of **Luis de Cieli** and María de Ochoa and he married Gerónima la Corazona in about 1586. As an adolescent, he confessed to having Islamized and took the Edict of

Grace offered to Deza's Moriscos. Later, he joined a local confraternity dedicated to the Most Holy Trinity and acted as its majordomo in 1597. In the same year Lope served on the town council as procurator. In June of 1608, he went to Cuenca to present a petition to the Holy Office on behalf of the Morisco Lope de Hortubia but found himself arrested and incarcerated instead on the basis of testimony offered against him by an inquisitorial informant and the confessions of other Moriscos. In 1610, he was reconciled to the Holy Office for Islamizing. He was punished with perpetual incarceration and the wearing of a *sanbenito*. That same year, he petitioned the Inquisition, was granted release, and was allowed to remove his *sanbenito* in order to locate his wife and son, Luis, and accompany them into exile. (Docs. 54–56.)

CIELI, LUIS DE (c. 1535–c. 1600): A Morisco canvas weaver from Deza, Luis is the brother of **Juan de Cieli**. He fathered at least nine children (including **Lope de Cieli**) and was husband to three successive wives: Agueda Romera, María de Ochoa, and Ana de Pazencia (also known as Ana de Deza). Around 1569, he moved to the Kingdom of Aragon for a time and lived in Terrer. He later returned to Deza, where he died. He appears never to have been investigated by the Holy Office. (Docs. 7, 48, 54–55.)

CONTRERAS, ANA DE (c. 1523–aft. 1581): A Morisca from Deza and the widow of Leonis de Saleros. She took the Edict of Grace offered to Deza's Morsicos and was reexamined by **Dr. Arganda** during his 1581 visitation. **Juan de Contreras** is her brother. (Doc. 50.)

CONTRERAS, JUAN DE (THE YOUNGER) (c. 1530–72): A Morisco from Deza who described himself as a farmer and wayfarer. He was the brother of **Ana de Contreras** and married to María de Molina from Ariza (Aragon). As a boy, he learned both Muslim prayers from Moriscos in Aragon and how to read and write from **Gonzalo de Santa Clara**, one of Deza's priests. The Holy Office tried Juan for Islamizing, first in 1558 and then again in 1570–71. The first time, he was reconciled (along with his wife) and ordered to wear the *sanbenito* for two years; the second time he was handed over to the secular arm. He was executed in July 1572. (Doc. 17.)

CORAZÓN, JUAN (1579–aft. 1616): A Morisco native of Deza who was the grandson of **Old Fadrique** and married into the Guerrero family. He described himself as "a poor day laborer who earns a *real* where he can find it." When he was a boy, his parents put him into service with his paternal granduncle, **Alexo Gorgoz**, with whom he lived until the latter's death in

1599. For his good service, Alexo left Juan about eight acres of land (most of which Juan sold) as well as 25 ducats to be paid in 1609 from property leased to the town. After Gorgoz's death, Juan moved into his mother's house and was soon joined there by his bride, Ana. The three lived there together until his mother's death c. 1607. The Holy Office arrested Juan in 1608 while he was delivering a cache of letters to Cuenca. After more than two years' imprisonment, he finally broke under torture in late 1610 and confessed to Islamic activities. He was reconciled to the Church and set to row at the oars of the royal galleys for a period of three years. Yet it was not until March of 1616 that he made landfall in southern Spain and was mustered out. He was thereafter incarcerated in the city of Cartagena's public jails, where he "suffered great need," before being released to comply with the royal order of expulsion. (Docs. 87–89.)

CUEVA, DR. CLAUDIO DE LA (d. 1611): Having formerly been an inquisitor at the tribunal of the Holy Office in Galicia, Claudio de la Cueva was appointed to the tribunal at Cuenca in May 1606. He took possession of the office the following month. By the early 1610s his health was failing, and from February 1611 he rarely attended inquisitorial audiences. He died in April of that year. (Doc. 88.)

DEZA, ALEJOS DE (d. 1584): A Morisco from Deza. **Antón de Deza**'s brother. Their father was also Antón (born c. 1531). Alejos married María de Truillo (or de Guzmán) around 1560. In 1570, the Holy Office began to gather testimony for a case against him, and in the summer of 1570 the prosecuting attorney requested Alejos's arrest and the confiscation of his goods. He was permitted to take the Edict of Grace offered that year and his trial was suspended. By 1581, Alejos had moved to Ariza (Aragon), but he returned to Deza soon thereafter and died a poor man in 1584. (Docs. 46, 67, 72.)

DEZA, ANTÓN DE (1556–1606): A Morisco from Deza. He was the son of Antón de Deza (born c. 1531) and the son-in-law of Juan de Fadrique (alias Juan de San Juan). His wife, María, bore him one daughter, who died young. Antón's wife predeceased him in 1602 and he died a poor man in Deza four years later. (Docs. 46, 68, 72.)

DEZA, JUAN DE (d. 1580): The son of **Miguel de Deza** and Gerónima la Manceba. Juan was a farmer from Deza and one of the wealthiest Moriscos in town. He confessed to Islamizing and was reconciled to the Church in 1571 by taking advantage of the Edict of Grace. He was married twice, first to María de Baptista and then to Ana de Hortubia (1536–c. 1590). A "Juan de Deza" served on Deza's town council in 1553, 1559, 1562, 1566, and 1574 and as magistrate in 1563, 1568, 1572, 1576, 1579 (although some of the earlier dates may refer to an older man by the same name). (Docs. 7, 57.)

DEZA, LOPE DE (1539–1611): A Morisco from Deza who worked as a muleteer and may have been reconciled by the Holy Office before 1569. As a younger man, he went by the names Lope del Sol and Pascual de la Pituerta—the latter because his father was named Pascual and his wife, **Ana de Arellano**, was club-footed (*pies tuertos*). He confessed to Islamic activities and received the 1571 Edict of Grace. **Dr. Arganda** examined him during the 1581 visitation. In 1608, Lope was arrested by the Holy Office on the basis of testimony offered by an inquisitorial informant and the confessions of other Moriscos. He was found guilty, charged as a relapsed heretic, and in May 1611 was handed over to the secular arm and executed. (Docs. 7, 9, 12, 18, 27–29, 57, 68.)

DEZA, MIGUEL DE (d. c. 1571): A Morisco from Deza. The father of **Juan de Deza** and **Alexo Gorgoz**'s father-in-law. He was married twice, first to Gerónima la Manceba in 1539 and then to Ines Burgueña in 1560. (Doc. 27.)

DEZA, ROMÁN DE (d. c. 1588): A Morisco from Deza. He is the son of Pascual de Deza (d. c. 1562) and Ana Ramírez (d. c. 1586). Román and his wife, Isabel de Miranda (d. 1608), had four children. He was involved in the illegal smuggling of livestock across the Aragonese border in the early 1570s. The judge, one Dr. Camargo, ordered Román arrested. Apparently, however, **Román Ramírez the younger**, his brother-in-law, was accidentally taken in his place. Román de Deza and **Juan de Deza** were first cousins (as well as brothers-in-law). (Doc. 73.)

DONOSO, JUAN (c. 1521–aft. 1584): An Old Christian miller from Deza. Married to María Escudero (d. 1584) and father to **Miguel Donoso**. (Docs. 47, 69–70.)

DONOSO, MATEO (b. c. 1536): An Old Christian tailor. Born in Deza but, in 1569, a citizen of Embid de Ariza about seven miles south of Deza in the Kingdom of Aragon. **Juan Donoso**'s brother. (Doc. 1.)

DONOSO, MIGUEL (b. 1561): An Old Christian shepherd from Deza. The son of **Juan Donoso** and María Escudera. (Docs. 47, 69–70.)

DUKE OF MEDINACELI, THE: *See Cerda, Juan de la.*

ERAS, FRANCISCO DE LAS (b. c. 1528): An Old Christian farmer. He married Isabel de Majan in 1551 and they had eight children before 1569. Francisco was raised in Deza but by 1569 moved to Cihuela (just south of Deza in Castile). A man by the same name held a position on the town council in 1562 and 1582, which may indicate that he later returned to town. But the de las Eras (or sometimes Desteras) family was large and the 1582 referent could be another person. (Doc. 3).

ESCUDERO, FRANCISCO (1538–1603): An Old Christian shepherd from Deza. He married Madalena Alcázar and fathered at least one child, a daughter named Francisca. He died poor in Deza. (Docs. 47, 69–70.)

ESTRADA, FRAY LUIS DE (c. 1518–88): A learned Cistercian monk who served as abbot of the monastery at Huerta from 1557 to 1559 and then as rector of the College of San Bernardo at the University of Alcalá de Henares from 1560. He collaborated with Arias Montano on the creation of the famous Plantin Polyglot Bible (or *Biblia Regia*), a project that occupied them between 1568 and 1573. He returned to serve as abbot of Huerta during the 1570s and early 1580s. (Doc. 58.)

FADRIQUE, OLD (d. bef. 1581): A Morisco native of Deza and the maternal grandfather of **Juan Corazón**. He was a "poor day laborer" but was also described as a potter. He married María la Marquesa with whom he had at least three children. Fadrique took advantage of the 1571 Edict of Grace. He married his son Juan de San Juan (or de Fadrique) to Ana de Cebea, daughter of **Luis de Cebea the elder**. (Docs. 7, 9, 12, 43.)

FAJARDO, RODRIGO (d. aft. 1611): A Morisco from Tarancón, 50 miles southeast of Madrid in Castile. Rodrigo was a *morisco granadino*, that is a Morisco who hailed from Granada in southern Spain. The government relocated him to Tarancón after the failed Morisco uprising that broke out in the late 1560s. His first contact with Deza's Moriscos appears to have occurred while they were in inquisitorial custody. He attempted to have his galley sentence commuted in 1611 but was unsuccessful. (Docs. 87–89.)

FERNÁNDEZ, FRAY MARTÍN (**"THE COMMANDER"**) (c. 1498–c. 1572): An Old Christian cleric in Deza who served as the town's inquisitorial commissioner during **Licentiate Reynoso**'s 1569 visitation. A member of the Old Christian Fernández-Abarca family, his father and brother served as wardens and chief magistrates of Deza. As the younger son, Martín became a professed member of the Knights Hospitaller, a medieval military order in which he held the rank of Commander of Almazán. Martín was supported financially by an endowed chaplaincy in the town's parish church for which he was made the "perpetual chaplain." (Docs. 5, 17–18, 27, 34.)

GARCÍA, MIGUEL (c. 1538–93): An Old Christian apothecary who held the office of inquisitorial *familiar* in Deza from at least 1571. He sat on Deza's town council in 1580 and 1581 and held the office of magistrate in 1584 and again in 1592. (Doc. 43.)

GARCÍA, PABLO (fl. 1560s–70s): A native of Cuenca who acted as an inquisitorial "Notary of the Secret" for the Tribunal of Cuenca during **Licentiate Reynoso**'s visitation to Deza in 1569. García first gained the office in 1560 and worked with the tribunal of Seville until, in 1563, he transferred to Cuenca. He temporarily was transferred to the tribunals at Toledo (1565), Llerena (1570), and Barcelona (1574), before being promoted to secretary of the *Suprema*. Working with multiple tribunals provided him with the experience necessary to write *Orden de processar* (1568), an important and frequently reprinted treatise, which helped reconcile the methods and procedures of the various tribunals. (Docs. 1–7, 9–33.)

GÓMEZ DE LA MADRIZ, DR. DIEGO (d. 1601): Born in Palencia and of noble lineage, he studied law at the University of Salamanca. As a young man, de la Madriz (or de Lamadrid) served as the *visitador* for Archbishop Pedro Guerrero of Granada. In 1566, he was made an inquisitor at Cuenca where he served until 1578. In that year, he was named bishop elect of Lima, Peru, but never crossed the ocean. Instead, in June of that year, thanks to the intercession of Queen Anne, King Philip II gave de la Madriz the bishopric of Badajoz. He remained in that office for 22 years, a model reforming bishop. (Doc. 34.)

GONZALO, FRANCISCO DE: *See Baptista, Francisco de.*

GORGOZ, ALEXO (c. 1534–99): A wealthy and influential leader in Deza's Morisco community and the younger brother of **Gerónimo Gorgoz**. Along with **Román Ramírez the younger** and **Francisco de Miranda**, Alexo was instrumental in brokering the 1571 Edict of Grace, which Alexo took after confessing to Islamic activities. He sat on Deza's town council in 1572, 1575, 1577, 1578, 1581, 1583, 1585, 1593, and 1598; he held the office of magistrate three times. Beginning in the early 1580s, he served as the parish churchwarden (*mayordomo de la iglesia*), in which capacity he loaned 400 ducats to the church building fund, a sum he forgave at his death. He married at least twice, the second time (in 1586) to a woman half his age. At his death, he possessed a substantial estate that included a wide variety of moveable property, business interests, and real estate. A portion of the estate went to his grandnephew, **Juan Corazón**, who had served him for years, but much of his wealth was joined to a pious work that his brother had established at his own death. Together, the endowments of the brothers Gorgoz continued to work into the nineteenth century, providing funds to help establish poor and orphaned girls in marriage. (Doc. 43.)

GORGOZ, GERÓNIMO (c. 1520–78): A leader in Deza's Morisco community and the elder brother of **Alexo Gorgoz**. He married Ana de Mancebo as a young man. Although they baptized a daughter named Catalina in 1546 and probably had at least one other child, they all died "very young." He was one of the few Moriscos who took the original 1570 Edict of Grace (although he does not appear to have been heavily fined or barred from office). Perhaps he felt obliged to do so since he was serving as town magistrate at the time. He held that office again in 1575 and additionally sat on the town council in various capacities in 1560, 1565, 1572, and 1577. Gerónimo claimed to have learned about Islam from one *Mosén* Sancho, an Aragonese Morisco. As he grew in wealth and influence, Gerónimo became increasingly cautious about practicing Islam overtly. At his death, he established a pious work though the parish church that provided dowries for poor and orphaned Moriscas. (Docs. 24, 27, 29.)

GUERRERO, FRANCISCO (1543–91): A Morisco from Deza who worked as an agricultural laborer and transporter of goods. He was married to María de Medina and was the son of Lope Guerrero and María la Ollera (alias María de Sepulveda). **Lope Guerrero the younger** is his son. (Doc. 27.)

GUERRERO, LOPE (THE YOUNGER) (1571–aft. 1611): A literate Morisco from Deza who worked as a farm laborer and a muleteer. He is the son of **Francisco Guerrero** and María de Medina. Lope married María de Ropiñón (d. 1606), the daughter of **Leonor de Hortubia**. He was arrested by the Holy Office in 1607 and immediately admitted to having practiced Islam along with his (deceased) wife. Over time, he confessed to additional offenses and by the end of 1610 he had offered testimony against many of his relatives and neighbors. He was reconciled to the Church and condemned to the galleys in 1611. His efforts to have the sentence commuted were unsuccessful. (Docs. 28, 84, 87–89.)

HORTUBIA, FRANCISCA DE (c. 1520–94): A Morisca from Deza and the wife of **Gabriel de Saleros**, a cobbler, whom she married around 1540. She bore at least six children, the last of them in 1558. (Doc. 1.)

HORTUBIA, FRANCISCO DE (1538–90): The chief bailiff of Deza from at least 1578 to 1581 and town magistrate in 1584. Francisco also served on the town council in various capacities in 1569, 1574, 1578, and 1582. Despite his aggressive treatment of **María de Medrano**, Francisco was, in fact, also a Morisco. (Docs. 37–38.)

HORTUBIA, ÍÑIGO DE ("THE SOLDIER") (1540–93): One of Deza's Moriscos, the son of Lope de Hortubia and Ana de Almatazán. He spent time as a soldier in Daroca (Aragon) in the 1550s along with **Juan de Cieli**, which earned him his nickname. After returning to Deza, Íñigo worked as a farmer and locksmith and held the office of town magistrate in 1577 and 1580. Around 1570, he married Cecilia de Cieli (b. c. 1550), **Lope de Cieli**'s sister. They had two children—a daughter, Cecilia, and a son, **Juan**, who inherited his father's nickname. (Docs. 48, 82.)

HORTUBIA, JUAN DE (b. 1529): A Morisco locksmith originally named Juan de Ropiñón. Born in Daroca (Aragon), he came to live in Deza around 1550. He knew how to read and write "a little" and may have served on the town council. In Deza, he married María de Hortubia. He claimed that he became known as "de Hortubia" because of his wife, and the name stuck even after her death, which occurred not long after they wed. He soon remarried to a woman named Tarba Tarba, a servant of the Countess of Haro (d. 1553). Tarba Tarba bore him three daughters before her own death. Finally, in 1568, he married Isabel la Manceba, the aunt of **Francisco** and **Román el Romo**. She gave birth to a daughter in 1570. Juan was arrested in 1569 by the Holy Office on suspicion of Islamizing and was reconciled to the Church the following year at a public ceremony. He was sentenced to three years' rowing on the royal galleys during which time he may have participated in the Battle of Lepanto. His fate is unknown. (Docs. 33, 58.)

HORTUBIA, JUAN DE ("THE SOLDIER") (c. 1583–aft. 1611): A Morisco from Deza, the son of **Íñigo de Hortubia** and Cecilia de Cieli. He married Ana de Fadrique in late 1606 or early 1607. His wife quickly became pregnant, but the child was stillborn. By early summer 1608, she was pregnant again. He may have inherited his nickname from his father or perhaps he actually spent some time as a soldier. He and his wife were arrested in

March of 1608 by the Holy Office and transported to Cuenca on the basis of testimony brought against them by an inquisitorial informant and the confessions of other Moriscos from Deza. Both Juan and Ana survived the ordeal and were reconciled to the Church by early 1611. Although his trial record has been lost, he was condemned to the galleys and a quarter of his goods were confiscated. (This sentence probably indicates that he resisted torture and refused to confess his guilt.) He attempted to have his sentence commuted but the efforts proved unsuccessful. (Docs. 79, 82–83, 87–89.)

HORTUBIA, LEONOR DE (1549–aft. 1611): A Morisca from Deza. She is the daughter of Lope de Hortubia and Ana de Almotazán and the sister of **Juan** and **Íñigo de Hortubia**. In 1575, Leonor married Alonso Ropiñón, who died only four years later. After his death she lived in their home and raised their daughter, María. Leonor confessed to Islamizing activities and took the Edict of Grace in 1571. She was examined by **Dr. Arganda** ten years later during his visitation. Her daughter married **Lope Guerrero the younger** but died around 1606. Leonor was arrested in 1608 and tried as a relapsed heretic. She suffered various forms of physical torture but refused to implicate herself or anyone else. At the end of 1610, she was once again reconciled to the Church and transferred from the inquisitorial to the royal jails. As part of her sentence, she was publicly exhibited riding on a horse, naked from the waist up, was exiled from Deza and Cuenca for four years, and a third of her goods were confiscated. (Doc. 84.)

HORTUBIA, LUIS DE (*EL JARQUINO*) (c. 1582–aft. 1611): A Morisco born in Morata (Aragon), but a citizen of Deza. The son of Luis de Hortubia the elder and **María la Jarquina**. He married María de Cieli, who died around 1606, probably in childbirth to a son who survived her by only two months. Luis was additionally the father of two daughters: María (b. 1601) and Ana (b. 1603). He was arrested in 1608 and tried by the Holy Office for Islamic activities on the basis of testimony from a Morisco visitor to Deza, an inquisitorial informant, and the confessions of other Moriscos from Deza. He was reconciled to the Church in 1611 but sentenced to serve five years in the king's galleys. He employed various strategies to have his sentence commuted but none were successful. (Docs. 79, 87–88.)

HORTUBIA, MARÍA DE (c. 1526–92): A Morisca born and raised in Deza. She married **Luis de Cebea the elder** in around 1544. In 1557, María was denounced to the Holy Office by an Old Christian servant for having expressed ideas and performed activities that smacked of Islam. María defended herself against the charge in Cuenca. Several influential Dezanos supported her cause against the servant—among them **Licentiate Páez** and his family, **Juanes Valles** (the church's lieutenant vicar), **Fray Martín Fernández** (the local commissioner of the Inquisition), and the town's former warden, a member of the powerful Fernández-Abarca family. Despite their support, she eventually confessed her errors under torture in June 1559. María was reconciled to the Church but ordered to serve one and a half years in Cuenca's perpetual prison as penance. In January 1561, having done her time, she requested and gained release and then returned to Deza to care for her seven children who had suffered "great fatigue and labor in her absence." She lived out the remainder of her days in town. (Doc. 68.)

HORTUBIA THE SOLDIER: *See Hortubia, Íñigo de.*

JARQUINA, MARÍA LA (c. 1568–aft. 1611): A Morisca born to Juan Jarquino from the town of Morata (Aragon) and Francisca de Deza, a native of Deza. She married Luis de Hortubia the elder (d. 1592) in Deza when she was about 15 years old. As a widow, she kept a shop in which she sold "fruit and other things" and she traveled to "various places in Aragon and Castile" to gather her wares. María bore four children; all but one predeceased her. She collected Islamic prayers and Arabic phrases. By 1608, she and her only living child, **Luis de Hortubia *el jarquino***, were arrested by the Holy Office. After some time, María confessed to having been a Muslim for more than 30 years and named many of Deza's Moriscos as associates. She suffered torture and was eventually reconciled to the Church. She was made to exhibit her shame by riding around town, naked from the waist up, and received 200 lashes. María was also sentenced to perpetual and irremissible incarceration in Cuenca and to wear the *sanbenito* for the rest of her life. Despite her suffering, she continued to work, even as a prisoner, by spinning thread and selling it. She showed charity not only to her "orphaned" granddaughters back in Deza but also to her fellow prisoners, giving of her own meager sustenance to help them. On 30 March 1611, María appealed to the inquisitors at Cuenca, asking to be freed and allowed to remove her *sanbenito* in order to prepare to comply with the royal expulsion decree. Her request was granted on 11 April by **Licentiate Diego de Quiroga**. (Docs. 79, 81.)

JUANA, WIFE OF JUAN DE LOZANO: *See Lorenzo, Juana.*

JUANA (NO LAST NAME): *See Muñoz, Juana (1569).*

LEONIS, THE OLD WOMAN OF: A Morisca from Deza reputedly able to perform curses. She may have been **Ana de Contreras**, the widow of Leonis de Saleros, a Morisco. (Doc. 23.)

LIÑÁN, ISABEL DE (1555–aft. 1608): A Morisca from Deza and the daughter of **Luis de Liñán** and Isabel Navarra. She married and had three children. In 1571 she confessed to Islamizing and took advantage of the Edict of Grace. **Dr. Arganda** reexamined her in 1581 during his visitation. She outlived her husband, and in 1608 the Holy Office ordered her arrest on the basis of testimony given against her by several incarcerated Moriscos from Deza. Although her son-in-law, **Luis de Cebea the youngest**, believed that she was still in Deza in 1611, her actual fate is unknown. (Docs. 58, 80, 85.)

LIÑÁN, LUIS DE (c. 1521–92): A Morisco potter from Deza known as "Old Liñán" by 1581. His family operated the pottery works on the northern edge of town. First tried by the Holy Office in 1557 for Islamizing, Luis relapsed into heresy and requested to be allowed to take the Edict of Grace in 1571. On the basis of the special terms of the Edict brokered by **Román Ramírez the younger**, **Alexo Gorgoz**, and others, the Council of the Inquisition (with one dissenting vote) allowed Luis to do so, and he was reconciled a second time. The terms of his reconciliation were remarkably lenient: abjuration of his heresy, three confessions per year in perpetuity, attendance at mass on Sundays and mandatory feast days with extra prayers, and 100 ducats to cover the costs of his case. In 1581, **Dr. Arganda** examined him yet again during his visitation and found irregularities in his confessional practice. Luis married Isabel Navarra (c. 1529–1605) of Ágreda, who survived him. He was Catalina and **Isabel de Liñán**'s father. (Docs. 26, 68.)

LORENZO, JUANA (bef. 1520–aft. 1569): A seamstress who was both poor and crippled. Her husband, Juan Lozano, was an agricultural laborer. Little is known about the couple, but Juana gave birth to at least four children between 1537 and 1548 and at least three of them survived to adulthood. (Doc. 4.)

LUISA, THE WIFE OF FRANCISCO DE BAPTISTA: *See Vizcaina, Luisa.*

LUNA, ÁLVARO DE (bef. 1517–1549): A Jewish New Christian from the town of Almazán. The father of **Beatriz Pérez de Luna**. The Inquisition opened a case against him in 1517 for Judaizing activities, but it was not until 1549 that he was relaxed to the secular arm. His fate meant that his descendants and relatives were excluded from the ranks of the nobility and prohibited from holding office, wearing fine clothes or precious stones, going about on horseback, or otherwise exhibiting the trappings of wealth or high social status. The Holy Office tried his son, Licentiate Simón de Luna of Almazán, in 1558 for having ignored those restrictions; he was penitenced. (Docs. 41, 60.)

LUNA, BEATRIZ PÉREZ DE: *See Pérez de Luna, Beatriz.*

LUNA, MARÍA DE (d. bef. 1569): The wife of **Román Ramírez the elder** and mother of **Román Ramírez the younger.** She was the daughter of Juan de Luna, an Aragonese Morisco with a reputation as a healer. María raised five children into adulthood. In 1556, she gave birth to her last child, Francisco. The birth was a difficult one, for he was baptized "at home out of necessity" instead of in the church, which was the norm. In 1599, long after her death, Pedro de Barnuevo, a member of one of the town's most important Old Christian families, claimed to have heard rumors that she had regularly conversed with a demon. (Docs. 13, 22.)

MADRIZ, DR. DE LA: *See Gómez de la Madriz, Dr. Diego.*

MANCEBO, JUAN (1567–aft. 1611): A Morisco from Deza who was arrested by the Holy Office for Islamic activities in October 1609. He is the brother of **Francisco** and **Román el Romo.** Juan was reconciled to the Church in 1610 and ordered to complete his penance by rowing in the royal galleys. To avoid this fate, he pursued a variety of different schemes from the royal jails in Cuenca and, in November of 1611, was released from prison in order to comply with the king's expulsion decree along with his brother Román, **Íñigo de Moraga,** and **Miguel Ramírez.** (Docs. 87–92.)

MANRIQUE, FRANCISCO (THE YOUNGER) (b. 1555): An Old Christian farmer from Deza. The son of Francisco Manrique and Mari Gonzalez. This Francisco sat on the town council in 1591, 1593, 1594, 1595, 1596, and 1603 and served as town magistrate in 1598, 1611 (the year of the expulsion), and 1616. (Docs. 43, 48, 54–56.)

MARCELO, FATHER [OR FRAY]: An Augustinian friar and an ordained priest from the town of Soria. He probably belonged to the convent dedicated to Our Lady of Grace. (Docs. 24, 34.)

MARTÍNEZ, GONZALO (THE ELDER) (c. 1499–1571): An Old Christian and citizen of Deza. **Francisca Borque**'s husband. Served as a royal scribe, notary public, and scribe of the town council from 1533 into the 1560s. (Doc. 3.)

MARTÍNEZ, GONZALO (THE YOUNGER) (b. c. 1542): The son of **Gonzalo Martínez the elder** and **Francisca Borque**. Like his father, this Gonzalo served as one of Deza's scribes and notaries public. (Docs. 36, 45.)

MARTÍNEZ NAVARRO, DR. DIEGO (b. 1556): An Old Christian from Deza, the son of Sancho Martínez and Magdalena Navarra. He attended the University of Salamanca but his subject of study is unknown. He may be the Diego Martínez who married Juana de Palencia in 1587. (Doc. 41.)

MEDRANO, MARÍA DE (c. 1547–aft. 1608): A Morisca from Deza married to **Juan Ramírez**, son of **Román Ramírez the elder**. María confessed to Islamic activities and took advantage of the Edict of Grace offered in 1571. In July of 1581, she confessed to **Dr. Arganda** that she had committed blasphemy in the midst of a dispute with **Francisco de Hortubia**, the town's chief bailiff. In 1608, her inquisitorial file was reopened and she was pursued as a relapsed heretic. Her fate is unknown. (Docs. 37–38.)

MELLAS, NICOLÁS DE (b. c. 1529): An Old Christian dry goods merchant from Deza. Husband to María Pecina. In the 1560s, he began the legal process of laying claim to *hidalgo* status, a case that dragged on until 1584. In 1592, when one Nicolás de Mellas (either this man or his son) served on Deza's town council, he held his seat as a member of the lower nobility. (Docs. 23–24.)

MIRANDA, ANGELA DE (1541–bef. 1594): **Román Ramírez the younger**'s first wife. Daughter of **Francisco de Miranda** and Isabel de Pineda. Like her husband and much of her family, Angela confessed to Islamic activities and took the Edict of Grace in 1571. She was examined again in 1581 during **Dr. Arganda**'s visitation. Her sister, Isabel, married **Román de Deza**. Angela gave birth to six children. (Docs. 34, 75–76.)

MIRANDA, FRANCISCO DE (c. 1521–c. 1571): A Morisco painter and native of Deza. Both his mother and father were reconciled by the Holy Office in 1530. He is the father of **Angela de Miranda**, the wife of **Román Ramírez the younger**. Francisco died before the Edict of Grace was offered in 1571. (Docs. 24, 34, 86.)

MOLINA, GERÓNIMO DE (c. 1550–bef. 1609): A Morisco tailor from Deza. He was arrested in 1570 in the wake of **Licentiate Reynoso**'s visitation. Having admitted to crypto-Islamic activities and having been denounced by several of his neighbors, he was reconciled to the Church. He was examined again in 1581 by **Dr. Arganda**. Gerónimo's wife, María Navarra (or Alman-zorre), who also took the Edict of Grace, gave birth to a son, also Gerónimo, in 1585. In subsequent decades, María and her son increasingly became part of Old Christian society. They moved out of the Morisco neighborhood and cut ties with their former neighbors. María was buried in Deza in 1627, years after the other Moriscos had been expelled. (Doc. 44.)

MONTERA, ANA (b. c. 1552): An Old Christian citizen from Deza and the sister of *bachiller* **Montero**. She worked for about two years as a servant in the house of **Mateo Romero the elder** and **Ana de Almoravi** in the mid-1560s. By 1569 she went into service with Martín Gutierrez, a farmer. She had moved away from Deza by 1581. (Docs. 11, 14.)

MONTERO, *BACHILLER* BARTOLOME (c. 1551–c. 1616): An ordained priest who served in Deza for decades. As a young man in the late 1560s he was the town's sacristan, but over time he gained a benefice and earned appointments as lieutenant vicar and, from 1606, commissioner of the Holy Office. He is **Ana Montera**'s brother. (Docs. 14, 40, 60, 62–65, 73.)

MONTERO, JORGE (d. bef. 1569): A Morisco formerly of Aragon, where he had been tried by the Holy Office. He came to live in Deza sometime around 1550. Purportedly, he performed circumcisions. (Doc. 18.)

MONTÓN, CATARINA (b. c. 1541): A citizen of Deza and the widow of Francisco de Arcos. Sister to **Madalena** and **María de Montón**. (Docs. 17, 51.)

MONTÓN, MADALENA DE (b. c. 1545): An Old Christian. The wife of Juan Cervero, a shepherd in Deza. Madalena is **María** and **Catarina de Montón**'s sister. (Docs. 17, 50.)

MONTÓN, MARI [OR MARÍA] (c. 1535–1610): Wife of Juan Sanz, a citizen of Deza. The Old Christian neighbor of **Mateo Romero the elder** and **Ana de Almoravi**. **Catarina** and **Madalena de Montón** are her sisters. (Docs. 7, 14, 17.)

MORAGA, GERÓNIMO DE: A Morisco from Ariza (Aragon) who weaves hemp and makes sandals for a living. He is engaged to **Ana Ramírez** [Ropi-ñón], a Morisca from Deza. (Docs. 45, 59.)

MORAGA, ÍÑIGO DE (d. aft. 1611): A Morisco originally from the town of Arcos de Jalón but living in Cuenca by the early seventeenth century.

Before his arrest by the Holy Office he acted as an informant to the Moriscos in Deza about inquisitorial activity. He was arrested by June of 1608 and lodged with his friends in the secret jails. Along with **Juan Mancebo**, **Miguel Ramírez**, and **Román el Romo**, he succeeded in having his galley sentence commuted and was released in 1611 to comply with the royal expulsion edict. (Docs. 90–92.)

MUÑOZ, BLASCO (d. 1588): An Old Christian from Deza. Town magistrate in 1569 during the visitation of **Licentiate Reynoso**. (Docs. 3, 47, 69–70.)

MUÑOZ, JUANA (1569) (b. c. 1556): A servant at the inn kept by Ana de la Torre and Alonso Pérez. She is the daughter of Pedro de la Torre, which suggests that she is related to her mistress, but oddly the inquisitorial scribe identified her as not having a last name. (Docs. 31–32.)

MUÑOZ, JUANA (1581) (b. 1563): An Old Christian from Deza; the daughter of **Blasco Muñoz**. (Docs. 47, 69–70.)

NIÑO DE GUEVARRA, CARDINAL DON FERNANDO (1549–1609): The Inquisitor General of Spain between 1600 and 1602. He studied law at the University of Salamanca. Don Fernando was not soft on heresy, but in 1600, he sent a memorial to the Council of State rejecting the notion of expelling the Moriscos as an "unjust and futile" action. Instead, he suggested that ongoing evangelization efforts be pursued. In 1601, he was made archbishop of Seville and the following year the pope pressured him to resign as inquisitor general in the midst of a row about papal authority. (Doc. 77.)

OBEZAR, GERÓNIMO DE (c. 1548–bef. 1581): A Morisco native of Deza who transported goods and worked as an agricultural laborer. **Román Ramírez the younger** claimed that **Mateo Romero the younger** had taught Gerónimo to practice Islam. He was arrested by the Holy Office in 1570 in the wake of **Licentiate Reynoso**'s visitation, subsequently confessed to Islamizing, and denounced others. Presumably he was reconciled to the Church but his trial record is lost. His fate is unknown, except that he died sometime before 1581. (Doc. 34.)

OBEZAR, LOPE DE (c. 1550–bef. 1594): A Morisco from Deza also known as Lope del Sol. As a boy, he was apprenticed to a cobbler in the Morisco town of Villafeliche (Aragon), but did not practice the trade in Deza. He was arrested and tried by the Holy Office in 1570. Transported to Cuenca, he admitted his own crypto-Islamic activities and denounced others. He was reconciled to the Church but had half his goods confiscated, was sentenced to four years in the galleys as penance, and strictly forbidden to enter the Kingdom of Aragon. He survived the ordeal and returned to Deza where he married María de Arellano. In 1578, Lope presented himself before the tribunal in Cuenca and informed them that he had traveled to Embid de Ariza (Aragon) to visit a dying cousin. The inquisitors **de la Madriz** and **Arganda** ordered him not to repeat the action but allowed him to return home without further punishment. During the 1581 visitation, Dr. Arganda examined Lope again. He was a member of Deza's confraternity of the Most Holy Sacrament and died sometime between 1588 and 1594. (Doc. 39.)

OCÁRIZ, GERÓNIMO DE (c. 1559–99): Son of Gerónimo de Ocáriz and **Beatriz Pérez de Luna.** He is of Jewish descent on both his mother's and father's side, and his maternal grandfather was condemned by the Holy Office for Judaizing. Nevertheless, the Ocárizes comprised one of the most important families in Deza and began pursuing legal recognition of their *hidalgo* status in the 1560s. It was probably this same Gerónimo whom the Duke of Medinaceli named chief magistrate and warden of the town's fortress between 1582 and 1584. (Doc. 41.)

OLD FADRIQUE: *See Fadrique, Old.*

OLD LIÑÁN: *See Liñán, Luis de.*

OZUEL, BACHILLER JUAN DE (d. 1605): One of Deza's ordained priests. He was of Jewish descent on his mother's side and studied at the University of Salamanca. (Docs. 40–41, 60, 62–63.)

PÁEZ, LICENTIATE ANTONIO (c. 1510–77): Born in the Castilian town of Atienza and of Jewish descent. His father was a physician whom the Holy Office absolved of "incredulity and concealment" in 1524. Páez came to Deza in about 1535 with a bachelor's degree and served as the town's physician. He married into the Rebolledo family (at least some of whom were considered *hidalgos*) and sired five children; he earned his licentiate around 1545 and remained in Deza until he died in August 1577, a decade after his wife. His daughter, María de Torres y de Rebolledo, married a local *hidalgo*, and in 1559 his granddaughter was baptized *doña* Isabela. (Docs. 3, 5, 7, 9, 12, 16, 25, 40, 60.)

PÉREZ [DE ULLIVARRI], PEDRO: An inquisitorial notary for the tribunal at Cuenca. He accompanied **Dr. Arganda** during his 1581 visitation and served in the office through the 1590s. (Docs. 34, 73, 75–76.)

PÉREZ DE LUNA, DOÑA[?] BEATRIZ: The daughter of **Álvaro de Luna** (from Almazán), who was condemned by the Holy Office for Judaizing in 1549. Beatriz married Beltrán de Ocáriz, a member of one of Deza's most important families. The Ocárizes claimed membership in the lower nobility. (Docs. 41, 60.)

PITUERTA, PASQUAL DE LA: *See Deza, Lope de.*

QUIROGA, LICENTIATE DON DIEGO DE (1564–1614): Originally from Lugo (Galicia), he held a variety of church offices before being appointed an inquisitor at Cuenca in December 1607. He took possession of the office the following May. Supposedly, Philip III offered him the bishopric of Ariano (Naples), but Quiroga refused to accept because of poor health. He served alongside of the ailing **Claudio de la Cueva** and died in Cuenca. (Docs. 88–89, 91.)

RAMÍREZ [ROPIÑÓN], ANA (b. 1561): A native of Deza who married **Gerónimo de Moraga,** a Morisco from Ariza (Aragon). Her mother was an Old Christian, her father a Morisco. (Docs. 45, 59.)

RAMÍREZ, JUAN (1544–aft. 1608): A Morisco farmer from Deza. He was the son of **Román Ramírez the elder** and married **María de Medrano.** In 1571, he confessed that he and his wife had fasted for Ramadan and took advantage of the Edict of Grace. Presumably, he was reexamined in 1581 during **Dr. Arganda**'s visitation, but the documents related to his trials have been lost. There is, however, evidence that the inquisitors became interested in him again in 1608, at which point they considered him a relapsed heretic. His fate is unknown. (Docs. 37–38.)

RAMÍREZ, MIGUEL (c. 1569–aft. 1611): A literate Morisco from Deza and the son of **Román Ramírez the younger** and **Angela de Miranda.** When his father married for the second time around 1594, Miguel moved in with his elder brother, Román, a muleteer and farmer. Miguel acted as chief constable for the duke of Medinaceli and moved into his own home when he married María de Almotazán in about 1603. By 1608, the couple had had two daughters: Ana (b. 1603) and Isabel, who died at eight months. Miguel inherited his father's legacy in a number of ways. He was literate, intelligent, strong willed, physically robust, and a leader. He took over the House of the Duke early in the seventeenth century and continued to use it as a base of operations for Islamic education, prayers, and as a way station for Moriscos traveling from Aragon. He was arrested by the Holy Office in

1608 but despite repeated interrogation, lengthy incarceration, and torture, refused to confess. He was nevertheless sentenced to three years' rowing in the royal galleys and a quarter of his estate was confiscated. Along with two other Moriscos from Deza, he succeeded in outmaneuvering the inquisitors at Cuenca and had his galley sentence commuted. In late 1611, he was released from jail and ordered to comply with the royal edict of expulsion. (Docs. 78, 81, 86–92.)

RAMÍREZ, ROMÁN (THE ELDER) (d. 1592): A farmer from Deza and a leader in its Morisco community. He performed acts of Islamic devotions through the 1560s, at least, and took the Edict of Grace in 1571. There is no record of his being reexamined during **Dr. Arganda**'s 1581 visitation, although he is likely to have been. He outlived his wife, **María de Luna**, who bore him six sons and a daughter, among them **Román Ramírez the younger** and **Juan Ramírez**. (Docs. 9, 12–13, 19, 22, 34, 43.)

RAMÍREZ, ROMÁN (THE YOUNGER) (1540–99): A Morisco from Deza, he was son of **Román Ramírez the elder** and **María de Luna**. Román married his first wife, **Angela de Miranda**, in 1558. She bore one daughter and five sons, among them **Miguel Ramírez**. His second wife, Ana de Uzedo, whom he married after 1594, bore two more children in the mid-1590s. Román's life is extremely complex and is obfuscated by the contradictory accounts of it that he provided to inquisitors, yet he clearly practiced Islam (more or less secretly) throughout much of his life. He worked as a farm hand, a guard at the dry port, a gardener, a healer, and a storyteller. He owned a library of medical books and chivalric tales—he even claimed to have received an advance of 300 *reales* for a story that he was composing entitled *Florisdoro de Grecia*. In his mid-twenties, he became associated with **Gerónimo de Salamanca**, at the time one of the wealthiest men in Spain. Román had a temper, which often got him into trouble (including a knife-fight with **Licentiate Páez** in 1570!), as well as an encyclopedic memory. In 1570–71, he traveled to Madrid to negotiate the Edict of Grace for Deza's Moriscos. Román was also closely connected to at least one duke of Medinaceli and was associated with the property known as the House of the Duke from at least 1570. He used the garden there to grow medicinal herbs; the house became a gathering place for Islamic instruction. In 1595, a group of men from Soria denounced him to the Inquisition for having made a pact with a devil, which explained his prodigious memory. He was allowed to remain in Deza on house arrest until April 1599, when he was transported to Cuenca. He admitted at least some of his Islamic activities but before the conclusion of his trial, his health began to turn. He was transferred to a local hospital and died in December of that year. In March 1600, an effigy of Ramírez and his bones were publicly burned in Toledo. In attendance were King Philip III, Queen Margaret of Austria, and the royal favorite the Duke of Lerma. Román became the inspiration for Juan Ruiz de Alarcón's play *Quien mal anda en mal acaba*. (Docs. 10, 34, 73–78, 90.)

RASA, MARÍA (LA) (b. 1548): The daughter of Juan Raso and Catalina de Almazul. An Old Christian from Deza sometimes known as María de Almazul. She married the weaver Francisco García Destaragan. (Docs. 42, 53.)

REYNOSO, LICENTIATE ALONSO JIMÉNEZ DE (d. 1607): Born in Mazuecos (Palencia). In 1569, he was an inquisitor at the tribunal of Toledo, having already served as the prosecuting attorney in the inquisitorial tribunal at Granada. Subsequently, he transferred to Valencia (in 1580), Cordoba (by 1590), and Valladolid (in 1600). Reynoso was reputedly the first person to officially suggest the expulsion of the Moriscos from Spain, in May 1581. His inquisitorial colleagues noted that he was a difficult man to work with and he seems to have been rather focused on the trappings of his office. In the 1590s, he became embroiled in a sexual liaison with one doña María de Lara, who lived in the company of Moriscas. In 1597, the celebrated poet Luis de Góngora y Argote (1561–1627) provided the Holy Office with written testimony about the affair. (Docs. 1–7, 9–28, 30–33, 86.)

ROBLE, FABIAN DE: A Morisco from Cuenca who interacted with some of Deza's Moriscos while they were in the royal jails in Cuenca, following their release from the secret jails of the Holy Office. He apparently was involved in delivering the illicit, ongoing correspondence between the incarcerated Dezanos and their friends and family back home. In March 1611, he deputized his adolescent son to carry the most recent cache of letters to Deza—a 250-mile round trip. The boy's mother, however, decided he was too young for such a journey and sent a priest to bring him home. The priest eventually discovered the letters and handed them over to the inquisitors at Cuenca. (Doc. 80.)

RODRÍGUEZ, DIEGO (b. c. 1533): An Old Christian carpenter from Cogolludo, about 80 miles southwest of Deza. He came to town to work on the construction of the House of the Duke. In some capacity or other, he was involved with the project from the late 1550s until at least 1569. (Doc. 15.)

RODRÍGUEZ, MARI (b. c. 1549): An Old Christian. A native of Alameda and, in 1569, engaged to Juan de Calataojar of Deza. Formerly, she worked as a servant to **Román Ramírez the elder** and his wife, **María de Luna**. (Doc. 22.)

RODRÍGUEZ, MARTÍN (bef. 1519–1571): One of Deza's Old Christians. He worked as a guard of the dry port along with **Román Ramírez the younger**. (Doc. 10.)

ROMERO, MATEO (THE ELDER) (c. 1530–aft. 1572): A literate Morisco originally from Terrer (Aragon). As a boy of about ten years old, he came to Deza to learn to read and write from **Gonzalo de Santa Clara**, but he later returned to Terrer, where he married **Ana de Almoravi**. In 1558, he fled his debtors by moving his family to Deza, and although he was poor when he arrived, he became at least moderately wealthy. He identified himself as a farmer and goat breeder. By 1569, he decided to return to Terrer and was in the process of transporting his goods when **Licentiate Reynoso** arrived. After spending some time in Terrer, Romero moved onto Valencia. His wife was arrested in September 1570 at which point Mateo returned to Terrer, where he was finally captured later that month. He was reconciled to the Church but his goods were confiscated and he was sentenced to four years' rowing on the royal galleys. While being transported, however, he slipped his guards and made an escape. Despite efforts to recapture him, Mateo remained at large. (Docs. 10–11, 14, 34, 46.)

ROMERO, MATEO (THE YOUNGER) (b. c. 1552): A Morisco born in Terrer (Aragon). Mateo was the son of **Ana de Almoravi** and stepson of **Mateo Romero the elder**. He married **Ana de Almanzorre**. According to **Román Ramírez the younger**, Romero was in the habit of teaching Deza's Moriscos about Islam and made several converts. Subsequent to **Licentiate Reynoso**'s visitation in 1569, Mateo was arrested in Deza in anticipation of being sent under guard to Cuenca. Remarkably, he succeeded in escaping twice. The first time, he broke out of his jail cell in Deza and made off to Aragon, where he was apprehended and returned to Deza. The second time, he escaped while in transit to Cuenca. In the absence of his body, his effigy was relaxed to the secular arm. Yet, based on the terms of the special Edict of Grace brokered by **Román Ramírez the younger**, **Alexo Gorgoz**, and others, when Mateo was captured a third time, he confessed his sins and was penitenced. (Docs. 10–11, 14, 34.)

ROMO, FRANCISCO EL (c. 1561–aft. 1611): A literate Morisco sandal maker from Deza who married Mari López (d. c. 1606). The brother of **Román el Romo** and **Juan Mancebo**. His father, also Francisco, died rowing in the royal galleys, part of the penance given to him upon being reconciled to the Church in 1571. This Francisco was arrested by the Holy Office on charges of Islamizing in 1608. Although his trial record has been lost, he was sentenced to serve in the galleys. To avoid this fate he pursued a variety of different schemes from the royal jails in Cuenca but Francisco's efforts proved less successful than his brothers'. (Docs. 78–79, 87–89.)

ROMO, ROMÁN EL (c. 1569–aft. 1611): A Morisco from Deza married to Isabel de Liñán (b. c. 1583). **Francisco el Romo** and **Juan Mancebo** were his brothers. Their father, Francisco, died in the galleys after being reconciled to the Church in 1571. The Holy Office arrested Román in 1608 after he had been accused by various other incarcerated Moriscos and by an inquisitorial informant. Although Román arrived at the jails intending to confess nothing, he soon admitted to Islamic activities and implicated others. In 1610, after undergoing torture, he was reconciled to the Church. As penance he was ordered to serve five years in the galleys. His wife wrote the inquisitors at Cuenca begging for mercy, pleading Román's poor health and her own "need and poverty" (as well as that of their children). Like his brother Juan Mancebo, Román avoided galley service. In 1611, he was released from the royal jails and ordered to comply with the expulsion edict. (Docs. 87–92.)

RUIZ, *BACHILLER* JUAN (d. 1589): A cleric originally from Almazul. When he arrived in Deza in 1557 he already held a university degree. When **Licentitate Reynoso** asked the vicar **Miguel Benito** about Ruiz in 1569, Benito said that he considered Ruiz to be "an Old Christian and a good cleric." But **Juanes de Altopica** informed Reynoso that Ruiz was a Judeo-converso on his mother's side. The Holy Office did not pursue the accusations made against Ruiz or his ancestry, but he left Deza a few months after Reynoso's visitation to become the parish priest at Pozuel de Ariza, a dozen miles southwest in Aragon (and outside of Reynoso's jurisdiction). Ruiz occasionally returned to Deza to participate in baptisms and some of Deza's Moriscos continued to confess with him. He returned to Deza in the 1580s and, as he had done before his interim in Pozuel, shared a home with his sister María, a *beata*. Ruiz held a chaplaincy at the Chapel of St. John in Deza's parish church. (Docs. 6–7, 73.)

RUIZ POLO, PERO [OR PEDRO] (d. 1568): One of Deza's clerics from the mid-1530s until his death. (Docs. 6, 8.)

SALAMANCA, GERÓNIMO DE: A royal financier, tax farmer, mineral speculator, procurator of Burgos, member of the royal council, and, in the last third of the sixteenth century, one of Iberia's wealthiest inhabitants. Salamanca went bankrupt toward the end of the century. **Román Ramírez the younger** worked for him. (Docs. 34, 73.)

SALEROS, GABRIEL DE (d. 1583): A Morisco cobbler and citizen of Deza and **Francisca de Hortubia's** husband. He served on the town council in 1559 and 1565. He died intestate "because he was poor." (Docs. 1–2.)

SANTA CLARA, *MOSÉN GONZALO DE* (d. bef. 1570): One of Deza's clerics from at least 1537. Gonzalo taught many Dezanos, especially Moriscos it seems, to read. In fact, his reputation was such that several Morisco families from other towns in the region sent their young sons to learn from him. One of his pupils explained that he taught them using a primer and they practiced reading poetry and copies of papal bulls. (Doc. 6.)

SOL, LOPE DEL: *See Deza, Lope de.*

TORRE [Y AYALA], DR. DON JUAN DE LA (d. 1638): A native of Burgos, he became an inquisitor at Cuenca in 1611 and later a member of the *Suprema*. In 1621 he was offered the bishopric of the Canaries but did not accept it. Instead, he became Bishop of Orense in 1622 and, in 1626, was promoted to the see of Ciudad Rodrigo. (Doc. 91.)

ULLIVARRI, PEDRO PÉREZ DE: *See Pérez [de Ullivarri], Pedro.*

UREÑA, GARCÍA DE (b. c. 1534): An ordained priest in Deza and a native of the town. (Doc. 33.)

VALLES, JUANES [OR JUAN] (c. 1506–85): An ordained priest in the town of Deza. He was sometimes called "the Prior" by locals and had formerly been a friar but "renounced his vows." He continued wearing what was described as "the habit of St. John," which may connect him to the military order of the Hospitallers (the Knights of St. John of Jerusalem). He served as a cleric in Deza from the late 1530s until his death in July 1585 and held the office of lieutenant vicar in the parish church from the late 1550s. (Docs. 6–7, 34, 40, 60, 73, 75–76.)

VILLOSLADA, JUAN DE (b. 1557): An Old Christian farmer from Deza. The son of Mingo de Villoslada and the brother of **Pascual de Villoslada**. (Doc. 44.)

VILLOSLADA, PASCUAL DE (b. 1560): An Old Christian from Deza. The son of Mingo de Villoslada and the brother of **Juan de Villoslada**. (Docs. 48, 54–56.)

VIZCAINA, LUISA (c. 1534–aft. 1594): A Morisca from Deza who married **Francisco de Baptista**. (Doc. 67.)

YLLANA, FRAY ALONSO DE (b. c. 1519): A legate from the Cistercian monastery in the Castilian town of Santa María de Huerta, about 20 miles southwest of Deza. (Doc. 20.)

ZAMORANO, PEDRO (1582–aft. 1611): A Morisco born in Cuenca. His parents moved to Deza when he was young and raised him there. As a youth, he started learning to read, but later in life he claimed to have forgotten how. After the death of his father, in about 1602, Pedro moved in with his cousin, **Luis de Hortubia**, and became a muleteer. At the time of his arrest by the Holy Office in 1609, he was single. Pedro was accused of Islamizing by some of his Moriscos neighbors as well as by an inquisitorial informant. After several months in the secret jails he confessed to a variety of Islamic activities. In 1610, he was reconciled to the Church and sentenced to row in the galleys for three years. He failed to have his sentence commuted. (Docs. 87–89.)

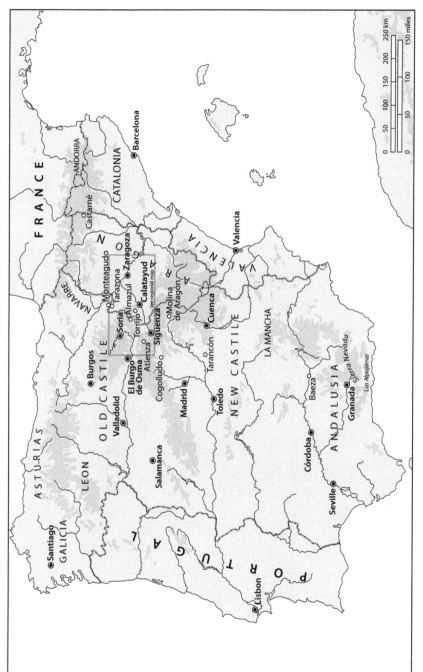

The Iberian Peninsula in the Early Modern Period

View of Deza

Looking northwest toward Deza with the parish church at center.
The Upper Neighborhood extends to the right and the Lower Neighborhood to the left.

Photo credit: Rachel A. O'Banion, 2013

Documents

1

The Visitation of Licentiate Reynoso (1569)[1]

*In the fall of 1569, as part of a regional visitation, Licentiate Alonso Jimé-
nez de Reynoso, an inquisitor from the city of Cuenca, made his way to the
small town of Deza. Before his arrival, a solemn Edict of Faith was read
in the parish church after high mass on Sunday. It listed specific heretical
activities and compelled all hearers to make known to the inquisitor any
knowledge of such infractions. Failure to comply would automatically result
in excommunication.*

*Between September 25 and October 11, dozens of Dezanos either pre-
sented themselves before Reynoso or were summoned by him. The inquisitorial notary, Pablo García, kept the official account of the visitation and
recorded 33 audiences (although marginal notes hint that several more
occurred). García's record of the visit to Deza is presented here in its entirety.*

*Reynoso received denunciations related to a wide variety of topics, but
most were tied to the behavior of the town's Morisco citizens, many of
whom were described as continuing to engage in Islamic religious practices
and cultural traditions despite being baptized Christians. In the months
that followed Reynoso's visitation, the Holy Office transported several of
the denounced Moriscos to Cuenca, where they were tried and punished
as heretics.*

1

In the town of Deza on September 25, 1569, a man appeared before the lord
Inquisitor **Licentiate Reynoso** without having been summoned. He was
sworn in and promised to speak the truth. He said his name was:

---

[1] ADC, libro 317, folios 448r–478v.

Witness: **Mateo Donoso**, a tailor, born in the town of Deza but now a citizen of Embid de Ariza. He said that he was about 33 years old. In order to unburden his conscience he declares that more than a year ago, during the summer (although he does not remember which month), he was in Deza at the house of **Gabriel de Saleros** (a cobbler and citizen of Deza who lives in the Neighborhood of the Vine). He was talking with **Francisca de Hortubia** (Gabriel's wife, both of whom are Moriscos) in the doorway to her house when a neighbor rode by on the street. Since this witness knew that she owned a horse, he asked her if that was hers. She responded, "No, mine has gone to pasture with Jesus Christ."

Mateo did not respond or ask anything else, but what she had said seemed wrong to him. When asked, Mateo said that he did not know if Francisca de Hortubia meant that the nag was dead or what she meant by it. He said that they were alone when this happened.

He swears this is the truth, and he does not say it out of hatred. He was charged to keep it secret and he promised to do so. This happened in my presence: **Pablo García**, notary.

2

In the town of Deza on September 26, 1569, a man appeared before the lord Inquisitor **Licentiate Reynoso** without having been summoned. He was sworn in and promised to speak the truth. He said his name was:

Witness: Francisco de Palencia, a farmer and a citizen of Deza. He said he was 65 years old, more or less. He does not remember when it happened—maybe during winter—but he was standing in Deza's church cemetery while they were digging a grave for a Morisco from Deza who had died. He does not remember who it was. The grave was very deep, and he thinks Francisco de Obezar, an itinerant Morisco laborer, was digging it, since he usually digs the graves for Moriscos.

Francisco de Palencia was amazed that the grave was so deep, and he said to **Gabriel de Saleros** (a Morisco cobbler and a citizen of Deza), "God help me! Why are you guys digging such a deep grave?" for it was almost as deep as a man is tall. Gabriel de Saleros responded, "That's how we do it amongst ourselves." Francisco de Palencia did not respond, although it seemed to him that they dug the grave so deep in order to reach virgin ground. For he has heard it said that Moriscos try to bury themselves in virgin ground. And based on the depth of the grave and what Saleros had said, it seemed to Francisco de Palencia that they had dug that deep.

When asked, he said that he did not remember if anyone else could have heard Gabriel de Saleros's words. He also said that it is typical for them to dig deep graves.

He swears this is the truth, and he does not say it out of hatred. He was charged to keep it secret and promised to do so. This happened in my presence: **Pablo García**, notary.

3

In Deza on September 26, 1569, a man appeared before the lord Inquisitor **Licentiate Reynoso** without having been summoned. He was sworn in and promised to speak the truth.

Witness: **Gonzalo Martínez [the elder]**, a scribe and citizen of this town. He said he was 70 years old, give or take a bit. He said that in order to unburden his conscience he declares that five or six years ago he was discussing matters related to the Holy Office with **Francisco de las Eras**.† Francisco (a farmer who was then a citizen of Deza but now lives in Cihuela) told this witness that one day when he was inside of the town's *humilladero*,[2] which is enclosed to about chest height, **Licentiate Antonio Páez** (a citizen of Deza) passed by. Páez removed his hat (or cap) from his head and, as he came riding along the road on a horse, he said, "I show you reverence because everyone else does it." He spoke these words just as he passed the cross in the *humilladero*.

And this witness told Francisco de las Eras, "Keep quiet and don't say a word to anyone," since it was a matter concerning the Holy Office. This happened between Francisco de las Eras and this witness.

When asked by the inquisitor, he said that Licentiate Páez is a *confeso*[3] and that his father came from Atienza.[4] He does not know the father's name, but he was a physician. He has heard that Páez's father had been tried by the Holy Office.

Item: He said that he, **Blasco Muñoz** (the town magistrate), Licentiate Páez, and other people whose names he does not remember were in his

---

[2] A *humilladero* was a place of devotion usually located along the roads going into or out of Spanish towns. They were often enclosed by a low wall and adorned with a raised cross or religious image. Deza's *humilladero* was located on the heights about a mile southeast of town and is currently the site of a shrine dedicated to Saint Roque.

[3] A synonym for Judeoconverso, that is, a convert (or the descendant of a convert) from Judaism to Christianity.

[4] About 60 miles southwest of Deza in Castile.

scriptorium about 15 or 20 days ago. When Gonzalo entered the room, he found the licentiate in conversation with Magistrate Blasco Muñoz and everyone else. This witness does not know what they were discussing, but as he sat down he is sure he heard the licentiate say that we were very much indebted to Our Lady but that Our Lady was even more indebted to us. For if there were no sinners, she would not be the mother of God. This witness heard him say this at least twice but did not respond to it, although it seemed wrong to speak that way.

And this is all he knows about the matter, and he swears it is the truth. He does not say it out of hatred. He was charged to keep it secret and he promised to do so. This happened in my presence: **Pablo García**, notary.

† On October 3, 1569, Francisco de las Eras, citizen of Cihuela, age 41 appeared and, as above, was examined under oath. When asked, he said that more than 12 years had passed since he was in the town's *humilladero* when Licentiate Páez (physician and citizen of this town) passed by on a horse. When Páez came alongside the *humilladero* he either said, "We Jews and Christians humble ourselves" or "Let us humble ourselves, Jews and Christians." He is not certain which of these Páez said. He heard nothing more.

Much later, Francisco told Gonzalo Herride (deceased) about this, and the Holy Office was notified of it when an inquisitor was here, staying in Pedro de la Huerta's house about 12 years ago. Francisco was summoned by that lord inquisitor and he told him that he did not know of anything else bad that anyone had said. No one else had heard Páez's words.

This is the truth under oath. He was charged to keep it secret. This happened in my presence: Pablo García, notary.

4

In Deza on September 26, 1569, a woman appeared before the lord Inquisitor **Licentiate Reynoso** without having been summoned. She was sworn in and promised to speak the truth. She said her name was:

Witness: **Gerónima del Castillo**, the wife of Juan Morales, who is a farmer and a citizen of the town of Deza. She said she was 30 years old, and in order to unburden her conscience she declares that about five years ago, give or take, she was on Net Street in Deza. And **Juana Lorenzo**, the wife of Juan Lozano (who is a farmer and a poor man), was sitting by the door to her house sewing. This witness does not remember the topic of conversation nor why Juana ended up saying what she did, but Juana said, "I believe in God and in Our Lady, but *that*," she said pointing to an image of Our Lady above the Net Gate, "is just a bit of varnish." This witness did not respond but what Juana said seemed very wrong to her. She does not remember who was present at the time.

When asked by the inquisitor, she explained that Juana never said that she had refused to honor the image. This witness considers Juana to be a good Christian, and she is a poor and crippled woman who makes a living by sewing.

This is the truth under oath, and she does not say it out of hatred. She was charged to keep it secret and she promised to do so. This happened in my presence: **Pablo García**, notary.

<hr />

5

In Deza on September 26, 1569, a man appeared before the lord Inquisitor **Licentiate Reynoso** without having been summoned. He was sworn in and promised to speak the truth. He was named:

Witness: **Juanes de Altopica**, a cleric. He said he was about 80 years old. He said that about three and a half years ago, more or less, he was in the town's plaza on the corner of New Street[5] with **Martín Fernández** (the commissioner of the Holy Office) and **Licentiate Páez** (a physician and citizen of Deza). Martín Fernández began describing how, when his father was on the verge of death, he had asked for a crucifix. (He heard all of this from a friar who had been present.) When they gave him the crucifix, he held it in both hands and adored it with such great devotion, bringing it up to kiss it; it was as if he wanted to draw it into his body.

When these words were spoken, Juanes de Altopica saw Licentiate Páez waving his arm and heard him saying, "That's worthless." He gestured with his fingers toward heaven and said, "Up, up! That crucifix profits nothing." Only the three of them were present, and it seemed very wrong to this witness. Later, when the licentiate had gone away, Juanes de Altopica told Martín Fernández, "Remember this. It was very wrong to say and is heresy."

When asked by the inquisitor, Juanes de Altopica said that the licentiate seemed to be of Jewish descent and he hailed from Atienza. His father was a physician who had been arrested by the Inquisition of Cuenca. He does not know where Páez's father was born nor does he remember his name.

This is the truth under oath, and he does not say it out of hatred. He was charged to keep it secret. This happened in my presence: **Pablo García**, notary. He promised to keep it secret.

<hr />

[5] Another name for Corrillo Street.

6

In Deza on September 28, 1569, a man appeared before the lord Inquisitor **Licentiate Reynoso**.[6] He was sworn in and promised to speak the truth. He said his name was:

Witness: **Juanes Valles**, a priest cleric born in Deza and about 60 years old. He said that in order to unburden his conscience he declares that perhaps three years ago, give or take, this witness was in the sacristy of Deza's church, and **Pero Ruiz Polo** (a cleric who is now deceased) asked him whether the soul of Christ our redeemer was in the Most Holy Sacrament.[7] Juanes Valles responded, "What kind of doubt is that? Yes, of course it is! Why would you even ask?" Pero Ruiz Polo explained that *bachiller* **Ruiz** (one of Deza's clerics) had asked, in the presence of **Gonzalo de Santa Clara** (another cleric) whether the soul of Jesus Christ our redeemer was in the Most Holy Sacrament. Gonzalo de Santa Clara had responded, "Yes, of course." But *bachiller* Ruiz had responded, "Well, no it isn't. Saint Augustine[8] or Saint Jerome[9] or one of the four doctors,"—Valles is certain now that he said Saint Augustine—"said that Christ's soul was not in the Most Holy Sacrament." Pedro [*sic*] Ruiz Polo responded, "Look, sir, it's possible for someone to read Saint Augustine and misunderstand him; he said no such thing."

And then he heard that **Jerónimo Barba** (a cleric studying theology in Valencia) and *bachiller* Ruiz had argued about this same matter. *Bachiller* Ruiz had stood his ground about what he had said and Jerónimo Barba took the contrary position.

This is the truth under oath, and he does not say it out of hatred. He was charged to keep it secret and he promised to do so. This happened in my presence: **Pablo García**, notary.

7

In the town of Deza on September 28, 1569, a man appeared before the lord **Inquisitor Reynoso** without having been summoned. He was sworn in and promised to speak the truth. He said his name was:

---

[6] Compare this account with Docs. 7–8.

[7] That is, the Eucharist.

[8] Saint Augustine of Hippo (354–430) was an influential theologian of the Western Church. He was one of the four great "doctors" (or teachers) of the Church, and during the sixteenth century he became one of Europe's most contested religious authorities as Roman Catholics and Protestants sought to claim him as their own.

[9] Saint Jerome (c.347–420) was an important Father of the Western Church. Although Jerome wrote extensively, his most influential work was a Latin translation of the Bible known as the Vulgate.

Witness: **Miguel Benito**, the town's vicar, who is about 50 years old. He said that in order to unburden his conscience, he declares that most of Deza's New Converts—the ones that were formerly Moors—neither eat pork nor drink wine. And not only them; they also keep their children from eating or drinking. Specifically, he heard the daughter of Bernardino Burgueño and Mari González say that she did not want to eat pork or drink wine because her mother (who is deceased) once punished her for doing so, striking her in the mouth, even though she was young and foolish. (He does not know the daughter's name, but she lives in the house of her brother-in-law, Francisco el Bueno, a citizen of Deza; Francisco el Bueno's wife is her sister.)

Item: He said that the Moriscos rarely take bulls of crusade nor do they get any of the other indulgences or jubilees.[11] If they went through the process of gaining them, he would know about it.

Item:[10] He said that, as for contracting marriages, the Moriscos do it differently than the Old Christians. After they seal a marriage agreement, the groom's father holds a family meeting and chooses two people to go in his name and in the groom's name to ask for the bride one more time. Miguel Benito has seen this happen, specifically, in the house of **Luis de Cebea the elder** (a Morisco citizen of Deza) when he was marrying his son [**Luis de Cebea the younger**] to [**Francisca de Baptista**], a daughter of Luis de Baptista (a Morisco), as well as his daughter [Ana de Cebea] to [Juan Fadrique], the son of [**Old**] **Fadrique** (another Morisco).

Since we never contract marriages in this way, it seems wrong to Miguel Benito. He has said this publicly in Luis de Cebea the elder's house, but Cebea did not respond.

Item:[12] He said Francisco de Uzedo (the son-in-law of Antonio de Melgosa, a citizen of Deza) told him about the wedding of **Gabriel Aliger**'s brother (a Morisco whose name he does not know, but who is a healer[13]) to Arévalo's wife's daughter, [**Ana de Arévalo**]. After they sealed the marriage agreement and went to ask for her in the manner described above—this was after they had published the marriage banns[14]—the bride and groom

---

[10] Compare this account with Docs. 9 and 12.

[11] Indulgences were a vital part of the spiritual economy of the medieval Church and of early modern Roman Catholicism. Many different types of indulgences existed, but they were granted by the pope and were used to remit the temporal punishment owed for sins. Jubilees were a particularly ample type of indulgence usually granted only every 25 or 50 years. Bulls of crusade, by contrast, were relatively cheap and abundant, which led millions of Spaniards to take them every year.

[12] Compare this account with Docs. 9 and 12.

[13] Gabriel's brother is **Alonso Aliger**.

[14] An announcement of a couple's intention to marry. The Council of Trent decreed that the banns were to be read from the pulpit for three weeks in a row in order to provide an opportunity for objections to be heard.

spoke the words ordained by the holy Council of Trent.[15] Then, **Lope del Sol** (a Morisco citizen of Deza whom they say has been reconciled by the Holy Office) said that once the banns had been performed and everything else had been done that was commanded by the holy mother Church *and by theirs*, they would be married (or words to that effect). Uzedo says that this seemed wrong to him.

Item: He said that he heard from Esteban Sanz de la Gorreta and others (but he does not remember whom) that when Gonzalo Bugueño was getting married, he placed an order for food for his wedding. Esteban Sanz asked him, "Will you be serving the wedding guests good mutton, good pork, and good wine?" And Gonzalo Burgueño, who is a Morisco, responded that he would rather die than serve that to his guests.

Later on, in the presence of **Juan de Deza** (a citizen of Deza and also a Morisco), Gonzalo Burgueño told Miguel Benito that it was true that he had spoken those words, but he had not meant anything bad by them. And Gonzalo Burgueño begged Miguel Benito, saying that if the episcopal *visitador*[16] came to Deza, Gonzalo would appear before him so that he could be given penance, if he deserved it. Miguel Benito does not know what became of this.

Item: He said that one of Deza's Moriscos goes to mass very rarely: Juan de Baptista, who lives on the *Corredero* and works as a laborer, but not often. On the many occasions when Miguel Benito has reprimanded him for missing mass, Juan de Baptista always gives excuses—that he is busy. In particular, this year Juan de Baptista's wife and daughters commemorated the first anniversary of the death of one of his daughters. Yet Juan de Baptista attended neither the office of mass nor vespers,[17] even though he was in town at the time. Miguel Benito looked into this as did *bachiller* **Juan Valles** (one of Deza's clerics).

Juan de Baptista's wife is an Old Christian. It seems to Miguel Benito that someone (but he does not remember whom) told him that she had commented about her husband not going to mass, saying, "To the devil with them! They're just as much Moors now as they've always been!"

---

[15] Miguel Benito is referring to the words of consent given in Session 24, Chapter 1 of Trent's *Canons and Decrees*, which states that "[t]he parish priest, after having interrogated the man and the woman, and heard their mutual consent, shall either say, 'I join you together in matrimony, in the name of the Father, and of the Son, and of the Holy Ghost;' or, he shall use other words, according to the received rite of each province."

[16] A representative of Deza's bishop who visited the diocese's parishes to determine whether they were complying with the procedural norms established by episcopal decree or at diocesan synods.

[17] Vespers is the liturgical service of worship conducted in the evening.

Item: He said that this past Lent, **Luis de Cieli** (a Morisco weaver of linen and citizen of Deza) received the Most Holy Sacrament, but Miguel Benito knows for certain that he had not confessed.[18] He made inquiries to determine with whom Cieli had confessed, and learned that he had not confessed with any of the town's clerics nor was his name recorded among the confessants. Then, a little while later, Cieli left town and has not returned, but they say he is in Aragon near Tarazona.

Item: He said that for the last twelve years—and for even longer, ever since he has lived in town—when they dig graves for the Moriscos, they dig them deeper than for the Old Christians. They try to bury them at the furthest edges of the cemetery, and none of them do the anniversary mass. The Moriscos themselves dig the graves and, what is more, they do not have masses said for dead Moriscos, except for the novena. (And then he said the fulfillment of the novena *and* the anniversary mass.)[19]

When asked by the inquisitor, he said he did not know of a specific case in which the grave had been dug in virgin ground but he suspects, since they dig the graves so deep, that that is their purpose.

The inquisitor asked Miguel Benito if he knew anything about a discussion regarding whether the soul of Jesus Christ is in the sacrament of the altar[20] and whether someone said, "Far be it. It's not," and whether this led to an argument.[21] He said he seems to remember that about two or three years ago he and **bachiller Juan Ruiz** (a town cleric) were standing in Deza's church cemetery—and there were other people there, but he does not remember their names. *Bachiller* Juan Ruiz and the others were debating the sacrament of the altar. He does not remember who else witnessed the debate (or discussion) but, while addressing the issue, *bachiller* Juan Ruiz concluded that the body and blood of Jesus Christ were not in the consecrated host—or words to that effect.

Now Miguel Benito remembers that **Jerónimo Barba**† (one of Deza's clerics, currently in Valencia) was there. And he thinks **Licentiate Páez**†† (physician) or the prior Juan Valles§ (a cleric) was present too.

---

[18] All Roman Catholic Christians were required to sacramentally confess their sins to a priest at least once a year. Usually, they did this during Lent in preparation for receiving the Eucharist at Easter. It was forbidden to take communion without having made a confession.

[19] During the Middle Ages and in the Roman Catholic Church during the early modern period, masses were said for the dead in order to speed the deceased on their way through purgatory and onto heaven. A novena is an act of religious devotion repeated for a period of nine days. It typically involves a series of set prayers and is performed in the hope of obtaining special intercessory grace. An anniversary mass was celebrated to commemorate an event, in this case, the death of a loved one.

[20] That is, the Eucharist.

[21] Compare this account with Docs. 6 and 8.

Exterior of the Parish Church of Deza
The parish church of Our Lady of the Assumption was constructed over
a period of several decades in the late sixteenth century. The tower was
completed only in 1612, the year after Deza's Moriscos were expelled.
Photo credit: Rachel A. O'Banion, 2013

Initially, they were discussing the material of the sacrament, but they moved on to the aforementioned topic. They addressed it by way of debate, and *bachiller* Ruiz's opinion was opposed from the beginning, as it seems to this witness. Then they consulted Chaves or Navarro,[22] or maybe both to see how they dealt with this matter. And the *bachiller* acknowledged that what they said was correct.[‡]

Miguel Benito does not remember if they consulted Chaves and Navarro on the same day that they debated the topic.

When asked, he said that he considers *bachiller* Ruiz to be an Old Christian and a good cleric. This is the truth under oath, and he does not say it out of hatred. He was charged to keep it secret and he promised to do so. This happened in my presence: **Pablo García**, notary.

[†] On January 9, 1570, [a representative of the inquisitorial tribunal of Cuenca] wrote to the Inquisitors of Valencia to have them examine Jerónimo Barba.

[††] On September 28, 1569, Licentiate Páez (physician) was formally examined, and he said he had not been present to hear such words nor had he heard what *bachiller* Ruiz (cleric) said. He was charged to keep it secret.

[§] Juan Valles was subsequently examined.

[‡] On October 1, 1569, this same Miguel Benito (vicar) appeared before this same lord inquisitor and clarified that, with reference to the books that they had examined, they consulted both Navarro *and* Chaves on the matter. And regarding what he had said about *bachiller* Juan Ruiz's proposal and argument: it was that only the body, but not the blood, of Our Lord Jesus Christ was in the consecrated host. And in everything else, he refers to what he has said. He was charged to keep it secret. This happened in my presence: Pablo García.

8

RECEIVED ON JANUARY 21, 1570[23]

In the City of Valencia on January 14, 1570, having been summoned, *mosén* **Jerónimo Barba** (who is a priest cleric, born in the town of Deza in Castile, which is in the diocese of Sigüenza, and who is currently a citizen of Valencia) appeared before the lord Inquisitor Licentiate don Joan de Royas in the senate room of the Holy Office during the afternoon audience. He said that he was about 30 years old, and by means of an oath, he placed himself in the hands and power of the lord inquisitor.

---

[22] Here "Chaves" probably refers to Tomás de Chaves's *Sum of the Sacraments of the Church*, a compilation of the work of his teacher, Francisco de Vitoria (d. 1546). The book was published originally in Latin beginning in 1560 and in Castilian translation from Madrid in 1565. "Navarro" is Martín de Azpilcueta (1492–1586), sometimes known as Dr. Navarro, whose *Manual for Confessors and Penitents*, first published in 1553, was one of the bestsellers of the early modern Roman Catholic world.

[23] Compare this account with Docs. 6–7.

When asked by the inquisitor, he said that he does not know nor did he presume the reason why he has been summoned to this Holy Office.

When asked, he said that as far as he recalls, he knows of no one who has either said or done anything against God Our Lord or the holy Catholic faith nor against that which our Holy Mother Roman Church preaches and teaches. Nor does he have any memory of any such thing.

He was told to think well about what he is saying and to scour his memory, for information exists suggesting that three years ago in a certain part of the diocese of Sigüenza a certain person said and insisted in his presence that only the body of our Lord Jesus Christ was in the consecrated host but not the blood. So, let him speak the truth and unburden his conscience. And thus he was charged to unburden his conscience.

He said, "Your lordship will know that I came to Valencia from my homeland around three years ago. And a man named **Pedro Ruiz Polo**, the uncle of one of my teachers,[24] told me that in the town of Deza, while they were alone....

The remainder of this document, which is written in a different hand than the rest, is missing.

9

In the town of Deza on September 21, 1569, a man who had been summoned appeared before the lord Inquisitor **Licentiate Reynoso**.[25] He was sworn in and promised to speak the truth. He said his name was:

Witness: Francisco de Uzedo, a citizen of Deza. He said he was about 32 years old. When he was asked if he knows or presumes why he was called before this Holy Office he said, "No."

He was asked if he knows, has seen, or has heard of anything contrary (or anything that might appear to be contrary) to our holy Catholic faith or anything that contradicts what the holy Mother Church of Rome holds to or teaches.

He said he does not recall any such thing, except that about three or four years ago—he thinks this is right, but is not certain of the time—he was in Deza at the house of **Gabriel Aliger** (a Morisco muleteer and farmer, a citizen of Deza). They had arrived at an agreement to marry Gabriel's brother, **Alonso Aliger** (who is a healer), to the daughter of a Morisco named Luis de Arévalo. He believes her name is María de Arévalo.[26]

---

[24] The teacher referred to here is a woman: *maestra*.
[25] Compare this account with Docs. 7 and 12.
[26] Francisco is mistaken. Her name is **Ana de Arévalo**.

The Moriscos have a custom: when one of them wants to marry, after negotiating the marriage contract, they either choose relatives or a couple of other people to act on the groom's behalf. They go to the bride's parents and ask them for her in the groom's name. Then, afterward, they eat food. Later, they perform the banns. So, in Alonso Aliger's name, the Moriscos **Lope de Deza** (also known as Lope del Sol) and **Román Ramírez [the elder]** went to the house of the bride's mother to ask for the bride. Then they returned to Gabriel Aliger's house, where this witness, **Juan Castro**, the **Licentiate Páez**[†] (physician), and lots of Moriscos had remained.

When they arrived, Lope de Deza declared that María[27] de Arévalo's mother said that she was delighted to give her daughter to be Alonso Aliger's wife. So they called Alonso Aliger, who was at his brother's house. When he arrived, Lope de Deza asked him, "Do you want María de Arévalo to be your spouse and wife as the holy Mother Church of Rome *and ours* commands?" Alonso Aliger said, "Yes." With that, they ate, and then they left and went out from there.

Later, Francisco de Uzedo mentioned to Juan de Castro[††§] what Lope de Deza had said. Juan Castro said that he had not heard it because he is hard of hearing. Moreover, because those words had seemed wrong to this witness, he told Deza's vicar about them.

Item:[28] He also said that about two months ago, **Luis de Cebea** (Morisco) married his son [**Luis de Cebea the younger**] to [**Francisca de Baptista**], the daughter of so-and-so de Baptista[29] (deceased). He also wedded his daughter [Ana de Cebea] to one of **Old Fadrique's** sons. (Francisco de Uzedo believes the son is named Juan.[30]) Once they had agreed on the marriage of Cebea's son with Baptista's daughter, Antonio de Melgosa, Leonis Cardenas, and Roman Ramírez[‡] went to ask for her on behalf of Luis de Cebea. And they returned with the answer: it would please her.

Then, Antonio de Melgosa said that Fadrique had asked for Luis de Cebea's daughter for his son. He replied that the marriage would make him very happy. Luis de Cebea said that he was content with it. And with that, they gave a meal. This is the truth.

The inquisitor asked him whether Deza's Old Christians follow the same ceremony as the Moriscos. Francisco de Uzedo said that he has not seen them nor is he aware of them doing so.

---

[27] That is, Ana de Arévalo.
[28] Compare this account with Docs. 7 and 12.
[29] Luis de Baptista.
[30] Juan Fadrique, also called Juan de San Juan.

And this is the truth on his oath, and he does not say it out of hatred. He was charged to keep it secret. This happened in my presence: **Pablo García**, notary.

† Licentiate Páez (physician) was examined under oath on [September 30, 1569] and he said that [...][31] Juan Castro and Francisco de Uzedo that he says he heard but that he did not hear such words. He was charged to keep it secret.

†† On September 29, 1569, Juan Castro was examined under oath and asked generally and specifically about this. He said that he had been present when they went to ask for Alonso Aliger's bride as well as when they returned with the answer—that she was delighted about it. He does not remember who went to ask for her let alone the exact words of the answer. He was charged to keep it secret, and he promised to do so. This happened in my presence: Pablo García, notary.

§ On September 30, 1569, Juan Castro said that he had remembered that the day after all this happened, Francisco de Uzedo said to him that Lope de Deza had said that [...][32] but that Juan Castro is deaf and did not hear him. That is how he replied to Uzedo.

‡ On October 1, 1569, Román Ramírez was examined under oath and said that he did not remember this. He was charged to keep it secret.

Alonso Aliger was examined under oath on [October 1, 1569] and he said *nihil*.[33] He was charged to keep it secret.

10

In the town of Deza on September 30, 1569, a man who had not been summoned appeared before the lord Inquisitor **Licentiate Reynoso**. He was sworn in and promised to speak the truth. He said his name was:

Witness: **Martín Rodríguez**, a citizen of Deza who works as a port guard.[34] He said he was more than 50 years old. In order to unburden his conscience, he declares that about four or five years ago, he was watching the town's goats. **Mateo [Romero the younger]** (son of **Mateo Romero [the elder]**, a Morisco and citizen of Deza) was walking with him, along with some of Mateo's father's goats. Mateo, who was then 13 or 14 years old, ate pork and lard and tallow with Martín and his sons. Everything that they ate, he happily ate.

Then, one day around that time, the lad's mother[35]—who is Mateo Romero's wife; Martín does not know her name—said to him, "For the

---

[31] Illegible.

[32] Illegible.

[33] Latin: "Nothing."

[34] Deza was a "dry port," where travelers could cross the border between the kingdoms of Castile and Aragon. Those who crossed had to register their horses and pay an import duty on any merchandise they were transporting. Thus, Martín Rodríguez worked as a sort of border guard who collected taxes under the oversight of a customs official.

[35] **Ana Almoravi.**

love of God, don't force Mateo to eat pork or lard against his will!" Martín told her that he was eating it of his own accord, but again she pleaded with him not to give him any of that stuff to eat. Since they do not eat it, she did not want Mateo to eat it.

After that, Mateo never ate pork or lard again although Martín and his sons did so in Mateo's presence, and he watched them. When Martín asked Mateo why he did not eat any, the lad replied that his mother had forbidden him.

When asked by the inquisitor, Martín Rodríguez said that they had been alone when Mateo's mother had spoken those words. Mateo is now married ~~and usually keeps goats~~, and they say that his mother and father want to move to Terrer because they come from there[†]. Mateo is married to [**Ana de Almanzorre**], a daughter of the Almanzorre woman.

This is the truth according to the oath that he took and he does not say it out of hatred. He was charged to keep it secret and promised to do so. This happened in my presence: **Pablo García**, notary.

[†] In Deza on October 1, 1569 before the lord Inquisitor, Licentiate Reynoso, Martín Rodríguez appeared, having been summoned. He swore the oath and promised to speak the truth. He was asked who told him that Mateo Romero was moving to Terrer, which is in Aragon, and when they had told him. Martín responded that **Román Ramírez the younger** (a Morisco who is a port guard in Deza) told him that Mateo Romero is moving to Terrer, which is where he comes from. Martín thinks that Mateo Romero has lived in Deza for ten or twelve years. And at night on Saint Michael's Eve [i.e., September 28], Mateo Romero moved two loads of household goods from his home in Deza to Aragon.

Francisco de Sevilla, Deza's customs agent, told Martín that Mateo Romero asked permission to move some goats—about 12 or 13, he thinks. All of this took place since the arrival of the lord Inquisitor to Deza. Mateo Romero is at least 40 years old by Martín's reckoning. Martín was charged to keep it secret and promised to do so. This happened in my presence: Pablo García, notary.

Item: He said that Mateo Romero is in Deza right now; he just saw him in the plaza.

11

In Deza, September 30, 1569, a young woman who had not been summoned appeared before the lord Inquisitor **Licentiate Reynoso**.[36] She was sworn in and promised to speak the truth. She said her name was:

Witness: **Ana Montera**, the daughter of Francisco Montero, who is a farmer and a citizen of Deza. She said she was 17 going on 18. In order to unburden her conscience she declares that she used to live in the house of

---

[36] Compare this account with Doc. 14.

Mateo Romero [the elder], a Morisco and citizen of Deza who is a farmer and often tends goats; he lives in Eugenio Hernández's house in what they call his "pen." Ana Montera worked for Mateo Romero for two years, but it has been two years (and going on three) since she left his service.

Two years ago on Shrove Tuesday, the son of Licentiate Miñana, a citizen of Miñana named Román, gave a hunk of cured beef to Mateo Romero's wife, an old woman named **Ana Almoravi**. He gave the meat to her in Miñana, which is where Mateo Romero and his wife were staying at the time. On Shrove Tuesday, they came to Deza and Ana Montera said to Ana Almoravi, "Let's throw that cured beef in a pot, Auntie." Ana Almoravi responded, "Why? There's plenty of other stuff to eat. This will be good for Easter, if God wills it." So she did not put it in the pot.[37]

Later, during Lent—she is not sure if two weeks of Lent had passed or more—Ana Montera saw that same hunk of cured beef soaking in a pot; it was in one of the pots from Almonacid in a kitchen cupboard. She dared not say anything to her mistress but instead went into the house of Juan Sanz (an Old Christian who lived next door) and told his wife **Marí [Montón]** about finding the cured beef in the pot. María told her, "Don't even let the ground know. But keep watch for anything else they do, because the inquisitors are coming." So, she kept her mouth shut and said nothing.

Then, on another day, Ana Montera saw that cured beef cooking in the pot over the fire, but saw nothing else happen. And she said to her mistress, "Auntie, I'd like to get something to eat from that pot." But Ana Almoravi said, "I don't want you to eat tonight. You can eat tomorrow." Later that night, at dinnertime, Ana Almoravi sent Ana Montera out to get some oil. When she returned, she found Mateo Romero and Ana Almoravi eating. She saw them take that meat from the plate and eat it. Their son, **Mateo Romero**, and his wife, **Ana de Almanzorre**, were there too, although she did not see them eat the meat.

When Ana Montera went in, Ana her mistress shoved the plate under the table. Her son Mateo Romero grabbed a bone from that cured beef—it was sitting on a cloak atop a chest—and he tossed it down the stairs. Ana Montera went upstairs to the kitchen and set down the oil cruet that she had fetched. Then, she went down to the front door, retrieved the bone that Mateo had thrown, and tossed it up to the kitchen. Her mistress said, "Annie,

---

[37] During Lent, an annual season of repentance and fasting that precedes the commemoration of Jesus Christ's resurrection, Roman Catholics refrained from eating meat. Lent begins on Ash Wednesday and lasts 40 days (plus Sundays) and culminates on Easter Sunday. Thus, the last day to eat meat before Lent begins is the Tuesday preceding Ash Wednesday, known as Shrove (or Fat) Tuesday.

what's that?" And she responded, "It's the bone from the eel, auntie." Then Mateo, her masters' son, found the bone and tossed it into the pen.

But Ana Montera knew that the bone was from that cured beef—it came from the fore shank and brisket. And when she washed their plates, she clearly saw that they had stewed the meat and eaten it; there was congealed fat on the plate and in the pot. She told Juan Sanz's wife María that her employers had eaten cured meat during Lent. María told her not to say anything to anybody. And nobody except for the people she mentioned saw what she has just described.

Item: She said that afterward, during that same Lenten season, she was in that same house and, for 15 or 16 days, she never saw Mateo Romero or his wife Ana eat during the day—neither in the morning nor at midday—not until night after bedtime, around nine or ten o'clock at night. Then, Ana Almoravi, Mateo Romero's wife, would get up and cook rice.

Ana Montera never saw her eat it, but the next morning she would find a large earthenware pot in the house that seemed to have been used to cook rice along with two bowls and a spoon that looked to have held rice. She asked her mistress, "Auntie, who put this here?" Ana Almoravi responded, "Shut up and wash them."

That whole time, she never saw Mateo Romero or his wife eat or drink anything. But her mistress gave her some sardines and bread to eat. And at the end of that time, Ana Montera saw them eat supper at midday—eel and fish, sardines and eggs, milk and other things. But during those 15 or 16 days, Ana Montera was never away from the house at mealtime. If they had eaten something, she would have seen it.

She also kept record of how much bread was in the house, and it seemed like they were not eating any of it. She always assumed that they were doing this on account of heresy—the law of Mohammed—for she had heard Old Christians say that Moriscos do not eat during the day, only at night.[38] When Ana Montera told Juan Sanz's wife María that her employers did not eat during the day but only at night, María responded, "Quiet, quiet. Don't even let the ground know that they are fasting for the law of Mohammed."

Item: She said that later, Ana her mistress went to Ágreda to sell cheese. That night, when she returned to Deza, the crucifix was being carried in a procession from the town's church. Ana her mistress said, "God help me! What a big Jesus! How can they carry him?!" Her husband Mateo Romero and Ana de Almanzorre, her daughter-in-law, were both present.

---

[38] Presumably, Romero and Almoravi were observing the Islamic fast of Ramadan, during which Muslims refrain from eating or drinking between sunrise and sunset.

Ana Montero said that this is the truth under the oath she swore. She does not say it out of any enmity that she has for them but rather because it is the truth and in order to unburden her conscience. She was charged to keep it secret and she promised to do so. This happened in my presence: **Pablo García**, notary.

12

In Deza on September 30, 1569 a man who was summoned appeared before the lord Inquisitor **Licentiate Reynoso**.[39] He was sworn in and he promised to speak the truth. He said his name was:

Witness: the **Licentiate Antonio Páez**, a physician and citizen of Deza. He said that he was 59 or 60 years old. When asked generally, he said that he neither knew nor presumed to know why he had been summoned, nor does he recall having heard anything said that should be revealed to the Holy Office.

He was asked if he had heard one person say to another, "Do you promise to marry so-and-so, once the banns have been performed as the holy mother Church of Rome and ours commands?" He said that he remembered no such thing.

Asked if he had come across some people somewhere going to ask for some woman's hand in marriage on behalf of some man. And whether, upon returning with the response, someone had spoken the words about which he has just been asked. He said, yes, he has come across some things of this sort, but he does not remember having heard those specific words.

Asked if he was present when **Alonso Aliger**, a Morisco healer, sent to ask for the hand in marriage of Luis de Arévalo's daughter?[40] And whether, after the men who went to ask for her returned, someone spoke those words to Alonso Aliger? Licentiate Páez responded that about three years ago he was at the house of **Gabriel Aliger** (a Morisco muleteer and farmer) along with Juan de Castro, Francisco de Uzedo (both citizens of Deza), Román Ramírez[41] (a Morisco), and other people. While Páez was there, two men went to ask for Luis de Arévalo's daughter's hand in marriage on behalf of Alonso Aliger, who is Gabriel Aliger's brother. **Lope de Deza** (also known as Lope del Sol, a Morisco whom Páez has heard was reconciled by

---

[39] Compare this account with Docs. 7 and 9.
[40] That is, **Ana de Arévalo**.
[41] This is probably **Román Ramírez the elder**.

this Holy Office) was one of them. And Páez thinks that maybe Román Ramírez was the other but is not certain. Yet, he does not remember anyone speaking the words about which he was asked.

Páez was told that the Holy Office has information that those words were spoken in his presence. Wherefore, he was admonished to scour his memory and speak the truth. He replied that he did not remember any such thing but that he would reflect on it, and if he does remember, he will return and declare it. He was charged to keep it secret and he promised to do so. This happened in my presence: **Pablo García**, notary.

Later, after the above occurred, on October 1, 1569, Licentiate Antonio Páez appeared before the lord Inquisitor without being summoned. He said that he has thought about what His Grace asked him yesterday. And [inserted: *under the oath that he swore*] he has recalled that while he and the others whom he mentioned were at Gabriel Aliger's house after Lope de Deza and his companion returned from asking for Luis de Arévalo's daughter's hand on behalf of Alonso Aliger, Lope de Deza told Alonso Aliger and everyone else that Luis de Arévalo's widow was content to give her daughter to him to be his wife. And Lope de Deza asked Alonso Aliger, "Do you, Alonso Aliger, promise that, once you perform the banns that the Holy Council commands, you will take Ana de Arévalo as wife and spouse according to the command of the holy Mother Church of Rome *and of ours?*"

To Páez this seemed poorly said. Lope de Deza should not have said "and of ours," but should have been satisfied to say only "the holy Mother Church of Rome." Since Lope de Deza is a Morisco, it sounds even worse. But Páez considers Lope de Deza to be a man of meager understanding— he does not grasp what the holy Mother Church of Rome is. It must have seemed to him that the "Church of Rome" was all the walls and altarpieces and images. So, it was necessary for his church in Deza to command it too. He is a man of limited capacity, as was said. This is why Páez did not pay attention to it.

He was asked if he had attended other Morisco marriage ceremonies. He said that he had attended many. He kept company with them in order to honor them.

He was asked if he has heard those words spoken at the other weddings. He said he does not remember having heard them from anybody.

He was asked about his experience with Moriscos in Deza contracting marriages. He said that over the last 35 years that he has lived in this town, he has seen the following: after reaching an agreement for a man and a woman to be married among the Moriscos, and after agreeing to the dowry and the vows, the groom's family and friends gather together in his father's or brother's house. Likewise, the bride's family and friends gather in her house. Both Old Christians and Moriscos attend these gatherings.

Two of the most honored and senior of those at the groom's house are chosen; sometimes they are Moriscos and at other times Old Christians. Whether Old Christians or Moriscos, they go to the bride's house and tell her parents that so-and-so has a son named such-and-such who is of age to marry. And it has occurred to them that they have a very virtuous and honorable daughter, and it seems good for the son to take her as wife. So, he asks, for mercy's sake, that the daughter be given and bestowed upon the son.

Then, two people on the bride's side stand up on behalf of her parents. And they say that, of course, they know such-and-such, son of so-and-so, and they consider him to be very honorable. And it goes without saying that they will give their daughter to him as a wife and that he honors them. Then they eat, and they take the answer back to the groom's house and report on what happened. Then they eat at the groom's house, and they inform his parents—if he has them and, if not, then they tell the groom himself—that once the banns are performed, he will marry the woman whom he has been pursuing.

This is the usual practice at all of Deza's Morisco marriages. And, specifically, he has seen it at the marriage that he mentioned as well as at two marriages that were performed three or four months ago. The first was between **[Luis de Cebea the younger]**, who is **Luis de Cebea [the elder's]** son and Luis de Baptista's daughter, **[Francisca de Baptista]**. The second was between [Ana de Cebea], the daughter of that same Luis de Cebea, and **Old Fadrique's** son. (All of them were Moriscos.) This is not typical among Old Christians.

This is the truth under the oath that he took and he does not say it out of hatred. He was charged to keep it secret and he promised to do so. This happened in my presence: Pablo García, notary.

13

In Deza on October 1, 1569, a man who had not been summoned appeared before the lord Inquisitor **Licentiate Reynoso**.[42] He was sworn in and promised to speak the truth. He said that his name was:

Witness: Juan de Santestevan, a farmer, citizen of Deza, and about 50 years old. He said that in order to unburden his conscience he declares that about a year ago he was traveling from Soria with Martín Prieto† (a muleteer

---

42 Compare this account with Doc. 21.

and citizen of Cihuela) and a son of Alonso Ropiñón (a Morisco conveyer of goods). Juan de Santestevan thinks the son is also named Alonso but is not certain. The lad is his father's only son and was maybe 16 years old.[††]

While they traveled between Almazul and Millana, Martín Prieto talked about the Aragonese Moriscos, about how they were bad. Alonso Ropiñón's son said, "What would it hurt the King to leave each one as he is in his own law?" Juan de Santestevan reprimanded him, saying, "Why are you talking about the things of God? That's what the Inquisition is for, so that no one talks about that sort of thing." And the lad shut his mouth and did not respond.

Item:[43] He said that a year ago he was harvesting with Rodrigo Navarro (a citizen of Deza) near the town's *humilladero*—they call that field the Campoalaves. Juan de Santestevan, Pedro Remarcha (a citizen of Deza who is a shepherd and keeps some rams for the town's butchers), Juan Blasco (a citizen of Deza), and the aforementioned Rodrigo Navarro were present. Pedro Remarcha said that one night around midnight, when he was returning from his livestock, he discovered **Román Ramírez the elder** (a Morisco and a citizen of Deza) bathing in the Argadil River.[44] He did nothing except recognize Ramírez and passed by without saying a word.

Item: He said that more than five years ago he was talking with Román Ramírez's wife, [**María de Luna**], who is now deceased. He does not know her name. They were talking about how the Turks had captured **don Gastón [de la Cerda]**,[45] the duke of Medinaceli's son. Juan de Santestevan said, "Ma'am, they will treat don Gastón as his father's son." But she responded, "May they treat him as you like, sir. The Turk knows how few of us are scattered around here and how poorly we are treated. Why would they treat a duke's son or anyone else well over there?"[46]

When she said it, the two of them were alone, this witness and the woman. This is the truth under the oath that he swore and he promised to keep it secret. This happened in my presence: **Pablo García**, notary.

[†] On October 2, 1569, Juan de Santestevan said that the lad to whom he is referring here is named Alonso Ropiñón, like his father. He said this in front of the Inquisitor. In my presence: Pablo Garcia, notary.

[††] On October 3, 1569, Juan de Santestevan said that it was not Martín but rather Miguel Prieto (a citizen of Cihuela) to whom Alonso Ropiñón told what Juan de Santestevan has declared. He said this under the oath that he swore.

---

[43] Compare this account with Doc. 19.

[44] It is not altogether clear how the witness interpreted Ramírez's actions, but the inquisitors would have recognized them as a sign of Islamic activity: the ritual ablutions known as *guadoc*, which Muslims performed before reciting their daily prayers (*azala*).

[45] The son of **Juan de la Cerda**.

[46] María de Luna's statement is grammatically garbled, but this seems the likely meaning.

The Argadil River
Flowing into town from the north, the Argadil provided Deza
with fresh water and carried away refuse. It was also used by
crypto-Muslims to perform the ritual ablutions known as *guadoc*.
Photo credit: Rachel A. O'Banion, 2013

14

In Deza on October 1, 1569, a woman who had been summoned appeared
before the lord Inquisitor **Licentiate Reynoso**.[47] She was sworn in and
promised to speak the truth. She said her name was:

Witness: **Mari Montón**, the wife of Juan Sanz, a mountaineer and citizen of Deza. She said she was more than 35 years old.

She was asked if she knew or presumed the reason why she has been
summoned to this Holy Office. She said, "Yes." She was told to declare it
and to speak the truth in everything.

She said that three years ago this coming Lent, there was a drought
around here—and elsewhere, too, they say. So, they took the crucifix from
the parish church and carried it in precession two or three times. Afterward,

---

[47] Compare this account with Doc. 11.

Ana [Montera] (Montero's daughter; he keeps the town's oxen) told her that when she was working for **Mateo Romero [the elder]** (a Morisco), his wife **Ana Almoravi** had said, "What are they trying to do? Why do they want to take out that big ol' god?" Then, Mari told Ana Montera, "Shut up. Keep your mouth closed until the holy Inquisition gets here."

Item: She said three years ago this coming Lent—it happened after what she just described but she does not remember exactly when in Lent— she and Ana Montera were talking in her house. (She was and is Mateo Romero's neighbor.) Ana Montera told her that during Carnival of that year Ana Almoravi, Mateo Romero's wife, brought a hunk of cured beef from Miñana on Shrove Tuesday.[48] And Ana Montera told her mistress to toss all the meat in a pot that day for Carnival, since it was the last day to eat meat. But her mistress said that they already had lots of meat in the pot, so she did not need to.

Then later, during that same Lent, Ana Almoravi set that meat to soak. And when she put Ana Montera to cleaning the pots, she found the meat in one of them. Ana Montera told Mari Montón that when her mistress saw her, she came running and asked if she had gotten to that one pot. Ana Montera told her that she had not.

On another day, Ana Almoravi cooked food to eat that night, and about the time that dusk fell, they sent the girl away from the house. (She did not say where.) Ana Montera returned quickly and found Mateo Romero and his wife Ana Almoravi and their son (also named Mateo, but she does not know his surname[49]) and his wife **Ana de Almanzorre** eating that meat.

When Ana Montera entered, they took the plate and quickly shoved it under the table. They were left holding slices of the meat! When she asked her mistress why she put the plate beneath the table, Ana Almoravi responded, "We finished eating." Mateo the younger tossed a bone down the stairs and the girl, to confirm that they were eating meat, went down to the door and searched for the bone. She found it and left it there. Then, Mateo came down to find the bone and tossed it onto a roof. This witness told the girl, "Keep quiet. Don't even mention this to the ground." After that she did not speak another word to her.

About 15 days ago or maybe a little more (but less than three weeks, because that is when the lord Inquisitor came to Deza; at this point His Grace was still in Almazán) the girl Ana, Montero's daughter, came to Mari Montón's house and said to her, "María, do you remember what I told you

---

[48] Carnival is an annual festive period before the season of Lent and culminates on Shrove Tuesday.

[49] **Mateo Romero the younger.**

about my mistress's house? About the crucifix and eating meat during Lent? Remember them, because you're going to be questioned."

Ana said this to her so that Mari Montón would know that Ana had told her brother, **Bartolome Montero** (the town's sacristan) that she had told Mari about what happened. But her brother said Ana was lying, that she had not told Mari her story and that Ana's brother would have to confirm it with Mari. But he never came.

Later, Ana Montera told Mari Montón that on certain nights—she did not say how many nor which—after her master and mistress, Mateo Romero and Ana Almoravi, went to bed, they got up again and cooked rice.[50] She did not say what time.

Ana Montera's mistress wore only a chemise while she cooked. And little by little she drifted over to where the girl was lying and looked to see if she was asleep. Ana pretended she was so that they would not know she was watching them. She saw them eat what Ana Almoravi had cooked, and they kept eating and eating, except when they got up and cooked.

Ana Montera never said whether they ate during the day as well. But Mari Montón told her, "Keep quiet. For the love of God, don't even let the ground know about this. Don't tell anyone." The girl did not respond. Mari Montón told all of this to her husband, who is currently in the mountains.

She was asked if she had heard anyone talk about people who refrained from eating during the day and only ate at night. She said that she had not heard such a thing from anyone.

She was told that the Holy Office has received an account that someone made that statement to this witness. Mari Montón responded that she has never heard of such a thing, except for what she has said.

She was told to understand the following: information exists that, when someone told her that certain people did not eat during the day but waited until night, she responded, "Keep quiet. They were fasting for the law of Mohamed." She said that she has never heard such a thing nor has she said that to anyone.

She was asked where Ana Montera is now and how long she has known her. Mari said that she has known her for more than ten years, and nowadays she lives in her father's house. But she has heard it said that they put her into service at the house of Martín Gutierrez, a farmer.

She was asked how long Ana Montera served Mateo Romero. She said, "Two years."

She was asked what sort of young woman Ana Montera is. She said that Ana is a good lass. She considers her to be a good Christian and the

---

[50] See footnote 38.

daughter of good Old Christian parents. Mari believed what Ana Montera said because Ana Almoravi is so evil; she just kept on doing and saying everything that Ana Montera said.

When asked, Mari Montón said that she has never seen Ana Almoravi do anything bad, only that twice she had seen her washing knit breeches on Sunday.[51]

She was asked how Mateo Romero and Ana Almoravi treated Ana Montera while she lived with them. Mari said that they treated her badly. They denied her food, preferring to let her starve. And she heard that the whole time Ana Montera had lived in their house, she never slept in a bed but on the floor instead. Mari Montón said she did not see any other mistreatment or punishment.

She was asked where Mateo Romero and Ana Almoravi came from. She said that they are natives of Terrer, five leagues[52] from here in the Kingdom of Aragon, and they are Moriscos. They have lived in Deza for 13 or 14 years already; they came here poor but now they are rich.

She said that this coming Monday they are moving back to Terrer, where much of their household is already located. A good four months ago they began talking about leaving. When Your Grace arrived in town, Ana Almoravi told her that she did not want to leave Deza while the inquisitor was in town, but she did not say why.

In addition to this, Ana Almoravi was on the verge of tears about leaving Deza. She does not want to move away from here. Mari Montón saw this and learned about it from Ana Almoravi after her husband started making plans to move to Terrer, which was more than four months ago, as she said.

This is the truth under oath and she does not say it out of hatred. She was charged to keep it secret and she promised to do so. This happened in my presence: **Pablo García**, notary.

15

In the town of Deza on October 2, 1569, a man appeared before the lord Inquisitor **Licentiate Reynoso** without having been summoned. He was sworn in and promised to speak the truth. He said his name was:

Witness: **Diego Rodríguez**, a carpenter from the north, a citizen of Cogolludo, who resides in the town of Deza working on the House of the

---

[51] For Christians, Sunday was set apart as holy and therefore typically not an appropriate day for labor.

[52] About 20 miles.

Duke of Medinaceli. He said that he is 36 years old. He said that in order to unburden his conscience he declares that more than 12 years ago he was in this town with the Duke of Medinaceli. He went hunting with his uncle Pedro de Nates (a carpenter from the north, deceased; a citizen of Nates in La Montaña near the Rada River), Francisco Burgueño (a potter whose nose has been cut off), and his brother. (He thinks Francisco Burgueño only has one brother; this one is married and is a potter.)[†] They released a hare in the area known as the Courts, at the edge of the town. And the greyhounds went after it and caught it under some crags. This witness went in under the crags and got the hare. He took it alive and wanted to kill it, but Francisco Burgueño told him not to, so he held back. Francisco Burgueño took out a little knife—he does not know where he was carrying it—and slit the hare's throat. He stuck the knife in its neck without cutting the hide open.[53]

Then they caught two other hares and Francisco Burgueño said, "Give me this one with the slit throat and do whatever you want with the others." So, Francisco Burgueño took the hare with the slit throat while he and his uncle kept the rest.

When asked, he said that he does not know why Francisco Burgueño slit the hare's throat nor did he hear him say anything. No one else was there except for the four people he mentioned. Francisco Burgueño and his brother are Moriscos.

Item: he said that at about the same time, while he and his uncle were staying in Deza, they wanted to cook some pork.[54] So, they went to Francisco Burgueño's house to cook it. While they were cooking, Francisco Burgueño and his wife (whose name he does not know) left the house. They never said anything to them, but they gave them a sauce in which to cook the pork.

He does not know where they went but suspected that they left the house to avoid the smell of pork. For they say that only a few of the Moriscos in this town eat it and even fewer drink wine.

This is the truth under oath and he does not say it out of hatred. He did not mention it earlier because he did not think there was anything wrong with it. And, moreover, he came twice and they told him that the inquisitor was busy. He was charged to keep it secret and he promised to do so. He was ordered to find out the name of Francisco Burgueño's brother. This happened in my presence: **Pablo García**, notary.

[†] On October 4, 1569, Diego Rodríguez told the lord Inquisitor that they told him that Francisco Burgueño's brother, whom he said accompanied them on the hunt, is called Bernardino Burgueño and is married. He was charged to keep it secret. In my presence: Pablo García, notary.

---

[53] Francisco appears to have been killing the hare in accordance with Islamic dietary practices.
[54] Muslims are forbidden to eat pork.

16

In Deza on October 2, 1569, a man appeared before the lord Inquisitor **Licentiate Reynoso** without having been summoned. He was sworn in and promised to speak the truth. He said his name was:

Witness: Pedro Raso, farmer, a citizen of this town, about 46 years old, more or less. He said that in order to unburden his conscience he declares that about six ~~or eight~~ years ago more or less by his reckoning, he and Miguel Pérez (farmer, Old Christian, a citizen of this town) were returning from having plowed. They were talking about the Day of Judgment and Miguel Pérez said that there was no judgment. This witness did not respond, but he continued to talk about it. He considers Miguel Pérez to be a good Christian and they were alone.

Item: He said that about eight or ten years ago, a bit more or less, he and the **Licentiate Páez** (physician, a citizen of Deza) were in this town of Deza in the house of Juan Ruiz's widow. They were talking about matters related ~~said~~ to death. This witness said that if he knew his works merited going to heaven, it would not bother him a bit to die. But the licentiate said that even if he knew that he would go to heaven right now, he still would not want to die, for even God—God Himself!—went about scrabbling to avoid death.[55] How much more we who are sinners? They were alone because even though Juan Ruiz's wife (who is called Agueda García) was in the house, she was going about her chores. He does not believe that she heard anything.

And when asked, he said that he has heard it said that the Licentiate Páez is a *confeso* of Jewish lineage. He considers him a good Christian. This is the truth under the oath that he took and he does not say it out of hatred. He was charged to keep it secret and he promised to do so. This happened in my presence: **Pablo García**, notary.

17

In the town of Deza on October 2, 1569, a woman who had been summoned appeared before the lord Inquisitor **Licentiate Reynoso**. She was sworn in and promised to speak the truth. She called herself:

Witness: **Madalena de Montón**, wife of Juan Cervero, shepherd. She is a citizen of this town of Deza, aged 25 or 26 years.

---

[55] Páez probably had in mind Jesus' prayer in the Garden of Gethsemane recorded in Luke 12:42.

Asked if she knows or presumes the reason why she was summoned before this Holy Office, she said, "Yes."

She was told to say it.

She said that about three years ago more or less one Friday between the festivals of Easter and Pentecost she was going to wash some clothes for the wife of **Juan de Contreras the younger** (a Morisco farmer who, along with his wife, had been held under arrest in Cuenca). It was a bit cold when she came to get the wash and while Juan de Contreras's wife gathered up the clothes, this witness went over by the stove. She noticed a pot on the fire and took the lid off to see what was cooking. She saw that it contained a mixture of eggs and cheese, fat and spices—a typical Morisco dish. And on top of it, there was a piece of meat.[56]

In order to make sure that it really was meat, she got a big spoon and stirred the pot to see what else was in there. At the bottom of the pot was the mixture that she mentioned. When she saw this, she turned to cover the pot and left it. She took the clothes and left to wash them. Before she left the house, Contreras's wife (who is called María) said that her husband was out plowing but was not well. This witness said nothing to her about the pot, which must have held more than enough for six bowls.

She has no idea what became of the stew because when she returned with the wash, she just put it in her house, charged what she was owed, and left. She told this to **Martín Fernández**, the town's commissioner of the Holy Office, which is why she had not come to speak with the inquisitor earlier. She thought that she had fulfilled her duty by telling Martín Fernández. She also told her sister [**Mari Montón**], the wife of Juan Sanz (mountaineer), and **Catarina Montón**, who is also her sister and Francisco de Arcos's wife. This is the truth under the oath that she swore and she does not say it out of hatred. She was charged to keep it secret. It happened in my presence: **Pablo García**, notary.

18

In the town of Deza on October 2, 1569, a woman appeared before the lord Inquisitor **Licentiate Reynoso** without having been summoned. She was sworn in and promised to speak the truth. She said her name was:

---

[56] Early modern Roman Catholicism considered Fridays to be days of fasting. In commemoration of Christ's death (on a Friday), the Church forbade the consumption of meat or dairy. Special permission to break the fast was sometimes granted to the sick, who needed extra nourishment.

Witness: María la Pola, wife of Juan de Santestevan (farmer, citizen of this town of Deza), aged 50 years. She said that in order to unburden her conscience she declares that about 20 years ago, more or less, **Jorge Montero** and his wife (whose name she does not remember, but she is a native of Arcos de Jalón and he is from Deza) came to live in this town. They had lived in Aragon but she does not know where. The Inquisition had punished Jorge Montero, so they say, because he circumcised Moors.[57] When they arrived, they had a boy with them named Jorge who would have been about a year and a half old. Currently, he is engaged to a Morisca from Medinaceli. (She does not know her name.) Nowadays they call him Jorge Montero and he is a farmer, but when Jorge was a little boy, not long after his parents arrived here, this witness ~~saw his~~ saw his member. It seemed to have been cut. This witness asked his mother, "Neighbor, why does this boy have such an ugly little thing?" She replied that it had been badly wounded; a barber had cured him but had cut it. And like she said before, back then he was just a baby, still nursing. His parents were Moriscos, now deceased.

Item: She said that about two or three weeks ago, on a holy day, she was at mass in Deza's church along with María de Guzman (the wife of Cisneros the tailor, citizen of this town), and a Morisca called the Queen (a servant of the Knight Commander **Martín Fernández**). The wife of Cisneros said that her son had told her what was happening in the Sierra Nevada Mountains between the Christians and the Moors. At this, the Queen left, saying, "All this trouble in Castile is the fault of the king's bad advisors. Why did the king make them wear different clothes and abandon their language? There have been Basques here for more than 20 years and they still speak their own language. But the king wanted to force the Moors to change theirs.[58] Yup, a fellow from Ateca, who was the warden, left from here to take slaves—both male and female—and he got his pay: a broken arm and a leg, too. And his lord stripped him of his wardenship."[59]

And this is the truth under the oath that she swore and she does not say it out of hatred. She was charged to keep it secret and she promised to do so. This happened in my presence: **Pablo García**, notary.

---

[57] Muslims, like Jews but unlike early modern Christians, circumcised their male children.

[58] The Queen is referring to the so-called Second War of the Alpujarras, which broke out in 1568 in the Kingdom of Granada. The conflict was ignited by efforts to eliminate the cultural and religious elements of the Moriscos' Islamic past. Among other things, Arabic and traditional dress were outlawed.

[59] This difficult passage lacks context, but the meaning appears to be that a former warden from Ateca, who had been involved in transporting Moorish slaves, ended up suffering a series of calamities. The Morisca known as the Queen apparently saw this as his just desserts.

19

In Deza on October 2, 1569, a man appeared before the lord Inquisitor **Licentiate Reynoso** having been summoned.[60] He was sworn in and promised to speak the truth. He said his name was:

Witness: Pedro Remacha, shepherd, citizen of this town of Deza. He said his age was just shy of 50 years.

Asked generally, he replied that what he had to say was that two years ago this past August, an hour or so before sunrise one morning, he was going out to harvest near the town's Argadil River. He saw a man in the river, standing with his legs splayed out. He wore a tunic but neither breeches nor underpants, for it appeared to him that the man's shirt was loose. In one hand he held a winnowing fork and with the other he was troubling the water; it looked like he was splashing it up between his legs.[61]

As this witness drew closer to him, the man turned his face toward the river, and, since it was morning and hazy, identifying him was difficult. But based on his clothing and gray hair, he appeared to be **Román Ramírez the elder**, a citizen of this town. But this witness did not solidly confirm the fact, for when he saw that the man was concealing himself, this witness did not get involved but continued on his way. Then, a few days afterward, he told the town's vicar and Rodrigo Navarro and some other people.

He had not come earlier to speak before Your Grace because he watches the livestock on his own and did not want to lose them. He imagines that this is why he was summoned, for he has nothing else to say. This is the truth under the oath that he took and he does not say it out of hatred. He refers back to what he has said about this before the town's vicar. He was charged to keep it secret and he promised. This happened in my presence: **Pablo García**, notary.

20

In the town of Deza on October 3, 1569, a man in a monk's habit appeared before the lord Inquisitor **Licentiate Reynoso** without having been summoned. He was sworn in and promised to speak the truth. He said his name was:

Witness: **Fray Alonso de Yllana**, a legate of the Order of Saint Bernard, resident in the monastery of Our Lady of the Garden of that same order.

---

[60] Compare this account with Doc. 13.
[61] See footnote 44.

He said he is around 50 years old. He said that in order to unburden his conscience he declares that about five or six years ago (although he is not absolutely certain of the time) he was in the aforementioned monastery of Our Lady of the Garden in conversation with Lope Román (a Morisco citizen of Ariza, a locksmith). This witness asked him how his law differed from ours, and Lope Román responded that his ancestors did not believe that Our Lady gave birth as a virgin. As they talked about his law—the law of the Moors—Lope Román said that the law of the Moors was better than that of Jews and gave various reasons why, none of which he now recalls since so much time has passed. They were alone.

This is the truth under the oath that he took and he does not say it out of hatred. He was charged to keep it secret and he promised to do so. This happened in my presence: **Pedro García**, notary.

21

In Deza on October 3, 1569, a man who had been summoned appeared before the lord Inquisitor **Licentiate Reynoso**.[62] He was sworn in and promised to speak the truth. He said his name was:

Witness: Miguel Prieto, muleteer, citizen of Cihuela, age 30 more or less.

Asked if he knows or presumes the reason why he has been summoned before this Holy Office. He said, "Yes."

He was told to say it.

He said that last winter—after Christmas he believes—he was traveling from Soria with Juan de Pasqual (farmer, citizen of this town) and two or three Moriscos from Deza. He does not know their names but one of them was a youth less than 20 years old—and if he was 20, he was no more than that—he thinks his name was Alonso Ropiñón. They had arrived at Almazul and were discussing how beautiful the women were in Almonacid,[63] which is a Morisco town in the Kingdom of Aragon.

This witness said he believed that within the domain of Épila, there are three or four little settlements of Moriscos where everyone is a Moor. Alonso Ropiñón (Morisco) responded, "The King won't leave everyone to be in his own law." But he is not sure if those were the words he spoke or if he said, "Each one wanted to follow his own law." He firmly believes that he said, "The King would not let each one be in his own law." Then this witness said to him, "What's that mean, to be in one's own law? So, you all

---

[62] Compare this account with Doc. 13.
[63] Presumably Almonacid de la Sierra.

don't believe in our law?" Seeing that he had made a mistake, the youth did not say anything in response, nor did he discuss the matter further.

Then, as he recalls, another Morisco said, "Can't you shut up, boy? You don't know what you're talking about. If I catch you, I'm gonna give you five or six smacks!" The Morisco who reprimanded the youth was called so-and-so Medrano, maybe Alonso, and he transports pots to market.

He did not mention this earlier because he was away from town.

This is the truth under the oath that he took and he does not say it out of hatred. He was charged to keep it secret and he promised to do so. This happened in my presence: **Pablo García**, notary.

22

In the town of Deza on October 3, 1569, a woman appeared before the lord Inquisitor **Licentiate Reynoso** without having been summoned. She was sworn in and promised to speak the truth. She said her name was:

Witness: **Mari Rodríguez**, a native of Alameda; she is engaged to Juan de Calataojar, a farmer. She said that she was more than 20 years old. In order to unburden her conscience she declares that about six years ago she was working for **Román Ramírez the elder** (Morisco) and his wife, [**María de Luna**], who is now deceased. One day during Lent, while his wife was ill, they cooked a bird for her and they also cooked some of the bird's tiny little eggs. She saw Román Ramírez, who was fit and healthy, eat the eggs.[64]

Item: She said that one day when she was in the aforementioned house, one of Román Ramírez's sons started sneezing. (She does not remember which of his sons it was.) She said to Román Ramírez, "He's sneezed so many times, and you didn't say, 'Jesus,' or cross yourself or commend yourself to God even once." Roman Ramírez replied, "Cross your own self, Miss Holier-than-thou." No one else was present but them.

This is the truth under the oath that she took and she does not say it out of hatred. She was charged to keep it secret and promised to do so. This happened in my presence: **Pablo García**, notary.

23

In the town of Deza on October 3, 1569, a woman appeared before the lord Inquisitor **Licentiate Reynoso** without having been summoned. She was sworn in and promised to speak the truth. She said her name was:

---

[64] Eggs were proscribed during Lent unless one was ill or had special permission.

Witness: María Pecina, the wife of **Nicolás de Mellas**, merchant, citizen of this town of Deza. She said she was 35 years old. She said that in order to unburden her conscience she declares that one day about four years ago by her reckoning, she was in her house in Deza on the Street of the Net Gate. And a Morisca from this town was with her. (She does not know her name but they call her the **Old Woman of Leonis**. She is very old.) She was helping this witness to wind flax, having just happened to have passed by that way at that time. Then, this witness said that she did not remember if the old woman had just passed by or if she had come specifically to talk with this witness about a girl named Ana, who is the daughter of Juan de Baptista (Morisco) and an Old Christian mother. This witness had known the girl when she was healthy and fit but then she had become ill and wasted away.

As they discussed the girl, the Morisca said, "You see her there, that one?"—or maybe she said "Juan de Baptista's girl and the other one, the cooper's daughter? Well, one day they were on the *Corredero*." As far as María Pecina recalls, the woman never explained why, but they all fell to quarrelling and the girls called her an "old bitch." When the woman complained to the cooper's wife, she whipped her daughter. But when she complained to Juan de Baptista's wife, she said, "Shut up, auntie. What do these girls have to do with you? What business is it of yours to talk about these girls?" The woman quarreled with her and cursed the girl.

María Pecina realized that the old woman's curses were the source of the girl's grave illness. Later, the girl died, and afterward, when this witness was talking about it with Juan de Baptista's wife, she looked sad. But when this witness commiserated, she responded that she was not crying over her daughter's death but rather because she suspected that the Morisca had done something to the girl.

When the Morisca had said what she said, Ana de Pecina, this witness's sister (who lives in the house of Hernán García, the apothecary, their father), had been present.

And this is the truth ~~Item: she said~~ under the oath that she swore and she does not say it out of hatred. She was charged to keep it secret and she promised to do so. This happened in my presence: **Pablo García**, notary.

24

In Deza on October 4, 1569, a man appeared before the lord Inquisitor **Licentiate Reynoso** without having been summoned. He was sworn in and promised to speak the truth. He said his name was:

Witness: **Nicolás de Mellas**, a dry good merchant and citizen of this town. He said his age is ~~more than~~ about 40 years. He said that in order to unburden his con [*sic*] conscience, he declares that on Holy Thursday of this past year[†], he was in the town church, after having eaten, praying before the most holy sacrament. He went out from the church into the plaza, where he ran into **Francisco de Baptista the younger** (a Morisco farmer who lives on the street they call the *Corrillo* in Deza). This witness asked Francisco de Baptista if he wanted to come see some saffron that this witness had planted. He said, "Yes," and that he would show him some that he had planted.

So they went to the saffron fields, and when they got to the road out of town, halfway past the threshing floors, at the bottom of the hill there, this witness said they should head back because he had to return for the Maundy Thursday service.[65] Then he began to talk about the Passion Monument in the town's church with its images and crucifix depicting the suffering of Our Lord Jesus Christ and his mercy, how he desired to suffer in order to redeem us. Francisco de Baptista—this witness saw it and heard it—said, "Explain how you could consent to it if you saw your son mistreated or killed?" And he waved his arm and shook his head and said, "Far be it! Don't say that." This witness replied to him, "Don't *you* say *that!* It's against the faith! How can you compare God with a human being? It's there, in Christ's sufferings, that you'll know the great power of God and his mercy toward sinners: that he desired his own son to die on the cross for them. You shouldn't have said what you did; nor did you have reason to. We can't even begin to understand the things that a human being does here, and yet you want to understand the supreme power of God." Francisco de Baptista, seeing that this witness refused to follow him on the path to ruin and temptation, did not engage him any more on matter of faith but rather on other things. So, they arrived at his house and discussed nothing else.

Afterward, maybe three months more or less, this witness brought a statue of the baby Jesus to the house of **Francisco de Miranda** (painter, Morisco, citizen of this town) so that he could touch up a few bits that had faded. When he brought the baby Jesus to be repainted, he held it in his hands and said, "O Jesus Christ, O Son of the living God. How lovely is this baby Jesus. It hasn't been many days since a dog,"—or maybe he said "someone from New Street." He does not remember which of the two

---

[65] Celebrated as part of Holy Week, Maundy Thursday (also known as Holy Thursday) commemorates the Last Supper shared by Jesus Christ and his disciples on the day before the Crucifixion. It specifically refers to Jesus' command (*mandatum*) that his disciples "love one another as I have loved you" (John 13:34).

things he said, but it was one of them—"said to me that Jesus Christ wasn't the Son of the living God." And the painter said, "That's bad." This witness said, "It doesn't have to be bad for me, but I promise you that it's a great wrong and a wicked thing. I think these Aragonese dogs no more believe in God than I do in Mohammed." And with that this witness left.

On Saint Michael's day this past September or a day just following it, when this witness was at the fair in Monteagudo de las Vicarías, **Luis de Cebea [the elder]** (Morisco, citizen of this town) told him that the painter wanted to come to the fair to speak to him. He did not know why the painter had not come nor what he wanted, but it had something to do with whether this witness had told anyone about this matter of faith.

He told Luis de Cebea, "That'll be the thing he'll want from me. If you see him, call to him and tell him that I'm here." So, Luis de Cebea left. He said that the painter would not be here, that he had gone to attend some weddings.

Last night, after returning from the fair as night was falling, this witness ran into Luis de Cebea and asked him if the painter was here. He said no, that he was attending some weddings but that he would come either that night or today. Today, when he got out of bed this witness came to the lord Inquisitor's dwelling but it was closed, so he went back to his house. Returning a second time to talk to the lord Inquisitor, he met Francisco de Baptista in the New Street plaza.[66] After greeting one another and discussing other matters, Francisco de Baptista told him that he needed to speak a couple words to him.

He went up Threshing Floor Street, toward Pedro de Melgosa's house, at which point this witness told him that he needed to return to his house; he was expecting his wife. Francisco de Baptista said that he only wanted to speak two words to him. So, this witness turned back along Threshing Floor Street, toward the *Corredero* in order to return to his house. When the two of them came to the street further on, next to the *Corredero* itself, Francisco de Baptista pressed this witness against a wall and said, "Look, I hear you already told the painter something you remember from when we walked toward the saffron fields." And this witness said, "I assure you that the painter won't repeat a single word that I've spoken to him. You've told me, and you don't have to say another word to me because matters of faith are very delicate things. I don't have to say anything to you. Consider what's in your best interests." And, so, he left for his house and this witness for his.

---

[66] That is, the *Corrillo*.

Asked what he thought Francisco de Baptista meant when ~~he said~~ they were discussing the death and passion of Our Lord Jesus Christ when he said, "How could you consent to it if you saw your son mistreated or killed? Far be it. Don't say that."

He said that based on Francisco de Baptista's words and, even more, his actions, this witness understood him to mean that he did not believe Jesus Christ was the Son of God and that he had not died on the cross. For if he were God's son, God would not have consented to let him die. This is what he understood Francisco de Baptista to mean. And this witness believes that if he had followed him down the path he would have said more. The two of them were alone.

Asked what kind of man Francisco de Baptista is, he said that he was about 34 years old, maybe as many as 40. He is a Morisco, as he said. By trade he is a farmer. He believes that he has previously been arrested by the Holy Office of the Inquisition in Cuenca but does not know anything about his release.

Asked if he has told anyone about this, he said that he has not spoken about it except to the town's vicar when he was confessing with him in confession and to an Augustinian friar, **Fray Marcelo** from Soria, who visited Deza last Lent. He named Francisco de Baptista to them, but he never mentioned the painter to anyone.

~~For~~ He has not previously spoken of the last matter that he mentioned. But he searched his memory and carefully recalled Francisco de Baptista's words to him; he held onto it in his heart in order to declare it. He is very certain and convinced that Francisco de Baptista said the words that he has here declared against him.

What he has said is the truth under the oath that he swore and he does not say it out of hatred or any enmity that he has nor has had with Francisco de Baptista, for he has never had any. He only says it to unburden his conscience.

Item: He said that about two or three years ago, although he is not absolutely certain about the time, this witness was keeping the vigil of Saint Andrew at the house of **Gerónimo Gorgoz**[††] (a Morisco citizen of this town who lives in the *Corrillo* plaza). This witness and Gerónimo Gorgoz went up to Gorgoz's house to the kitchen. His wife (he does not know her name) was preparing dinner then and when she saw this witness standing above her, she took the food she was cooking in a pan and hid it under a bench or a table. He spent a little time talking with Gerónimo Gorgoz but since he wanted to get back, Gerónimo Gorgoz got the pan and said, "Look here, sir! Isn't she a good wife?" She was cooking breadcrumbs in fat. This witness replied that he believed it. Then he left the house.

This is the truth under the oath that he took and he does not say it out of hatred. He was charged to keep it secret and he promised to do so. This happened in my presence: **Pablo García**, notary.

---

† On this same date, October 4, 1569, at night, Nicolás de Mellas returned to the audience of the lord Inquisitor and said that as he was scouring his memory, he remembered that the events about which he had testified in this testimony concerning Francisco de Baptista happened on Holy Thursday of the year 1568. He is sure of this. This was the truth under the same oath and he was charged to keep it secret. In my presence: Pablo García, notary.

†† In Deza, October 8, 1569, Nicolás de Mellas appeared before the aforementioned lord Inquisitor and said that since having said what he said in this Holy Office, he has remembered that what he says he saw in the house of Gerónimo Gorgoz happened ten years ago more or less. This is the truth under the oath that he took. He was charged to keep it secret. This happened in my presence: Pablo García, notary.

25

In Deza on October 4, 1569, a man appeared before the lord Inquisitor **Licentiate Reynoso** without having been summoned. He was sworn in and promised to speak the truth. He said his name was:

Witness: Juan Delgado, farmer, citizen of Cihuela. He said his age was sixty years more or less. He said that in order to unburden his conscience, he declares that more than 25 and maybe even 26 years ago, he, Diego de Antón the elder (farmer, citizen of Cihuela), Catalina de Nieve (deceased), and some other women (he does not remember who) were in Ciheula, but he does not remember where exactly. They were talking about the virginity of Our Lady, the Virgin Mary, how she had given birth to Our Lord Jesus Christ and remained a virgin. Diego de Antón said, "Sure, she remained a virgin, and she gave birth through her knee!" This witness said to him, "Don't say that! It's badly said." He does not remember how Diego de Antón responded.

When asked, he said that Diego de Antón is an Old Christian and an honorable farmer. This witness and the rest of the town take him to be a good Christian, which is what he seems to be. This is the truth under the oath that he took and he does not say it out of hatred.

Item: He said that more than 15 or 16 years ago, this witness was in the town of Deza near the Cubo Mill at the door of the house of **Licentiate Páez** (physician), right next to the licentiate himself. This witness had come to bring him some of his daughter's urine. Just then, there was a very cold gust of wind and the licentiate said, "They say that God doesn't make any ugly thing. I say that if this weather is bad, God made it." The two of them were alone.

When asked, he said that he takes Licentiate Páez to be a good Christian and he has heard it said that he is the offspring of *confesos*,[67] although he does not know for sure.

This is the truth under the oath that he took and he does not say it out of hatred. He was charged to keep it secret and he promised to do so. This happened in my presence: **Pablo García**, notary.

26

In the town of Deza on October 4, 1569, a man appeared before the lord Inquisitor **Licentiate Reynoso** without having been summoned. He was sworn in and promised to speak the truth. He said his name was:

Witness: Martín Portero, farmer and plasterer, a citizen of this town. He said he was 40 or 41 years old. He said that in order to unburden his conscience he declares that about a year and a half ago, he and his brother Francisco Portero were at the edge of town in a place they call the hocino.[68] They were grinding gypsum for the House of the Duke of Medinaceli and a Morisco from Deza named Lope de Baptista was hauling the gypsum on his donkey to the House of the Duke.[69]

One day, he said to the Morisco Lope de Baptista, "These Moors that the duke has gotten, they were bought and captured." Around that time the duke had traveled from Sicily and brought Moors back with him, both males and females. Lope de Baptista responded, "They're captive chattel now, except for a traitor who still lives there." He never indicated about whom he was talking, and this witness did not understand him. "The traitor brought the Moors to a celebration. They thought they were taking another trip, but instead he cast them, along with all the riches they carried, into Sicily into the hand of the duke."[70] Lope de Baptista cursed that person, saying, "An unsettled grave to the mother who bore him and the father who sired him!"

This all seemed very wrong to this witness because it seemed like Lope de Baptista favored the Moors. But he said nothing in response to him except, "It wouldn't take much for the one who had betrayed his own kind

---

[67] See footnote 3.
[68] The hocino is a little less than a mile northeast of town.
[69] The House of the Duke was a large building with gardens constructed in the mid-sixteenth century just north of town and outside of the town walls.
[70] The context of this passage is unclear, but the meaning is that a group of Moors were betrayed by someone in their midst, who tricked them into becoming slaves and sold them to the Duke of Medinaceli.

to betray the duke." Lope de Baptista responded, "Well, if you put it like that, it would be easy." And the whole time he was spouting curses.

Item: He said that this past May, he was getting gypsum in Carabantes,[71] but he returned to his house on Saturday nights. One day, he and **Juan de Cieli** (a Morisco bricklayer, citizen of Deza, and the son-in-law of **Luis de Liñán**) were traveling from Deza to Carabantes. They traveled along the road talking about the farms and ended up discussing the farm that the holy Inquisition had confiscated from his father-in-law Luis de Liñán.

Juan de Cieli said that this had cost his father-in-law more than 200 ducats. He claimed that when Luis de Liñán was in custody, being transported to the Inquisition, he had joined up with a scribe from Almazán. (He did not name the scribe nor does this witness know his identity.) The scribe told Liñán that the holy Inquisition just demands that he agree with whatever they say.[72] If he refuses, they will torture him badly, in ways unfit for a man. The scribe said he had been arrested two or three times and that this had been his strategy.

This witness said to Juan de Cieli, "So, your father-in-law confessed out of fear?" And he replied, "Believe it. That's how it is." He and Juan de Cieli were traveling alone.

This is the truth under the oath that he took and he does not say it out of hatred. He was charged to keep it secret and he promised to do so. This happened in my presence: **Pablo García**, notary.

27

HEARSAY—AGAINST AGUSTÍN DE BAPTISTA, FRANCISCO DE BAPTISTA THE YOUNGER, FRANCISCO DE BAPTISTA THE ELDER, FRANCISCO GUERRERO, AND PASQUAL WHO TRANSPORTS GOODS[73]

In the town of Deza on October 4, 1569, a young man appeared before the lord Inquisitor **Licentiate Reynoso** without having been summoned. He was sworn in and promised to speak the truth. He said his name was:

Witness: Juan Martínez, son of Pablo Martínez, native of Abión, in the region of Soria. He lives with **Gerónimo Gorgoz**, a Morisco citizen of Deza. He said he was 23 years old, more or less. He said that in order to

---

[71] Carabantes is about six miles (as the crow flies) north of Deza in Castile.
[72] That is, the scribe advised Liñán to confess to anything of which he was accused.
[73] Compare this account with Docs. 28–29.

unburden his conscience he declares that about six months ago—then he said in February or March of this year—this witness and Francisco de la Plaza (farmer, citizen of this town) were at the Gloomy Cave on the edge of the town gathering firewood.[74] They were discussing the Moriscos from the Kingdom of Granada who have risen up. Francisco de la Plaza said that he had a son in service to a New Christian in this town named **Agustín de Baptista**. His son is 12 or 13 years old and told him that one night while he was sleeping sitting up in the bed, Agustín de Baptista had jostled his head with his hands. The boy woke up and saw five or six men in the kitchen. One of them was **Francisco de Baptista the younger** and another was Francisco de Baptista the elder. One of Lope el Guerrero's sons, named **Francisco Guerrero**, was there, and so was Pasqual[75] who transports goods and lives in the Plaza of the *Corrillo* (but he does not know his surname). **Miguel de Deza** was there too. He does not know if there were any others. All of them are Moriscos and citizens of Deza.

When the boy woke up, the men moved to another room. While they were there, the other men asked Agustín de Baptista if he thought they should go to Granada. Agustín de Baptista responded that they were few in number. One of the men—he does not know which—said that he dared to go in ten days. Another man asked—he does not know who it was—why they shouldn't go and die alongside of their friends.[76] The boy had heard this because they spoke loudly, since Agustín de Baptista was and is going deaf.

This past Thursday (or Saturday), this witness asked Francisco de la Plaza if he had reported this to the holy Inquisition. Francisco de la Plaza responded that he had not believed the boy because he often lies. This witness said that it made him uncomfortable and he wanted to come tell it, but Francisco de la Plaza did not respond to him at all. This witness gave an account of it to **Martín Fernández** (cleric) last night. For, when he came here on a previous night they had refused to let him enter. Martín Fernández said that he would notify them so they would let him in tonight. So, he came to declare it.

This is is [*sic*] the truth under the oath that he took and he does not say it out of hatred. He was charged to keep it secret and he promised to do so. This happened in my presence: **Pablo García**, notary.

This testimony against Francisco de Baptista and Agustín de Baptista and Lope de Deza the lad was extracted.[77]

---

[74] The Gloomy Cave is about three and a half miles northwest of town.

[75] Pasqual is also known as **Lope de Deza**.

[76] The men are discussing joining the Moriscos of Granada in the uprising known as the Second War of the Alpujarras. See footnote 58.

[77] That is to say, it was used as evidence in inquisitorial trials.

28

In the town of Deza on October 5, 1569, a boy who had been summoned appeared before the lord Inquisitor **Licentiate Reynoso**.[78] He was sworn in and promised to speak the truth. He said his name was:

Witness: Miguel de la Plaza, the son of Francisco de la Plaza, farmer, citizen of this town. He said he was 11 years old and going on 12. He lives with **Agustín de Baptista**, a Morisco citizen of this town and has lived with him for a year and four months.

Asked if he knows or presumes why he has been summoned to the Holy Office. He said, "Yes."

He was told to say what he had to say.

He said that during Lent of this year, one night he was lying down in the house of Agustín de Baptista, his master. In the house's stable, which is near where this witness was lying, were Lope el Guerrero, his son **Lope [Guerrero the younger]**, **Pasqual de la Pituerta**, Lope[79] the brother-in-law of Pasqual (then he said that Pasqual is married to Lope's daughter[80]), Francisco de Baptista [the elder] (who lives on the *Corrillo*), Francisco de Gonzalo[81] (who is married; his father is named Gonzalo and he lives right next to Pasqual de la Pituerta's house), and **Agustín de Baptista** (Miguel de la Plaza's master).† They are all Moriscos and citizens of Deza. (Later this witness claimed that he was sitting on a bed made out of a wooden board with a pack on it; and then he said that he was sitting on the ground; then he said he was lying on his side on top of the board.)

He was half asleep when he heard Pasqual de la Pituerta and Lope, the son of Lope el Guerrero, say they wanted to go to the Sierra Nevada and die with their friends. He heard no response at all from any of the others and then they left. This occurred between 10 and 11 o'clock at night. ~~After they all left, his master kicked him out~~ before those men entered the house, this witness's master had kicked him out of it, but he remained in the doorway. The men must have entered through the door of the house that opens onto the *Corrillo*, although the house's main door opens onto the *Corredero*.†† This witness never saw any of the men gesturing, but rather was awakened by the noise they made when they were talking in the stable. He knew them by their voices.

---

[78] Compare this account with Docs. 27 and 29.
[79] There is some confusion here. Pasqual de la Pituerta's given name is Lope de Deza.
[80] Pasqual de la Pituerta (aka Lope de Deza) is married to **Ana de Arellano**.
[81] That is, **Francisco de Baptista the younger**.

Asked, he said that the stable or barn is about two strides from where he was. The door of the stable is right next to the door to a big house. The men did not exit through the main door. They used the other one.

Asked what this witness did after the men left and where he slept that night. He said that that night, because it was very late, he stayed and slept at his employer's house. He slept on top of a table at the feet of his master and mistress. On the nights before and after this happened, he slept at his father's house.

Asked where his master's wife was when all this was going on in the stable, while they were discussing the matter he described. He said she was upstairs making the bed. He knows this because he could hear the bed boards.

Asked how many times he saw the men together or heard them discuss the matter he described. He said just the one time.

Asked whom he told what he heard the aforesaid people say. He said that he has told his father and Calvo de la Rosa, farmer, citizen of this town.§ He told them exactly what he heard the men say.

Asked if anyone spoke to him or persuaded him to say what he has declared (even though it is not true) or to leave out any of the details he witnessed or knows. He said no one has told him to say anything or to leave anything out. What he has said is the truth. He is not lying about it.

Asked if he heard the men say any other words besides the ones that he has declared. He said that he heard nothing more than what he has declared because he was asleep.

Asked if anyone came to check whether he was asleep or awake or if someone shook his head. He said no one came to him.

Asked if he heard anyone of them say he "dared to go to Granada in ten days." He said he heard Pasqual de la Pituerta and Lope son of Lope el Guerrero say to the others that they dared to go to Granada in ten days. He had forgotten this or else he would have mentioned it. Now that he has been asked, he has remembered. The others, especially Lope el Guerrero the elder and Lope the brother-in-law of Pasqual de la Pituerta, said that they did not dare so much. He does not remember anything else.

Asked if he was treated well or poorly in his master's house. He said, "As they like. Sometimes poorly and sometimes well." His mistress, who is named **Isabel de Baptista**, beats him if he is not quick enough in following her orders. His master treats him better than she does.

Asked if what he has said is true. He said that he cannot say anything else; he understands it to be the truth.

Asked if he says it out of any hatred or enmity. He said that he does not want to see them any more than he wants to see the devils. And that is why he said it and because it is what he heard said. He was charged to keep it secret and he promised to do so. This happened in my presence: **Pablo García**, notary.

This testimony against Francisco de Baptista the lad and Agustín de Baptista and Lope de Deza the lad was extracted.

† Deza

˜ Lope el Guerrero

˜ Lope his son

˜ Pasqual de la Pituerta—they say that they call him that because his father was named Pasqual de Deza and his wife is lame; but his given name is Lope and he transports goods.

˜ Francisco de Baptista—this one is the eldest

˜ Francisco de Gonzalo—this one is called Francisco de Baptista the younger, and he is the one who was arrested by the Holy Office. **Nicolás de Mellas** testified against him earlier. They call him de Gonzalo because his father was named Gonzalo de Baptista. Martín Fernández gave this explanation on October 6, 1569.

˜ Agustín de Baptista

†† On October 6, 1569, Martín Fernández, cleric commissioner of this Holy Office, was sworn in to speak the truth before the lord Inquisitor Licentiate Reynoso. He said that he knows that Agustín de Baptista's house has two doors—the main one onto the *Corredero* and the other that goes out to the *Corrillo*, which is where the oven is located. This is the truth under oath. He was charged to keep it secret and he promised to do so. This happened in my presence: Pablo García, notary.

§ On October 6, 1569, Juan Calvo, an Aragonese farmer whom some call de la Rosa because he has a red mark on his face, was examined under oath and formally questioned about what Miguel de la Plaza claimed to have told him. He said that no such person had spoken to him nor had he heard such things from anyone. He was charged to keep it secret. This happened in my presence: Pablo García, notary.

29

In Deza on October 5, 1569, subsequent to the examination of Miguel de la Plaza, a man who had been summoned appeared before the lord Inquisitor.[82] He was sworn in and promised to speak the truth. He said his name was:

Witness: Francisco de la Plaza, citizen of this town of Deza, farmer. He said he was at least 45 years old.

Asked if he knows or presumes the reason why he was summoned.

He said that he presumes that it has to do with certain things that he heard from one of his sons.

He was told to make them known, speaking the truth under the oath that he spoke.

He said that he has a son named Miguel whom he thinks is 12 years old. He is employed by **Agustín de Baptista** (Morisco, citizen of this town) and has been for 15 months. As he recalls, one night this past Lent his son came to sleep at his house at 9 or 10 o'clock at night. It was unusual for him to go so late. This witness asked him, "Why are you coming so late?" He responded, "They didn't kick me out, father. There were some men inside the stable at my master's house, and I heard them ~~that~~ talking about the

---

[82] Compare this account with Docs. 27–28.

Sierra Nevada." He heard nothing else and the boy did not tell him who the people were nor did this witness ask him. He does not have anything else to say.

Asked if his son usually slept in his house or in his master's house and whether he left he left [*sic*] to sleep in this witness's house one night.

He responded that his son came and slept in his house every night until this past May. At that point, this witness told Agustín de Baptista not to send him home; his son was a rascal who just wanted to stay in bed. Since then, he had not slept a single night outside of Agustín de Baptista's house. This witness is certain of this because he never allowed him to sleep in his house.

Asked if this witness has told anyone about what his son says that he told him.

He replied that he told a young man who lives with **Gerónimo Gorgoz**, Morisco. He does not know his name but he believes he hails from Cáraves or Abión in Soria. He did this while they were gathering firewood in the Romerales over by the shallow fertile plain.[83] He told him nothing more than what he has already stated his son told him. He has told no one else.

He was informed that in this Holy Office information exists indicating that, in a manner other than that which he has stated, he discussed this matter with someone and spoke to him and that he named the people who had been present, the people who spoke the words that he says his son told him. Therefore, out of reverence for God, he is admonished to tell the truth without hiding a single thing. He responded that his son did not tell him anything beyond what he has declared. As far as he recalls, he said nothing more to the lad.

Asked if this witness has told someone that one of the people who was part of the group that he says his son told him about said he had to "leave here for Granada in ten days."

He said that now he remembers that his son told him that one of the persons—he does not remember who it was—said that in nine days he would go to the Sierra Nevada. This witness might have mentioned it to the aforesaid young man, but he does not remember very well.

Asked if his son Miguel is a boy of good sense.

He said that when he is given orders, his son understands and has ability. But he is somewhat dishonest. For this witness has caught him in a few lies and never believes anything from him unless he sees it himself. Even

---

[83] About a mile and a half southwest of town.

his master has complained to this witness that he is a liar. He is not sure how to determine whether or not his son told the truth about what this witness said that his son told him that he heard in his master's house.

What he has spoken is the truth under the oath that he took. He does not say it out of hatred. He was charged to keep it secret and he promised to do so. He was ordered to think about what he has been asked and, if he remembers anything else, to come and make it known.

Asked where Agustín de Baptista lives.

He said, in the neighbourhood of the *Corredero*, right next to the *Corredero* itself.

Asked how many doors that house has.

He said, it has one that goes out to the street of the *Corredero* and he has heard that another door goes out toward the oven. But he has never seen it because he has never entered that way. This is the truth. This happened in my presence: **Pablo García**, notary.

This witness was examined with regard to the statement made by his son, Miguel, who is the preceding witness. Regarding what Juan Martínez said, it is on folio 472 [i.e., Doc. 27].

This testimony against **Francisco de Baptista**, Agustín de Baptista, and **Lope de Deza** the lad was extracted.

30

AGAINST FRANCISCO DE BAPTISTA (OR DE GONZALO)

In the town of Deza on October 5, 1569, a woman appeared before the lord Inquisitor **Licentiate Reynoso** without having been summoned. She was sworn in and promised to speak the truth. She said her name was:

Witness: Madalena Gutierrez, wife of Antonio de Cuellar, a tailor. She is a citizen of Deza and she says she is perhaps 22 years old. She said that in order to unburden her conscience she declares that one day about half a year ago, **Francisco de Baptista** (who is also known as Francisco de Gonzalo, Morisco) and Melchior López were in her house. (Melchior López is the brother of Gaspar López, the scribe for Deza's customs house; Melchior López is not married; and he lives with his brother and this witness.)

Francisco de Baptista asked Melchior López why he had sent his son to tell Francisco that Melchior López would not be returning the platter Francisco de Baptista had sent him. For while it once contained honey, now there was bacon on it. Melchior López sent this message even though none of his ~~parents and his~~ grandparents ~~had not~~ had eaten bacon![84] Melchior López responded, "Truly, Francisco, when any part of me touches a Morisco, it's a nuisance and I want to cut it off." Francisco de Baptista replied, "Well, hold onto your Jewish bits if you prefer them. I'm of Moorish descent and it doesn't bother me in the least."

Nothing more happened nor was anyone else present except this witness and María Gutierrez (wife of Gil de Hercoles, a farmer who lives in Monteagudo). What Francisco de Baptista said seemed wrong to this witness, but she said nothing to him in response.

She did not say anything earlier because she had forgotten about it until two days ago.

And asked, she said that Francisco de Baptista (or de Gonzalo) is a farmer. She does not know where in town he lives.

This is the truth under the oath that she took and she does not say it out of hatred. She was charged to keep it secret and she promised to do so. This happened in my presence: **Pablo García**, notary.

Extracted

31

AGAINST JUAN DE MIGUEL'S WIFE[85]

In Deza on October 6, 1569, a woman appeared before the lord Inquisitor **Licentiate Reynoso** without having been summoned. She was sworn in and promised to speak the truth. She said her name was:

Witness: Ana de la Torre, wife of Alonso Pérez, an innkeeper. She is a citizen of this town of Deza and says she is 60 years old. She said that in order to unburden her conscience she declares that this past summer during either May or June, her husband was hunting quail. The town's vicar told him to send a pair of them to Juan de Miguel's wife who was ill at that time. The woman is a Morisca, but this witness does not know her first name.

This witness sent the quail with a girl whom she keeps at her house named **Juana Muñoz**, who is 12 or 13 years old. When the girl returned from

---

[84] This is difficult a passage, but the meaning seems to be that Baptista sent some honey to López, who responded by sending his son to tell Baptista that he was keeping the plate, which now held bacon. The assumption being that Baptista was a crypto-Muslim who would not eat from a plate that had been contaminated by pork. Baptista, for his part, is all the more upset at the response since López himself was descended from Jews, who did not eat pork either.

[85] Compare this account with Doc. 32.

delivering the pair of quails she said that Juan de Miguel's wife refused to accept them because they were already dead. She had said that if they send her quails, let them be alive. This witness never sent her any more, living or dead.

This witness suspects that, because the woman is a Morisca, she wanted to kill the quails in the Moorish way, although she does not know how they kill them.

This is the truth under the oath that she took and she does not say it out of hatred. She was charged to keep it secret and she promised to do so. This happened in my presence: **Pablo García**, notary.

32

AGAINST JUAN MIGUEL'S WIFE[86]

In the town of Deza on October 6, 1569, a girl who had been summoned appeared before the lord Inquisitor **Licentiate Reynoso**. She was sworn in and promised to speak the truth. She said her name was:

Witness: Juana,[87] who has no last name. She is the daughter of Pedro de la Torre and Antona his wife, who are citizens of this town. She said she was between 12 and 14 years old.

Asked what she wants.

She said that this past summer—she does not exactly remember what month it was but they had not yet harvested the barley—Ana de la Torre told her to deliver a pair of dead quails to the house of Miguel (Morisco) and give them to his wife, who was sick. She does not know her name and they live on the *Corrillo*.

This witness took them and asked Miguel's wife if she wanted to buy the pair of quails that she had with her. She showed them to her and the woman responded that she did not want dead ones. She said that if they brought some live ones she would take them because she wanted to keep them in case they could not eat them. Miguel, the woman's husband (who is a farmer), was present.

This witness conveyed her answer to her mistress and she took no more quails to her, neither living nor dead.

This is the truth under the oath that she took and she does not say it out of hatred. She was charged to keep it secret and promised to do so. This happened in my presence: **Pablo García**, notary.

---

[86] Compare this account with Doc. 31.
[87] This seems to be the **Juana Muñoz** mentioned in the previous audience.

33

AGAINST JUAN DE HORTUBIA, LOCKSMITH

In the town of Deza on October 9, 1569, a man who had not been summoned appeared before the lord Inquisitor **Licentiate Reynoso**. He was sworn in and promised to speak the truth. He said his name was:

Witness: **García de Ureña**, cleric priest, a native of this town. He said that he was 35 or 36 years old. He said that in order to unburden his conscience he declares that maybe four years ago, although he is not fully certain about the time, on a summer day he and **Juan de Hortubia** went hunting out toward Bordalba at the edge of town. Hortubia is a Morisco locksmith and a citizen of Deza. He is married.

There is a cross on the left hand side of the road to Bordalba, and they flushed a hare out from under it. Then they sent the hounds after the hare and they caught it just there. But before the hounds killed it, they both got to the spot. And Juan de Hortubia took the hare, which was not quite dead, and he drew a little knife out of a dagger that he was wearing to slit the hare's throat. He cut its hide from the neck, piercing the throat. This witness did not hear him speak any words nor does he remember how he held the hare while slitting its throat. But he did it quickly—he took it and slit its throat, like he said.

Later, they caught another hare, which this witness kept. Juan de Hortubia carried the one with the slit throat.

And asked, he said that he could not say if Juan de Hortubia said that he wanted to take the one with the slit throat. But, indeed, he took it. This witness never said a word to Juan de Hortubia about the throat slitting nor did Juan de Hortubia say anything about it to him.

This is the truth under the oath that he took and he does not say it out of hatred.

And asked, he said that he had not come to speak earlier because he was not sure about it. But then he was thinking about the very paths that they had walked on that hunt and then he remembered. He is very certain that what he described happened and it is the truth under that same oath.

He was charged to keep it secret and he promised to do so. This happened in my presence: **Pablo García**, notary.

Asked, he said that no one else saw what he described happen. He and Juan de Hortubia went alone.

Later, on October 11 of the same year, García de Ureña was summoned before the aforementioned lord Inquisitor. Having sworn to speak the truth, the lord Inquisitor asked him his opinion about Juan de Hortubia slitting the hare's throat.

He said that he never saw anyone with whom he hunted do such a thing. For that reason it seemed wrong. Since then, he has suspected that it was wrong because Juan de Hortubia is a Morisco, but he does not know why he did it. The Edict that was read aloud mentioned something about slitting throats, so he came to disclose it.[88] But he does not know if Moors slit necks.

This is the truth under the same oath. He was charged to keep it secret and he promised to do so. This happened in my presence: Pablo García, notary.

Extracted.

Focus Questions

Doc. 1: What was "wrong" with Francisca's statement? Why did Mateo feel compelled to mention it to the inquisitor?

Doc. 2: What is the significance of the Moriscos digging such deep graves? Is this a religious practice (indicating adherence to Islam) or merely a cultural tradition?

Doc. 3: Drawing upon the references to Licentiate Páez in this document and in others, sketch his personality. (Compare with Docs. 5, 7, 9, 12, 16, 25, 40, and 60, as well as the information in the Cast of Characters.)

Doc. 4: How do Gerónima's and Juana's perspective on the image of the Virgin differ? How does Gerónima attempt to moderate her denunciation of Juana? Why is it significant that Juana is not identified as either a Judeoconversa or a Morisca?

Doc. 5: Why might Juanes de Altopica's past experiences (described in the Cast of Characters) have inclined him to keep a careful watch on someone like Páez?

Docs. 6–8: What role does authority (of individual priests, saints, creeds, or contemporary theological authorities) play in the debate about the presence of Christ's soul in the sacrament? Was there room for theological debate in late-sixteenth-century Deza? If so, under what conditions? If not, why?

---

[88] García de Ureña is referring to the Edict of Faith read from the pulpit before Licentiate Reynoso's arrival.

Doc. 7: Why does the inquisitor keep pressing Benito to give specific examples of offenses when the witness seems more inclined to speak in generalities?

Doc. 7: Is it surprising that Juan de Baptista (a Morisco) married an Old Christian woman? Why or why not?

Doc. 7: Why is Benito's testimony so much longer than most others?

Doc. 8: Why did the inquisitors send all the way to Valencia in order to get Gerónimo Barba's testimony? What do you think the missing pages would reveal?

Doc. 9: What is distinctive about the Morisco marriage ceremony? How does the Church fit into their practice? Is it surprising to see respected Old Christians (like Francisco de Uzedo and Juan Castro) and Judeoconversos (like Antonio Páez) attending a Morisco wedding? (Compare with Docs. 7 and 12.)

Doc. 10: Why did Mateo Romero move his family to Deza? Why are they leaving in such a hurry? (Compare with Doc. 14.)

Doc. 11: Why is Ana Montera so focused on the role of food? Why does she try to recover the beef bone? Is she a trustworthy witness?

Doc. 12: What are the possible meanings of Lope de Deza's use of the phrase "and ours"? How and why does Páez attempt to explain the statement away?

Doc. 13: What does María de Luna's comment mean? Why might it have been a particularly shocking statement for her to make?

Doc. 14: How does Mari's description of these events differ from Ana Montera's in Doc. 11? Where do they agree? How do you explain the differences and similarities?

Doc. 14: Mari Montón tells the inquisitor that she never said, "Keep quiet. They were fasting for the law of Mohamed." Why might Mari have been reluctant to admit that she made this statement?

Doc. 14: Mari Montón is asked "what sort of young woman Ana Montera is." Compare this question with the one asked of Francisco de la Plaza (Doc. 29) about his son's character. Why do you think the inquisitor asked these questions about Ana and Francisco?

Doc. 15: Why did the inquisitor ask Diego if he knew why Francisco Burgueño had slit the throat of the hare?

Doc. 16: Why didn't Pedro respond to Miguel's comment about the Day of Judgment?

Doc. 17: Was Madalena just being curious or was she trying to get Juan de Contreras's wife in trouble?

Doc. 18: Why does María la Pola describe an event that happened two decades previously?

Doc. 18: Why does the Queen make a comparison between the Basques and the Moriscos of Granada? Is the analogy convincing?

Doc. 19: Why might Pedro have been reluctant to identify with certainty the man who was bathing in the river?

Doc. 20: Why did Lope focus on the virgin birth when asked to describe the difference between Islam and Christianity?

Doc. 21: Why did the Morisco threaten to hit Alonso? What was so troubling about his statement? (Compare with Doc. 13.)

Doc. 22: Throughout the documents, as here, there are several examples of Old Christians working for or living with Moriscos. What does this suggest about how the different groups interacted?

Doc. 23: Why might the Old Woman of Leonis have cultivated the idea that she had the ability to curse others?

Doc. 24: Why was Francisco so forthcoming with Nicolás about his unorthodox beliefs?

Doc. 25: Why does the inquisitor keep asking witnesses about Páez's ancestry? Doesn't he already know that Páez is a Judeoconverso? What does it matter whether his neighbors think he is one? (Compare with Docs. 3, 5, 16, 40, and 60.)

Doc. 26: Why might confessing to the Inquisition "out of fear" be a matter of concern?

Docs. 27–29: What evidence is there that the conversation described by Miguel actually took place? Why might these denunciations have been of particular concern to the Holy Office?

Doc. 28: Why does the inquisitor seem so concerned with seemingly inconsequential details, such as where Miguel was sleeping or the number of doors in Agustín de Baptista's house?

Doc. 28: Why might the inquisitor have asked Miguel about how his master and mistress treated him?

Doc. 29: Francisco seems almost intentionally obtuse in his interview. Why was he so reluctant to reveal what his son had told him about the Moriscos?

Doc. 30: How does this interaction between a Morisco and a Judeoconverso differ from the interactions that Licentiate Páez (another Judeoconverso) had with the town's Moriscos (Doc. 12)? How do you account for the difference?

Docs. 31–32: Were Ana and Juana charitable neighbors or self-serving gossips?

Doc. 33: How did the Edict of Faith read in preparation for the inquisitor's arrival function in this case?

2

The Confession of Román Ramírez the Younger for the Edict of Grace (1571)[1]

In the wake of Licentiate Reynoso's visitation, the Holy Office arrested a handful of Deza's Moriscos. They, in turn, denounced others, leading to more trials—34 in all in 1570. Later that year, the inquisitor Dr. Diego Gómez de la Madriz arrived in town and proclaimed an Edict of Grace. Any Moriscos who voluntarily confessed and abjured their Islamic activities would be reconciled to the Church without undergoing a full inquisitorial trial. Some of their property might be confiscated as punishment and they would no longer be permitted to hold local office, but they would be safe from the denunciations of their neighbors. Few of Deza's Moriscos jumped at this opportunity.

Instead, supported by the Duke of Medinaceli, several Moriscos entered into negotiations with the royal court for the promulgation of a special, revised Edict of Grace. Those who took the new Edict in early 1571—which included most of the adult Morisco population—were reconciled to the Church, exempted from the confiscation of their property, and allowed to hold office in the future. Of course, if they were ever convicted again, they would be treated as "relapsed heretics" and subject to the harshest penalties.

Below is the confession of Román Ramírez the younger, who had personally traveled to Madrid to broker the deal for the second Edict of Grace. Later in life, Román became known as a great storyteller and claimed to have performed "many times" before King Philip II himself. Something of that talent comes across in this description of Román's religious journey.

---

[1] ADC, legajo 343, expediente 4876, folios, 192r–195r.

34

The confession of **Román Ramírez the younger**, a citizen of Deza, for the grace that was granted to the Moriscos of that place in the year 1571 ~

~ In the town of Deza on January 22, 1571, the lord Inquisitor **Dr. de la Madriz** was in his afternoon audience. A man appeared there who had not been summoned. He swore an oath and promised to speak the truth. He said he was called:

~ Román Ramírez the younger, son of **Román Ramírez [the elder]**, a citizen of the town of Deza. He is married to **Angela de Miranda**, the daughter of **Francisco de Miranda**—all citizens of this town of Deza. He is one of the Moorish New Converts and said that he was 30 years old, a little more or less.

~ He said that he desires to avail himself of the grace that has been conceded to the Moorish New Converts. In order to unburden his conscience he declares that five years ago he was traveling for the harvest to Fuentes along with **Mateo Romero the younger** (the son of a woman[2] who is currently in inquisitorial custody) and **Gerónimo de Obezar**. (Fuentes is in Aragon;[3] it belongs to the Count of Fuentes and is inhabited by *convertidos*.[4]) They harvested at the home of Juan de Fuentes, a *convertido,* and while they were reaping one Saturday, on the eve of Trinity Sunday, this witness said to Mateo Romero and Gerónimo de Obezar, "Today is a fast day." And Mateo Romero responded, "Why do you need to keep that bad fast? It's ~~beware~~ causing you to stumble. Some Dezanos don't care much for you because you're in error, and you can't be saved if you continue along the path you've been walking until now. I'm telling you so that you'll know: Ramadan is the fast you need to keep."

And so, they called over to Juan de Fuentes, who was a distance away in the same field where they were reaping. And Mateo Romero said, "Let's call Román over here so that you all can tell him what I've shared with you." So, they called to him and all four of them walked off toward [inserted: *an irrigation canal*] that flowed out of the Ebro. Then Juan de Fuentes told this confessant, "Look, brother, you're in error. That fast that you were talking about, it doesn't matter at all. For I want you to see that you have to fast without eating or drinking from star to star. What I'm explaining to you will save your soul. And tomorrow, if God wills it, I'll tell you how to pray."

---

[2] **Ana Almoravi**, who was arrested by the Inquisition in September of 1570.
[3] Presumably they were traveling to Fuentes de Ebro, southeast of Zaragoza.
[4] *Convertido* is another term for a New Christian, in this case a Morisco.

This confessant replied, "Sounds good, boss. Let's do the harvest and we'll see about tomorrow."

And so, on Sunday morning, Juan de Fuentes (along with Gerónimo de Obezar and Mateo Romero) came to this confessant's bed while he was sleeping. Juan de Fuentes brought a washtub with water and washed his own arms, legs, and whole body. Then he lowered his head and said they were going to pray. Mateo Romero asked this confessant if he wanted to begin praying, and Juan de Fuentes told this confessant, "Look, Román, Mateo Romero will teach you what you need to do here." And this confessant said, "Sounds good. We'll see what happens when we're back in Deza."

And so, when they were on the road, Mateo Romero told him that he had introduced Gerónimo de Obezar and two others in Deza to the Moorish life. And although this confessant asked him who the others were, he did not tell him—he told him he would tell him, but he never did.

And so, they came to Deza. When Lent was approaching—not that this confessant viewed Lent as either good or bad, but he had gone to Madrid and when he returned it was nearly Lent—Mateo Romero approached this confessant in the plaza and told him, "I'm telling you so you'll know: I've seen the moon, and now you have to do what you promised. Don't eat or drink until the star comes out and then only until it goes away." And this confessant said that he would do it; Mateo Romero could relax.

And so, this confessant began to fast, and he fasted 20 days during Lent—four years ago this coming Lent—and he fasted the 20 days, neither eating nor drinking all day until the star came out at night and then he dined. He went to Castar[5] and he only ate at night, then fasted again until the next night. While he was fasting, at the end of the 20 days, **Gerónimo de Salamanca** sent for this confessant, and he was with him in Medina[6] for 12 or 13 weeks.

When he returned, Gerónimo de Obezar and Mateo Romero asked him, both of them together while they were walking in the plaza, whether he had completed his fast during the month of Ramadan. This confessant told them, "No," he had only fasted for 20 days. Mateo Romero told him, "I'm telling you so you'll know: I've spoken with my mother and she's told me that it won't do you any good if you don't fast another ten days." And he also told him, "Don't eat pork or drink wine while you're doing it," because this confessant eats and drinks them. This confessant replied that he would

---

[5] Perhaps Castarné, 200 miles northeast of Deza, in Aragon.
[6] Probably Medinaceli, 40 miles southwest of Deza, or perhaps Medina del Campo, 170 miles due west.

complete the fast but would not stop eating pork or drinking wine because the day he did, he would die.

And so, on the day of Saint John,[7] this confessant finished the ten days that he lacked and broke his fast. On the day after the vigil of Saint Peter, Mateo Romero and Gerónimo de Obezar approached this confessant while he was in the Argadil and told him, "I'm telling you so that you'll know: there are more than six people in Deza who really care for you because you've turned to the good. But don't go to mass so often. Why do you want to attend mass so often?" And this confessant skipped mass on four or five festival days and Sundays in a row because of what Gerónimo and Mateo told him, although they never told him why he should avoid attending mass. Later he resumed going because it seemed to him a good thing.

And so it was until Lent came again, and one night Mateo Romero brought him to his mother's house. And Román's mother[8] told him, "I'm pleased to hear from my son that you fasted for Ramadan last year and that you're living as a Moor. Make your wife do it too." And this confessant ~~asked~~ promised that he would make her do it.

And so, the moon appeared for the month of Ramadan more than ten days earlier than in the previous year and Mateo Romero told this confessant, "I'm telling you so that you'll know: I've seen the moon and the time has come for you to correct last year's mistakes. And make your wife do it, even if she doesn't want to. When you want, I'll introduce you to what I promised you in Fuentes." And while we were in the middle of this, Gerónimo de Obezar arrived, and he said, "Mateico,[9] you're absolutely right about what you're saying. I'm telling you so that you'll know: we harvested in Osera[10] this year and our boss there reminded us about you several times, and I asked Mateico to teach you to pray. He'll teach you so that you won't neglect the prayers; he taught them to me also." And since time was passing, this confessant said that he should tell him what he had to do.

And so, this confessant went home and told his wife, "I'm telling you so that you'll know: I fasted the moon last year and I have to do it this year, and you're doing it with me." His wife did not want to but, from what this confessant saw, she did fast; this confessant never saw her eat while it was day and she told him that she was fasting. This confessant and his wife kept that fast together for fifteen days, neither eating nor drinking all day until it was night.

---

[7] That is, John the Baptist, whose feast day is celebrated on June 24.
[8] Presumably, this is an error and should read "Mateo's mother."
[9] A diminutive of Mateo, "Matty."
[10] Probably Osera de Ebro, just northeast of Fuentes de Ebro.

Then, an Augustinian friar called **Father Marcelo** came here to Deza, and he requested that Francisco de Sevilla (the customs agent for this dry port) permit this confessant (who was a port guard) to travel with him.

And so, this confessant went with Father Marcelo to Torre Loizaga[11] and Serón.[12] And while they were on the road, coming and going, he told this confessant all sorts of things from the holy Scriptures. Because of what he said, this confessant decided for himself never again to keep that fast nor to do Moorish things. And he went to his wife and told her, "Get ready to eat! I don't want you to fast any more because if you do it, I will break your head. And just like I told you to do it, now I'm telling you not to do it. Know this: God has miraculously breathed upon me. The trip with the friar has illuminated the way for me." And his wife told this confessant, "Oh, how unfortunate for me! For Mateo Romero's mother asked me if I was fasting and I told her, 'Yes.' And now if we don't do it she's going to find out." But this confessant said, "Well, we'll tell her that we did it. But this fast won't be of service to God and I don't want us to do it. Yet, we need to have some masses said because, you know, we've greatly offended Our Lord Jesus Christ in this." And, weeping, she embraced him and said that on account of this confessant she had not dared say anything, but that it seemed good to her. And she said that she had four *reales* over there and she wanted to take them to the Prior[13] so that he would say masses, and she took them. Then, eight days later, Mateo Romero's mother asked them whether they were fasting. And this confessant and his wife told her, "Yes."

This past Lent marks a year since **Mateo Romero [the elder]**, Mateo Romero the younger, and Gerónimo de Obezar came and told this confessant and his wife to fast for the month of Ramadan. And this confessant and his wife told them that they would, but they didn't do it. They told this confessant and his wife that, if they wanted, they would teach them to do Moorish ceremonies. But this confessant told them that he had already learned a few, and they left and never said anything to him ever again.

And this confessant kept those fasts as a Moorish ceremony and because he considered them to be good and because they told him that they were Moorish fasts and that he would go to heaven if he did them. And so, because of what they told him, at that time this confessant considered the law of the Moors to be better than that of the Christians. And, at that time, he believed that if he were to die, he would go to heaven, and he kept the fasts in order to abide by the law of the Moors. He has not done any

---

[11] In the Basque lands, about 180 miles north of Deza.
[12] Probably Serón de Nágima, a dozen miles west of Deza.
[13] **Juanes Valles**, who was known as "the Prior."

other Moorish ceremonies. And although he told the others that he knew some Moorish ceremonies, he only said that to be done with them. He does not know any. He has neither discussed nor talked about this with anyone other than with those whom he has declared. He does he not know of anyone else who might be performing or might have performed Moorish ceremonies, nor has he heard any mentioned.

His former belief endured until Marcelo told him what he did. Since then, since what he has declared happened, he has been a Christian and that is what he wants to be. The fact that he embraced the Moorish sect is a burden to him. And if he were able to set it right with tears of blood, he would do so. From here on out, he intends to live and die in the faith of Jesus Christ. And, from here on out, if temptation leads him to action, may the lord inquisitors show him no mercy but instead burn him in that plaza. He asks God's pardon and for penitence with mercy from His Grace.[14] He has nothing more to say.

~ He was told to continue thinking upon the unburdening of his conscience and, if he remembers anything, let him come and make it known. When they read what he had declared, he said that it was well written and set down. He was charged to keep it secret and he promised to do so. This happened in my presence: Juan Rodríguez de los Rios, notary.

~ In the town of Deza on February 19, 1571, the lord Inquisitor Dr. de la Madriz was in the afternoon audience. The aforementioned Román Ramírez the younger appeared, having been summoned. When he was present, he was told that if he has remembered anything about his business to say it under the oath that he took. ~

~ He said that he has nothing more to say.

~ Then his confession was read to him, which is that which was given above.

~ He said that it is well written and set down and he acknowledges it. This confessant does not know the date on which the month of Ramadan falls. He is prepared to complete whatever penance is imposed upon him and to abjure his errors. ~

~ He was told to think well on the unburdening of his conscience and was charged to keep it secret. He promised to do so. This happened in my presence: Juan Rodríguez de los Rios, notary.

~ The confessions made by Román Ramírez the younger, a citizen of Deza, having been seen by us, the Inquisitors against the heretical depravity and apostasy in the dioceses of Cuenca and Sigüenza with the support

---

[14] That is, from the inquisitor.

of and acting as the ordinary for this diocese of Sigüenza, by virtue of
the power that we have from the most Illustrious lord cardinal bishop of
Sigüenza, Inquisitor General,

~ Xρ[ist]i nomine Invocato[15]

We rule that we should declare and we do declare that the said Román
Ramírez has been an apostate heretic and as such has kept the sect of the
Moors, believing he could be saved in it and, on account of it, he has fallen
and incurred a sentence of greater excommunication and all the other
punishments and ineligibilities into which heretics fall and which heretics
incur who, under the title and name of Christians, perform and commit
such like sins. And howsoever that, with good conscience, we could well
condemn him unto those, yet being attentive to the fact that in his confessions before us, the aforesaid Román Ramírez showed signs of contrition
and repentance, asking pardon for his sins from God our Lord and penance from us with mercy, declaring that henceforth he wants to live and die
in our holy Catholic faith, and that he is prepared to comply with whatever
penance is imposed upon him by us and to abjure his said errors and that
he confessed during a period of grace. If the said Román Ramírez turns
himself toward our holy Catholic faith with a pure heart and an unfeigned
faith and if he has entirely confessed the truth, not hiding anything about
himself or about another person, whether living or dead, then, desiring
to exercise mercy on him and grace, we should administer it and we do
administer it unto reconciliation.

And we command that, in the chamber of this Holy Office, he abjure
the errors he has confessed and every other type of heresy and apostasy
and we command that he, having completed this abjuration, be absolved
and we absolve him of whatsoever sentence of excommunication he has
incurred as a result of the above, and we unite and reincorporate him into
the association and union of the Holy Mother Catholic Church, and we
restore him to participation in the holy sacraments and the communion of
her faithful and Catholic Christians.

As punishment and penance for what the said Román Ramírez did and
committed, we should command and do command him to confess his
sins at each one of the three holy days[16] each and every year and to retain a
receipt for having completed them, and to receive the most holy sacrament
of the Eucharist with the approval and advice of his confessor, and hear
mass every Sunday and mandatory feast days, and on the said Sundays and

---

[15] Latin: "Invoking the name of Christ."
[16] That is, Easter, Pentecost, and Christmas.

feast days let him pray the Pater Noster with the Ave Maria five times with great devotion, beseeching Our Lord to pardon him his sins.

All of this we command be thus done and completed under pain of relapsed impenitence. And we dispense with all of the ineligibilities that the said Román Ramírez might have incurred as a result of his sins, according to the said grace. And by this we pronounce and prescribe our definitive sentence.

[Signed:] Dr. de la Madriz ~

PRONOUNCEMENT
~ The said sentence was given and pronounced by the lord Inquisitor and ordinary in the town of Deza on the first day of the month of April of the year one thousand five-hundred and seventy-one, the said Román Ramírez being present, to whom notice was given. And he said that he consented to it. ~

ABJURATION
~ And then the said Román Ramírez the younger publicly abjured the sins of heresy that he had confessed in his confessions and, in general, all other species of heresy whatsoever according to and by means of the form that is contained in the abjuration that is in the book of abjurations of this Holy Office. He was formally absolved and he was declared and advised to keep himself from that which he had abjured because, doing otherwise, if he turns again and falls into some heresy, he will incur the punishment for relapsing and, without any mercy, he will be relaxed to the secular arm and the same if he does not keep the remainder of what is contained in his sentence. He responded to this saying that he had already heard and understood. He signed with his name, being present as witnesses: **Martín Fernández**, the commissioner, **Juanes Valles**, and Francisco Clara, ordained priests of Deza. This happened in my presence: Juan Rodríguez de los Rios, notary.

[Signed:] Román Ramírez ~

The words "asked" and "beware" are crossed out and the phrase "an irrigation canal" was inserted in the margin of the first page.

~ This copy was corrected and compared with the original from which it was taken, with which it agrees. In Cuenca under the secret of the Holy Office of the Inquisition, being witnesses thereto: the Licentiate Juan

Ochoa, prosecutor, and Simón Ángel, notary of the said secret, and me, **Pedro Pérez de Ullivarri**, notary.[17]

Focus Questions

How does Román's description of his conversion to Islam compare with his re-conversion to Christianity? Do you find his account of these events believable? Why or why not?

How do men and women interact with one another in Román's testimony? Who exercises authority? And how?

What "punishment and penance" did the inquisitor impose upon Román? Why did he choose that sentence? What did the Holy Office hope it would accomplish?

---

[17] This final paragraph references the fact that this document is a copy of Ramírez's original 1571 confession. The copy was probably made in 1599 and was included in his inquisitorial docket for a subsequent trial.

3

The Visitation of
Dr. Arganda (1581)[1]

In the summer of 1581, a decade after the Edict of Grace, the inquisitor Dr. Francisco de Arganda departed Cuenca and ventured on another visitation of the region. As in 1569, an Edict of Faith was read from the pulpit in preparation for the inquisitor's arrival, and the townsfolk were summoned to denounce any known incidences of heresy. And, once again, the town's Moriscos became a major focus of concern. Many of the same individuals who first appeared in Licentiate Reynoso's visitation reappear here—both as denouncers and as denounced. But a new generation of Dezanos has come on the scene as well.

Curiously, although many of the denunciations that follow raised serious concerns, none of them developed into full-blown inquisitorial trials. Below are the 38 audiences recorded by Pedro Pérez, the inquisitorial notary.

--------------------------------- **35** ---------------------------------

In the town of Deza on June 19, 1581, the lord Inquisitor **Dr. Arganda** was in the chamber for the morning audience. A person entered therein without having been summoned, was sworn in, and promised to speak the truth:

Witness: Young Juan, a citizen of Judes.[2] He said he was 54 years old. He said that in order to unburden his conscience he comes to make known to this Holy Office that this August will mark two years that Catalina Moraga (who is Antonio Moraga's daughter, a citizen of Arcos, and Pedro Benito's wife) has lived in Judes. This witness asked Pedro Benito how he was and he said, "Reasonably well, except that I had to eat a chicken all alone." This witness asked him why he had not shared it with his wife.

---

[1] ADC, libro 318, folios 94r-124v.
[2] Judes is about 30 miles south of Deza in Castile but near the Aragonese border.

Pedro Benito replied that all he had done was buy a chicken and wring its neck. But because he had failed to slit its throat, his wife Catalina Moraga had refused to eat it.[3]

This is the truth under the oath he took and he does not sign it because he said he does not know how. His statement was read to him and he said that it was what he said. He was charged to keep it secret and he promised to do so. The lord Inquisitor signed it. This happened in my presence: **Pedro Pérez**, notary.

[Signed:] Dr. Arganda

36

In the town of Deza on June 21, 1581, the lord Inquisitor **Dr. Arganda** was in the chamber for the morning audience.[4] A person entered therein without having been summoned, was sworn in, and promised to speak the truth:

Witness: **Gonzalo Martínez [the younger]**, the town's notary public before whom the business of the Holy Office is conducted. He said he was age 39. He said that in order to unburden his conscience he comes to make known to this Holy Office that three or four days before the lord inquisitor arrived in town, which was the fifteenth day of the present month, Francisco Sánchez (an Old Christian citizen of this town) was in this witness's house. He asked this witness when the lord inquisitor was coming and this witness told him that he understood he was coming that week. And Francisco Sánchez told him, "Now the people who live on New Street will be afraid. The ladies who live near me told me they saw them going from house to house at night, crying, with a dog wrapped in a shroud."

This witness told him, "Watch what you say and remember which neighbors these were. Be aware that you need to go to **Miguel Benito**, the town's commissioner of the Holy Office, and reveal this." For if he failed to do it, then he and the neighbor ladies would be excommunicated. And he told him to keep it secret. Francisco Sánchez said that he went and told the aforementioned neighbor ladies not to forget what happened.

---

[3] Although the text does not explain why Catalina Moraga's behavior might have been a problem, it seems likely that the witness was responding to the Edict of Faith read before the arrival of the inquisitor. The Edict listed a number of behaviors that might have suggested Islamic behavior, and among them was the practice of slitting the throat of an animal to drain its blood in accordance with Islamic dietary practices. It is not clear whether Catalina is a New or Old Christian.

[4] Compare this account with Docs. 42, 48, and 54–56.

This is the truth about what happened under the oath that he took. He asked no more questions to avoid being scandalized. He signed it with his name and promised to keep it secret. Before me: **Pedro Pérez**, notary.

[Signed:] Gonzalo Martínez

37

In the town of Deza on June 21, 1581, the lord Inquisitor **Dr. Arganda** was in the chamber for the morning audience.[5] A person entered therein, was sworn in, and promised to speak the truth:

Witness: **Juan Ramírez**, farmer, 28 years old.

Asked, he said that he does not know anything that he should reveal to this Holy Office except that four years ago, when this witness arrived home, **María de Medrano** (his wife) said that she had been arguing with a bailiff[6] and had told him, "May the evil Inquisition enter your house!"

This is the truth under the oath that he took and he did not sign it because he said he does not know how. He was charged to keep it secret and he promised to do so. This happened in my presence: **Pedro Pérez**, notary.

[Signed:] Dr. Arganda

38

The following audience provides further information about María de Medrano's quarrel with the bailiff, Francisco de Hortubia. María apparently made a trip to Medinaceli, where Dr. Arganda was staying before he arrived at Deza, and voluntarily made this confession to him a few days before her husband was summoned to make his statement. This audience was not included in the record of Arganda's visit to Deza, but rather in a different dossier of trial documents.[7]

In the town of Medinaceli on June 19, 1581, the lord Inquisitor **Dr. Arganda** was in the chamber for the afternoon audience.[8] A woman entered without being summoned. She was sworn in and promised to speak the truth. She said her name was:

---

[5] Compare this account with Doc. 38.
[6] **Francisco de Hortubia**, who is a Morisco.
[7] ADC, legajo 370, expediente 5232.
[8] Compare this account with Doc. 37.

María de Medrano, a Morisca, the wife of **Juan Ramírez**, a farmer. She said that she was 34 years old and that she had accepted the Edict of Grace that they granted the Moriscos of this town and that she was reconciled in it. In order to unburden her conscience she comes to make known to this Holy Office that two and a half years ago, **Francisco de Hortubia** (bailiff) had taken some collateral at the command of Dr. Camargo, the Port Judge.[9] What he took was worth more than ~~for~~ twice the four *reales* ~~on which had been made~~.

Although the debt was satisfied, he returned to her house and took a pot. When she saw how they were insulting her and because she needed the pot for her house, she exited the house arguing with the bailiff, both of them holding onto the pot. At the end of a street he grabbed it and threw it so it rolled down the street until it finally came to a rest in the plaza.

Hurt and saddened at seeing her goods mistreated, she said, "May it please God that just as you wrong me by taking more surety than necessary [...][10] to God that just as you wrong me, may the evil Inquisition sell off your goods." Her intention was not to offend God our Lord or the Holy Office of the Inquisition, before which she receives holy and righteous justice. If she has offended in what she said, she requests pardon and penance with mercy.

This is the truth under the oath that she took. And when she said what she said, there were many people about. But because she was so upset, she could not see who they were. Yet she did see that a crowd of people gathered while they were arguing. She promised to keep it secret. The words "for" and "on which had been made" were deleted. This happened in my presence: **Pedro Pérez**, notary.

39

In the town of Deza on June 21, 1581, the lord Inquisitor **Dr. Arganda** was in the chamber for the afternoon audience. A person appeared therein without having been summoned, was sworn in, and promised to speak the truth:

Witness: Pedro Sánchez, dyer, an Old Christian citizen of the town, age 46 years. In order to unburden his conscience he comes to make known

---

[9] The context to these events appears to be that María de Medrano and her husband had failed to make good on a debt and the town bailiff was ordered to take possession of household goods, which had been pledged as collateral.

[10] This phrase is illegible but probably, "I swear ..."

to this Holy Office that one year ago this coming August, this witness was going to Bordalba (which is in Aragon). He came upon **Lope de Obezar**, also known as Lope del Sol (a Morisco reconciled by this Holy Office, a citizen of this town).[11] And as this witness caught up to him, he said, "Mr. Pedro, I'm trusting you not to reveal that I come this way in order to save myself a league of travel.[12] For you know that we can't enter Aragon or this place, Bordalba."

Then, he said that he had responded that there were neither Moriscos nor any other suspicious people there. He also said that he commended him to his wife and said he hoped matters improved.

When they came to Bordalba, this witness went in but Lope de Obezar went on by way of Monteagudo.[13]

This is the truth under the oath that he took and he does not sign it because he said that he does not know how. He was charged to keep it secret and he promised to do so. The lord inquisitor signed it. This happened in my presence: **Pedro Pérez**, notary.

[Signed:] Dr. Arganda

40

In the town of Deza on June 23, 1581 the lord Inquisitor **Dr. Arganda** was in the chamber for the morning audience.[14] A person appeared therein without having been summoned, was sworn in, and promised to speak the truth:

Witness: **Juanes Valles**, an ordained priest of the Order of St. John, from the town of Deza. He said that he was age 75 and that in order to unburden his conscience he comes to make known to this Holy Office that six years ago, more or less, he was inside of the town's church along with **Miguel Benito** (the commissioner of the Holy Office) and **Licentiate Páez** (a physician, originally from Atienza).[15] Earlier that day they had heard a friar preach on Christ's humanity, and Licentiate Páez said that Christ was the Son of God only insofar as he was man. This witness responded, "Lord Jesus! I'm appalled that your honor would say such a thing! For Christ was

---

[11] As part of his reconciliation to the Church, Lope had been forbidden to cross into Aragon, which inquisitors viewed as exerting a corrupting influence on Deza's Moriscos.

[12] A distance of about four miles. A league is traditionally defined as the distance a person can walk in one hour.

[13] That is, Monteagudo de las Vicarías, seven miles southwest of Bordalba, in Castile.

[14] Compare this account with Doc. 60.

[15] Atienza is about 60 miles southwest of Deza in Castile.

the Son of God both insofar as he was man and insofar as he was God."
Licentiate Páez replied, "I say this *su correctione sancte matris eglesie*."[16]

This witness took up a breviary and showed him the statement in the
Athanasian Creed that says Christ is equal to *pater secundum divinitatem*.[17]
But he refused to believe what this witness told him until he came to the
verse that reads, *equalis patris minor pater secundum humanitatem*.[18] Then
Licentiate Páez said, "Now it's clear!"

But this witness was greatly scandalized because Licentiate Páez was an
old and learned man. He was a very genteel physician and a philosopher
and had very good judgment and was well natured.

Asked, he said that the licentiate was a native of Atienza and that he
considered him to be of Jewish descent. Nothing more happened beyond
what he has said and declared.

Item:[19] He said that about two weeks ago, *bachiller* **Bartolome Montero**
(one of Deza's clerics) told this witness that he had heard **Juan de Ozuel**
(another of Deza's clerics) say and strongly insist that many of the saints to
whom they prayed were in hell.

Miguel Benito (the commissioner) and the young vicar[20] were both
there. Some other people were also present whom Miguel Benito and the
young vicar will name.

This is the truth under the oath that he took and he does not say it out
of hatred. He signed his name after it was read to him and said that it was
well written. He was charged to keep it secret and he promised to do so.
This happened in my presence: **Pedro Pérez**.

[Signed:] Juanes Valles

41

AGAINST LUIS DE LEÓN, MORISCO

In the town of Deza on June 23, 1581, the lord Inquisitor **Dr. Arganda**
was in the chamber for the morning audience. A person appeared therein

---

[16] This Latin phrase, which contains some grammatical errors, means: "subject to the correction of the holy mother Church."

[17] Latin: "the Father according to his divinity." The Athanasian Creed is an important early Christian credal statement that helped to formulate the doctrines of the Trinity and of Christ's dual natures.

[18] Latin, from the Athanasian Creed: "equal to the Father and inferior to the Father according to his humanity." The quotation (accidentally?) leaves out a key part of the formula, which should read: Equal to the Father according to his divinity and inferior to the Father according to his humanity.

[19] Compare this account with Docs. 60 and 62–63.

[20] A reference to **Licentiate Miguel Benito**, the nephew of the commissioner, whose name he shares.

without having been summoned, was sworn in, and promised to speak the truth:

Witness: **Dr. Diego Martínez Navarro**, a citizen of this town and an Old Christian. He said he was 25 years old and in order to unburden his conscience he comes to make known to this Holy Office that when he was traveling from the University of Salamanca,[21] Luis de León (a Morisco muleteer originally from Arévalo and a citizen of Terrer in Aragon) was with him. They discussed a certain married woman from Deza, saying that a certain man kept her as a "friend"—it was Luis de León who mentioned it to this witness. This led Luis de León to tell this witness that he needed to get *that* kind of a woman to be his friend. This witness replied that he would do no such thing and also said, "Don't you see that that's a mortal sin?" Luis de León denied that it was a sin and they discussed that business no more. Not another word was spoken about it.

Item: He said that about ten or eleven years ago he was in Deza in the presence of *bachiller* Juan de Cisneros and Pedro Borovia, who is in Alessandria della Paglia.[22] **Juan de Ozuel** (one of Deza's clerics) said that when he was in Salamanca he fell in love with a woman and he ran into an old lady (he does not remember what she said her name was) who told him that she could tell from his face that he was in love. She said that if he wanted to get what he was hoping for, that apparently he should take a hoopoe[23] to a field where he could hear neither a dog bark nor a rooster crow and boil it until a bone rose to the top of the boiling pot. While doing this he must not turn his head to look behind him. And if he used that bone to draw some blood from the woman he loved, she would love him back.

Juan de Ozuel also said that he had taken the bone out of the pot and stirred up the hoopoe's remains because he wanted to see if the old woman would know—and she did. It seemed to this witness that *bachiller* Ozuel had claimed this was a surefire solution.

AGAINST *BACHILLER* JUAN DE CISNEROS

Item: He said that in the same conversation *bachiller* Juan de Cisneros told him that waving a handkerchief perfumed with certain things under the nose of a woman would make her fall deeply in love with the man who

---

[21] Salamanca, about 200 miles east of Deza, boasted one of the most important universities in Spain.

[22] A diocese in Piedmont, Italy.

[23] A hoopoe is a colourful medium-sized bird with a distinctive crest of feathers. They appear in spells and magical recipes with some frequency.

did it. He also said that an old woman in Salamanca had given him this remedy and when he went to confess, they had ordered him to burn the handkerchief, which he did. It seemed to this witness that Juan de Cisneros said that this had worked or that it was true.

AGAINST BEATRIZ PÉREZ DE LUNA— DISQUALIFIED[24]

Item: He said that ~~lady~~ **Beatriz Pérez de Luna**, the daughter of **Álvaro de Luna** (condemned by this Holy Office, who was a citizen of Almazán) lives in Deza as do her children **Gerónimo de Ocáriz**, Francisco Beltrán de Ocáriz, and Beatriz de Ocáriz. They wear silk and fine cloth, and Francisco and Gerónimo ride around on horseback.

AGAINST JUAN HERNÁN MARTÍNEZ

Item: He said he has read the special edict regarding simple fornication.[25] About two years ago more or less, in the presence of this witness and don Juan Cerbados del Castro (a citizen of Baeza who was then in Deza), Juan de Hernán Martínez (a citizen of Deza) was discussing a certain married woman who had been "friendly" (in a wicked way) with a friar.

Consequently, Juan de Hernán Martínez pointed to the house of that woman's mother and said, "I know it's not a sin for *me* to go into that house." This witness understood these words to mean that it would not be a sin for him to have carnal knowledge of that married woman. This witness told him to take it back and to watch what he said. And, like an embarrassed man who had made a mistake, Juan de Hernán Martínez said something that this witness does not remember and retracted his comment.

---

[24] The meaning of the word "disqualified" here is ambiguous and no explanation is provided. Presumably, it indicates that inquisitorial authorities determined that this denunciation lacked credibility or did not fall under their jurisdiction. It is likely, however, that the inquisitors chose not to pursue the denunciation because, in spite of having multiple lines of Jewish blood in the family, the members of the Ocáriz clan were influential local nobles who virtually everyone agreed should be regarded as Old Christians. See the Cast of Characters for more information about Beatriz Pérez de Luna, Álvaro de Luna, and Gerónimo de Ocáriz.

[25] Fornication is sexual relations between two unmarried people. The edict referred to here is the Edict of Faith read before Dr. Arganda's arrival in Deza. It enumerated the offences that fell under the authority of the Holy Office and obliged witnesses to reveal any knowledge of such offences to the inquisitor.

This is the truth under the oath that he took and he does not say it out of hatred.

AGAINST THE DUKE OF MEDINACELI

Item: He said that he heard Hernando Ochoa (the secretary of the Duchess of Medinaceli) say that when **Duke don Juan Luis de la Cerda** contracted malaria he had said, "O most harsh God."

This is the truth and he does not say it out of hatred. He signed it with his name and when it was read to him, he said that it agreed with what he said. He was charged to keep it secret and he promised to do so.

Item: He said that *bachiller* Juan de Cisneros [inserted: *said*] to him that an old woman from Salamanca had told him that in order to enter a house without being seen, one apparently should take a black cat and plant a fava bean in its corpse. Then put one of the beans that grows out of it in your mouth. If you keep it with you, you can enter without anyone seeing you. He told this witness that they should try it, but they have not done so.

This happened in my presence: **Pedro Pérez**, notary. The insertion "said" is correct.

[Signed:] Dr. Martínez Navarro

42

AGAINST ISABEL DE BAPTISTA, MORSICA[26]

In the town of Deza on June 26, 1581, the lord Inquisitor **Dr. Arganda** was in the chamber for the morning audience. A person appeared therein without having been summoned and swore to speak the truth:

Witness: **María la Rasa**, an Old Christian, the wife of Francisco García Destaragon, a weaver and a citizen of Deza. She said that she was 30 years old and that in order to unburden her conscience she comes to make known to this Holy Office that nine years ago—this was after the Edict of Grace was granted to the town's *convertidos*[27]—she was on her way to the

---

[26] Compare this account with Doc. 53.

[27] *Convertidos* (meaning "converted ones") usually refers to Jewish converts to Christianity in Spain but, as is the case here, the term can refer to Moriscos as well.

fountain at about midday. She ran into one of the town's *convertidas* named **Isabel de Baptista**, the wife of so-and-so de Baptista,[28] the deaf guy, who lives in [inserted: *the*] town's *Corrillo* in the house of a *convertido*.

Isabel de Baptista was drawing water from the fountain with her hand and washing her private parts.[29] Then, as this witness approached, she stopped what she was doing. This witness does not remember if she said anything to her. Then this witness ran int [*sic*] into *mosén* Hernando García (a surgeon) and told him what she had seen. Yesterday, he spoke to this witness and reminded her of what had happened; he had very nearly seen it too. And he told her that she had to come and make it known.

Item:[30] She said that a few days ago she heard Mari Martínez, wife of Martín Gutierrez (a farmer and citizen of Deza), say that the town's *convertidos* were playing with a corpse. They carried it from here to there, but Mari Martínez said nothing more.

This is the truth under the oath that she took. She did not sign it because she said she does not know how. When it was read to her, she said that it agreed with what she said. She was charged to keep it secret and promised to do so. The lord inquisitor signed it. The insertion "the" is correct. This happened in my presence: **Pedro Pérez**, notary.

[Signed:] Dr. Arganda

43

AGAINST OLD FADRIQUE, MORISCO

In the town of Deza on June 26, 1581, the lord Inquisitor **Dr. Arganda** was in the chamber for the morning audience. A person entered therein without having been summoned, was sworn in, and promised to speak the truth:

Witness: **Francisco Manrique**, an Old Christian farmer and citizen of Deza. He said that he was age 31 and that in order to unburden his conscience he says that about ten years ago, more or less, Juan Martínez (a citizen of Aliud in the region of Soria) told him that he had heard that **Old Fadrique** (a Morisco and citizen of Deza, now deceased) claimed Our Lady could not have given birth as a virgin.

---

[28] **Agustín de Baptista**.

[29] Presumably Isabel was performing Islamic ritual ablutions in preparation for daily prayers. Why she decided to do so at the fountain in the town's main plaza at midday is unclear.

[30] Compare this account with Docs. 36, 48, and 54–56.

When this happened, this witness gave an account of it to Deza's inquisitorial *familiares*.[31] A week ago yesterday, which was Sunday, he went back to see **Miguel García** (an apothecary and a *familiar* of this Holy Office) ~~and that~~ about it and asked him if he had record of what he had said. **Román Ramírez the elder** (a Morisco citizen of Deza) saw this witness talking to Miguel García and approached him, saying, "What are you looking for over here with Miguel García? Are you looking for some mule that came this way?" This witness responded that he was not, but rather had gone to ask Miguel García to be patient about this witness's brother paying for some medicine. Román Ramírez turned to him and said he thought perhaps this witness knew something about someone who lived up here (speaking with reference to the town's *convertidos*).[32]

At that moment, **Alexo Gorgoz** (also a Morisco) arrived and asked this witness what he wanted around there, if he wanted something around there. He responded that he kissed his hands[33] and wanted nothing. With that, they left.

This is the truth under the oath that he took. He signed it with his name after it had been read to him and he said that it agreed with what he said. He was charged to keep it secret and he promised to do so. The phrase "and that" was struck out. Juan Martínez is also deceased. This is the truth and he does not say it out of hatred. This happened in my presence: **Pedro Pérez**, notary.

[Signed:] Francisco Manrique

44

AGAINST ÍÑIGO DE SALEROS AND GERÓNIMO DE MOLINA

In the town of Deza on June 26, 1581, the lord Inquisitor **Dr. Arganda** was in the chamber for the morning audience. A person entered therein without being summoned, was sworn in, and promised to speak the truth:

Witness: **Juan de Villoslada**, an Old Christian farmer and citizen of Deza. He said his age was 27 years and that in order to unburden his

---

[31] *Familiares* were lay representatives of the Inquisition. Deza had several, and they worked alongside the local commissioner, receiving denunciations from others and making denunciations of their own. *Familiares* had to prove that they were Old Christians, and while they received no pay for their work, the office gave them a degree of prestige and authority.

[32] Most of Deza's Moriscos lived in the Upper Neighborhood.

[33] A Spanish formula of courtesy that suggests respect.

conscience he comes to make known to this Holy Office that two or three years ago, more or less, he was in the house of Íñigo de Saleros (a Morisco and a citizen of Deza) who has been and is this witness's friend. He entered his house at about 9 o'clock at night without knocking and found Íñigo de Saleros seated on a bench with his head bowed. And in front of him, on his knees, was **Gerónimo de Molina** (a tailor and a Morisco). When they noticed this witness, Íñigo de Saleros stayed where he was, but Gerónimo de Molina sat down on the ground, pretending.

No one else was there and they were alone in a small kitchen, and it was summertime. This seemed wrong to this witness, since one of the men, Íñigo, was very old and Gerónimo was young and because both of them have previously been in the custody of the Holy Office.

Item: He said that Hernando de Sevilla[†], a native of Deza, told this witness that four or five years ago a Morisca woman (a citizen of Deza) went to communion. But after she had received the most holy sacrament, when they gave her the wine she spat it out.[34] This witness remembered it just this past week.

When asked, he responded that he had not mentioned this to anyone.

This is the truth under the oath that he took and he does not say it out of hatred. He signed it with his name after it had been read to him and said that it corresponded with what he had said. He promised to keep it secret. This happened in my presence: **Pedro Pérez**, notary.

[Signed:] Juan de Villoslada

[†] Hernando de Sevilla was examined on July 16, 1581, and he had nothing to say.

45

AGAINST GERÓNIMO DE MORAGA[35]

In the town of Deza on June 26, 1581, the lord Inquisitor **Dr. Arganda** was in the chamber for the afternoon audience. A person appeared therein without having been summoned, was sworn in, and promised to speak the truth:

Witness: **Francisca Borque**, the widow of **Gonzalo Martínez**, a scribe. She said that she is a citizen of this town and is more than 40 years old. In order to unburden her conscience she comes to disclose to this Holy Office that about five months ago more or less she had a young woman in her

---

[34] According to Roman Catholic doctrine, in the sacrament of the Eucharist the bread and wine are miraculously transformed into the body and blood of Jesus Christ.

[35] Compare this account with Doc. 59.

service named **Ana Ramírez**, who was engaged to **Gerónimo de Moraga** (a Morisco hemp weaver and a citizen of Ariza).[36]

Gerónimo de Moraga came from Ariza to see Ana Ramírez, who later confided to this witness something that seemed wrong to her: she gave her fiancé a clean shirt, but he told her he did not want to wear it. As Ana kept pestering him about it, he finally agreed but only if she gave him a jug of clean water and if she and her younger sister left the house. So, she brought the jug of water, gave it to him, and left the house with the girl. When she returned, she found that he had gotten part of the floorboard wet.[37] Ana also informed this witness that Gerónimo her fiancé had said to her that her parents told him that she had been sold to him.[38]

On the eve of a feast day, this witness gave Ana a small loaf of bread for her to give it as an offering. But Ana returned the next morning and asked this witness for another one. When she asked her what had happened to the first one, Ana responded that her fiancé had come in at midnight and eaten it. Ana told this witness that she had a bad feeling about all of this. And, furthermore, on another night, Gerónimo ate at two in the morning, according to what Ana had told this witness.[39]

Ana also said that one night while she was praying, Gerónimo said to her, "Why are you praying? We already know that you know how pray." She also told this witness, as she recalls it, that she had told Juan Ramírez[40] about this—he is her brother, whom they call "the Friar"; he is currently in service to **Gabriel Aliger**, the town alderman, and is a New Christian. And Ana told this witness that, afterward, Gerónimo her fiancé had asked her, "Did you tell your brother something about what I said that caused you to stop laughing?" For, although the three of them had been enjoying themselves together, Juan's mood had turned gloomy. Gerónimo had left the room and when he returned he found that her brother (the Friar) was gloomy.

This is the truth under the oath that she took and she does not say it out of hatred. Ana is an Old Christian on her mother's side. When it was read to her, she said that it was well written. She did not sign it because she said she did not know how. The lord inquisitor signed it. She was charged to keep it secret and she promised to do so. This happened in my presence: **Pedro Pérez**, notary.

[Signed:] Dr. Arganda

---

[36] Ariza is about 15 miles south of Deza in Aragon.

[37] The concern is probably whether Gerónimo was performing ritual washings in preparation for Islamic prayers.

[38] This seems to be the intended meaning of the manuscript.

[39] The concern is probably whether Gerónimo is fasting for Ramadan.

[40] This is a different Juan Ramírez from the man included in the Cast of Characters.

46

In the town of Deza on June 26, 1581, the lord Inquisitor **Dr. Arganda** was in the chamber for the afternoon audience.[41] A person entered therein without being summoned, was sworn in, and promised to speak the truth:

Witness: María Barba, the wife of Martín Estaragan, a rope maker and citizen of Deza. She is 40 years old, more or less, and said that in order to unburden her conscience she comes to make known to this Holy Office that she heard Francisco Donoso (a miller and citizen of Deza) say that a New Christian lad was out gathering firewood on Holy Thursday morning last year. (The lad is a native of Terrer in Aragon and she does not know his name, but he serves a tile maker from Terrer who is working in Deza; she does not know his name either but he is very well known.) [inserted: *Do*]noso told the lad that they should get back soon because it was nearly time for them to seal up the most holy sacrament.[42] And the Morisco lad had asked him what it meant to seal up the most holy sacrament. Francisco Donoso said that they would enclose the most holy sacrament in a tabernacle, then preach the Maundy Thursday sermon at midday, then at night they would have a procession and preach the Passion sermon. The lad asked him what he meant by "the Passion" and said that in Terrer they had no Passion.[43]

Moreover, ~~Francisco Donoso, miller~~ he told Martín Ruiz (a citizen of Deza) that when he went to chop firewood with the Morisco lad, he had told him that they should hurry up so that they would get back in time to release a soul out of purgatory, for they were releasing one that day. The Morisco lad asked him, "How do you release a soul from punishment?" and "How is a soul taken from purgatory?" and "Where had it been taken from?" and "Where did they release it from?"

AGAINST ALEJOS DE DEZA, THE SON OF ANTÓN DE DEZA[44]

Item: She said that she heard Juana (Francisco Donoso's wife's cousin) tell some of her neighbors that Cristóbal Ruiz (a citizen of Deza and a farmer)

---

[41] Compare this account with Doc. 71.

[42] The "most holy sacrament" is a reference to the consecrated bread used in the Eucharist and preserved in an ornate vessel known as a tabernacle.

[43] The passion refers to the suffering of Jesus Christ on earth and especially in the days leading up to his crucifixion, which are often known as Passion Week.

[44] Compare this account with Doc. 72.

had seen **Alejos**, the son of **Antón de Deza**, a Morisco, kneel in front of the father of the aforementioned tile maker when he was in town. He had kissed his hand.

The morning after they read an edict from the Holy Office in Deza's church against **Mateo Romero**,[45] that Morisco left town. He is the father of the tile maker and was very old.

This is the truth under the oath that she took. She does not say it out of hatred but rather in order to unburden her conscience. She did not sign it because she said she did not know how. When it was read to her, she said that it agreed with what she said. She was charged to keep it secret and promised to do so. The lord inquisitor signed it. "Francisco Donoso, miller" was struck out; the inserted "Do" is correct. This happened in my presence: **Pedro Pérez**, notary.

[Signed:] Dr. Arganda

--------------------------------- 47 ---------------------------------

AGAINST FRANCISCO ESCUDERO[46]

In the town of Deza on June 26, 1581, the lord Inquisitor **Dr. Arganda** was in the chamber for the afternoon audience. A person entered therein without having been summoned, was sworn in, and promised to speak the truth:

Witness: **Juan Donoso**, a miller and a citizen of this town of Deza. He said he was 60 years old and that in order to unburden his conscience he comes to make known to this Holy Office that five weeks ago, more or less, **Francisco Escudero** (a citizen of Deza) was at the Duke's Mill.[47] Several times, he angrily repeated, "I swear to God" because of the lumber they had brought him. When this witness told him that he should not swear to God, he turned and said, "I swear to God that I have to swear to God, even if it means being put in the devil's house." **Miguel Donoso** (this witness's son) and María or **Juana** (**Blasco Muñóz's** daughter) were present.

This is the truth under the oath that he took and he does not say it out of hatred. When it was read to him, he said that it was well written. He did

---

[45] Mateo Romero the elder had escaped from his captors while being transported to serve his sentence in the galleys. On May 28, 1581, in the lead-up to Dr. Arganda's visitation, a pronouncement of Romero's condemnation from the Holy Office had been read in the pulpit of Deza's parish church after high mass.

[46] Compare this account with Docs. 69–70.

[47] That is, the Cubo Mill.

not sign it because he said that he did not know how. He was charged to keep it secret and he promised to do so. The lord inquisitor signed it. This happened in my presence: **Pedro Pérez**, notary.

[Signed:] Dr. Arganda

48

AGAINST ANA DE PAZENCIA THE WIFE OF LUIS DE CIELI AND CECILIA DE CIELI THE WIFE OF ÍÑIGO DE HORTUBIA THE SOLDIER[48]

In Deza on June 27, 1581, the lord Inquisitor **Dr. Arganda** was in the chamber for the morning audience. A person entered therein without having been summoned, was sworn in, and promised to speak the truth:

Witness: Juana Sánchez, the widow of Francisco de Palencia, a farmer. She is a citizen of Deza and said that she was more than 43 years old. In order to unburden her conscience she comes to make known to this Holy Office that more than two months ago Berlandino de Palencia (her daughter [*sic*]) told her what happened when he was in the town plaza with four of his companions. He said that he was there late one night with Francisco de Villoslada [the younger], **Francisco Manrique [the younger]**, **Pascual de Villoslada**, and one other whom she does not remember. While they were there, they saw Ana de Pazencia leave the house of her husband **Luis de Cieli** (a Morisco) carrying a bundle about the size of a dead child. Then she entered the house of Cecilia [de Cieli] (her sister-in-law, the wife of [**Íñigo de**] **Hortubia** the soldier). They went out from there, and a man accompanied them into the house of Amador (a Morisco). They were crying and making lamentations as they went, going with the man from house to house amongst the town's Moriscos.

AGAINST ANA DE MOLINA, WIFE OF GABRIEL DE ALIGER

Item: She said that about three months ago, they opened the crypt in the main chapel of Deza's church. She was there giving thanks to our Lord for keeping it in such good condition. This witness happened to turn her head and saw the wife of **Gabriel Aliger** (the town alderman), who

---

[48] Compare this account with Docs. 36, 42, and 54–56.

is a Morisca. (She thinks the woman is called Ana de Molina and is the daughter of Old Molino, a Morisco.) This witness considers her a very treacherous woman in her actions. The woman was gesturing as if she was mocking the crypt that had been uncovered, putting her hand on her face and her nose between her fingers, like she was "giving the figs." [49] It seemed very wrong to this witness, as if she were poking fun at the temple of God.

This is the truth under the oath that she took and she does not say it out of hatred. When it was read to her, she said that it agreed with what she said. She did not sign it because she said she did not know how. She was charged to keep it secret and she promised to do so. The lord inquisitor signed it. This happened in my presence: **Pedro Pérez**, notary.

[Signed:] Dr. Arganda

49

AGAINST ANTONIO MORAGA THE LAD

In the town of Deza on June 27, 1581, the lord Inquisitor **Dr. Arganda** was in the chamber for the morning audience. A man entered without having been summoned, was sworn in, and promised to speak the truth. He said his name was:

Witness: Pedro de Sotomayor, a citizen of the town of Cihuela. He said he was more than 50 years old and that in order to unburden his conscience he comes to make known to this Holy Office that about five or six years ago more or less he was in the town of Molina. Gerónimo de Heredia (a citizen of Sotodosos who is at His Majesty's court) told this witness that Antonio Moraga the lad (son of Antonio Moraga, a citizen of Arcos de Jalón) had told him and recounted in front of others that when his grandfather or grandmother died, they washed the body, formed a circle, and showed reverence to the ancestor.

Then, at the burial, they put raisins, figs, honey, and other foodstuffs in the grave. They buried it next to an elm tree outside of the church at Arcos. And Gerónimo de Heredia called on Antonio Moraga the lad once or twice to repeat what he had said in the presence of this witness, but he told them to

---

[49] An obscene gesture, usually made by putting the thumb between the index and middle fingers of a closed fist. Here, Ana de Molina forms the gesture by putting the fingers of her hand around her nose.

leave him alone, saying he would repeat it later. It was wrong for him to have said what he did, for other *convertidos*[50] from the town of Arcos were present.

AGAINST JUAN DE GONZALO, CITIZEN OF CIHUELA[51]

Item: He said that Juan de las Eras (parish priest of Escobosa de Alamzán) told this witness that Antón de las Eras believed the following: while Antón de las Eras was sitting somewhere in Cihuela with Juan de Gonzalo (a citizen of that town; a *convertido* on his father's side and a native Dezano), Pedro de Chahorna, who was sick, joined him. When Chahorna stood up from his seat, Antón de las Eras said to him, "I swear to filthy Mohammed! You're hardy and can stand up!" The sick fellow went into his house, but then Juan de Gonzalo said to Antón de las Eras that he swore to the same thing that if he had a dagger on him, he would stab him for having done such a wicked thing to Mohammed as call him "filthy Mohammed."

This is the truth under the oath that he took. He signed it with his name after it was read to him and he said that it was well written and set down. He does not say it out of hatred. He was charged to keep it secret and promised to do so. This happened in my presence: **Pedro Pérez**, notary.

[Signed:] Pedro de Sotomayor

50

AGAINST FRANCISCA, THE WIFE OF GABRIEL DE LA GARZEZA

In the town of Deza on June 27, 1581, the lord Inquisitor **Dr. Arganda** was in the Chamber for the morning audience. A woman entered without having been summoned and was sworn in and promised to speak the truth. She said her name was:

Witness: **Madalena de Montón**, an Old Christian and the wife of Juan Cervero. She said she was more than 30 years old and that in order to unburden her conscience she comes to make known to this Holy Office that about seven or eight years ago this witness was leaving the town church after vespers.[52] **Ana de Contreras** (~~wife of Gabriel de Saleros~~ widow),

---

[50] See above, footnote 27.
[51] Compare this account with Doc. 52.
[52] Vespers is the liturgical service of worship conducted in the evening.

Interior of the Parish Church of Deza
The magnificent parish church—with vaulted ceilings and columns—
was constructed to accommodate Deza's growing population. It was an
important center of the town's religious and social life.
Photo credit: Rachel A. O'Banion, 2013

Francisca (wife of Gabriel de la Garzeza, deceased), and another woman
(whom she does not remember—but all three of them were Moriscas) were
walking along in front of her down the road. And Francisca said to the
women who were walking with her, "When I'm in vespers it sure seems like
they're setting me on fire."

AGAINST THE MORISCOS OF DEZA
Item: She said that when one of the town's *convertidos*[53] is buried, she has
seen the other Moriscos stand over the grave in an arc. And the women
walk on the top of the deceased's grave. At times, because they know that

---

[53] See above, footnote 27.

the Old Christians are watching them do it, some Moriscas walk on it but not others.

Asked, she said that so many Moriscas do this that she does not remember any of them in particular.

This is the truth under the oath that she took and she does not say it out of hatred. She was charged to keep it secret and she promised to do so. After it had been read to her she said that it corresponded with what she said. The lord inquisitor signed it. The phrase "wife of Gabriel de Saleros" was struck out. This happened in my presence: **Pedro Pérez**, notary.

[Signed:] Dr. Arganda

51

In the town of Deza on June 27, 1581, the lord Inquisitor **Dr. Arganda** was in the chamber for the afternoon audience. A person entered without having been summoned, was sworn in, and promised to speak the truth:

Witness: **Catarina Montón**, the widow of Francisco de Arcos, a citizen of this town. She said that she was 40 years old and that in order to unburden her conscience she comes to make known to this Holy Office what she has seen at the burials of the town's *convertidos*.[54] Every woman in attendance walks right up to and over the top of the graves of the deceased. They stomp on them. In particular, María la Roma (widow of Gabriel Corazón) does it, but so do the rest of them.

This is the truth under the oath that she took and she does not say it out of hatred. When it was read to her she said that it was well written and set down. She promised to keep it secret. The lord inquisitor signed it because she said she did not know how. This happened in my presence: **Pedro Pérez**, notary.

[Signed:] Dr. Arganda

52

AGAINST JUAN DE GONZALO, A CITIZEN OF CIHUELA[55]

In the town of Deza on June 28, 1581, the lord Inquisitor **Dr. Arganda** was in the chamber for the morning audience. A man entered without having

---

[54] See above, footnote 27.
[55] Compare this account with Doc. 49.

been summoned, was sworn in, and promised to speak the truth. He said he was called:

Witness: Antón de las Eras, a farmer and a citizen of the town of Cihuela, which is near Deza. He said he was 35 years old and that in order to unburden his conscience he comes to make known to this Holy Office that last year on the feast of Saint Michael this witness was near his front door with Juan de Gonzalo de Liñán. And Pedro de Aparicio de Chahorna, who was very ill and thin, was right next to them. One of Pedro de Aparicio's daughters came out and told him to come eat and to lean on her so as not to fall. Pedro de Aparicio got up to go into his house, but he stumbled on a stick and nearly fell. This witness said to him, "Have courage! I swear by filthy Mohammed that you won't fall!" And so he went into his house.

Then Juan de Gonzalo de Liñán thrust out his hand behind this witness, as if he were stabbing with a knife and punched this witness on his left side. And this witness asked what he was doing and why he was doing it. Juan de Gonzalo told him that he swore to the same that if he had a dagger or a knife he would stab this witness because of the ~~aforementioned~~ oath he had sworn. This witness responded, "To the devil with you! Go stab yourself!" He saw him become a heretic and grow very angry with this witness because he spoke ill of Mohammed.

Since then, he has considered Juan de Gonzalo to be a bad Christian for having turned from one of the saintly ones into a devil. Juan de Gonzalo is a descendant of Moriscos. This witness went into his own house marveling at what had happened because as soon as he said, "I swear by the filth of Mohammed," he struck him on the left side.

Later when this witness was with Diego de las Eras or Pedro de las Eras (deceased; citizens of Cihuela), he ran into Juan de Gonzalo. He told whichever one of them it was, "You don't know how much that rascal wanted to kill me. It was because the other day I said, 'I swear by filthy Mohammed.'" And Juan de Gonzalo grabbed some pebbles for this witness.[56] But they ended up leaving together and they drank in a house[57] belonging to Juan López (Marco López's widow's son). They have always been friends because Juan de Gonzalo is married to this witness's cousin, the daughter of his father's brother.

This is the truth under the oath that he took and he does not say it out of hatred. When it was read to him he said that it was well written but that when he said, "because of the oath he had sworn," he also asked this

---

[56] Perhaps Juan meant to throw the stones at Antón.
[57] Presumably this was a public house, or pub. It is unclear whether Juan de Gonzalo is included in the "they" who went to drink.

witness why he said "filthy Mohammed." This is the truth and he does not sign it because he said that he does not know how. As a sign of good faith that this witness does not say this out of hatred but rather in order to unburden his conscience, he was charged to keep it secret and he promised to do so. And the lord inquisitor ~~goes~~ signed it with his name.

Then this witness said that 15 or 20 days ago, when the lord inquisitor was in Arcos very nearby, he had been sick. Juan de Gonzalo came to visit this witness and told him that if he needed anything or if there was something to be done for this witness, he would do it and may God keep us. The words "aforementioned" and "goes" were struck out. This happened in my presence: **Pedro Pérez**, notary.

[Signed:] Dr. Arganda

53

AGAINST ISABEL DE BAPTISTA, A MORISCA, DECEASED[58]

In the town of Deza on June 28, 1581, the lord Inquisitor **Dr. Arganda** was in the chamber for the morning audience. A person entered therein without having been summoned, and was sworn in, and promised to speak the truth:

Witness: *Mosén* Hernando García, a surgeon and citizen of Deza. He said that he was 70 years old and that in order to unburden his conscience he comes to make known to this Holy Office that four or five years ago, early one morning in August, he ran into [**María Rasa**], the wife of Francisco Destaragon the lad. She told this witness about a *convertida*[59] from this town washing her private parts in the fountain and this witness continued on, having told her to disclose it to the Inquisition, since it was their business. But he did not imagine that he would actually find the Morisca doing what the woman had said.

Nevertheless, he found **Isabel de Baptista** (now deceased, the wife of **Agustín de Baptista**, a deaf *convertido* who made poultices) and she was washing herself, drawing water from the fountain's basin with her hand and bringing it up under her skirts, washing her private parts or some such thing, as it seemed to him. She stood there, completely lost in what she was

---

[58] Compare this account with Doc. 42.
[59] See footnote 27.

doing and, out of embarrassment, this witness continued on without saying anything to her. Isabel was a *convertida* from Ágreda.[60]

This is the truth under the oath that he took and he does not say it out of
hatred. He signed it with his name after it had been read to him and he said
that it was well written. He was charged to keep it secret and he promised
to do so. This happened in my presence: **Pedro Pérez**, notary.

[Signed:] Hernando García

54

AGAINST LOPE DE CIELI, A MORISCO CITIZEN OF DEZA, AND OTHERS[61]

In the town of Deza on June 30, 1581, the lord Inquisitor **Dr. Arganda** was
in the chamber for the morning audience. A young man entered without
having been summoned, was sworn in, and promised to speak the truth.
He said his name was:

Witness: **Pascual de Villoslada**, the son of Mingo de Villoslada, a citizen of this town. He said that he was 20 years old and that in order to
unburden his conscience he comes to make known that last Christmas
around 9 or 10 o'clock at night he was in the town plaza with Francisco de
Villoslada (Francisco de Villoslada's son), **Francisco Manrique the lad**,
and Berlandino de Palencia. This witness and Berlandino de Palencia saw
Lope de Cieli the younger, [Gerónima la Corazona] his wife, and others
(about six) leave the house of **Luis de Cieli** (a Morisco citizen of this town).
They went to the house of [Ana de Almotazán], Lope de Hortubia's widow;
they were really carrying on as they entered. Lope de Cieli was carrying
a big bundle underneath his cape, and when they left Lope de Hortubia's
widow's house, Francisco Manrique went over to Lope de Cieli and pulled
back his cape. He saw that he was carrying a bundle, like the corpse of a
child; the shroud was white. And then ~~Luis~~ [inserted: *Lope*] de Cieli and the
rest who were with him went back to ~~Lope~~ [inserted: *Luis*] de Cieli's house.

When asked by the inquisitor, he said: What can this confessant know
of their hearts? He imagined they had done it for fun and a laugh, but they
might well have been performing some ceremony of their sect.

This is the truth under the oath that he took and he does not say it out
of hatred. He was charged to keep it secret and he promised to do so. After

---

[60] Ágreda is 80 miles east of Deza in Aragon.
[61] Compare this account with Docs. 36, 42, 48, and 55–56.

it was read to him, the lord inquisitor signed it. This happened in my presence: **Pedro Pérez**, notary. The corrections to "Lope" and "Luis" are correct.

[Signed:] Dr. Arganda

55

AGAINST LOPE DE CIELI, MORISCO, AND OTHERS[62]

In the town of Deza on June 30, 1581, the lord Inquisitor **Dr. Arganda** was in the chamber for the morning audience. A person entered therein without having been summoned, was sworn in, and promised to speak the truth:

Witness: **Francisco Manrique the lad**, a citizen of this town. He said that his age was 24 years and that in order to unburden his conscience he comes to make known to this Holy Office that one night around Christmas of last year—it was about 10 o'clock—this witness, Francisco de Villoslada the lad, **Pascual de Villoslada**, and Berlandino de Palencia were in the town plaza. They saw [**Lope de Cieli the younger**], son of **Luis de Cieli** (a Morisco citizen of this town), and Luis de Cieli's wife[63] as well as two other people (whom this witness did not know) pass through the plaza to the house of [Ana de Almotazán], Lope de Hortubia's widow. Cieli's son— his only grown son—was carrying a big bundle under his cape.

And when they left the widow's house, this witness decided to go over to ~~Lope de Cieli~~ Luis de Cieli's son and lift up the cape. And he saw that he was carrying a white bundle, like the corpse of a two-year-old child. He was holding it in his arms like one would carry a child to bury it. That's how this witness's companions saw it.

The Moriscos returned to Luis de Cieli's house and neither Luis de Cieli's son nor any of those who were with him said anything to this witness. He doubts that they recognized him. It seemed wrong to this witness and must have been some Moorish ceremony—making a joke of and ridiculing the dead.

This is the truth under the oath that he took and he does not say it out of hatred. He was charged to keep it secret and promised to do so. When his statement was read back to him, he said that it was well written. The lord inquisitor signed it. The phrase "Lope de Cieli" was struck out. This happened in my presence: **Pedro Pérez**, notary.

[Signed:] Dr. Arganda

---

[62] Compare this account with Docs. 36, 42, 48, 54, and 56.
[63] Ana de Pazencia, Luis's third wife and Lope's stepmother.

56

In the town of Deza on June 30, 1581, the lord Inquisitor **Dr. Arganda** was in the chamber for the morning audience.[64] A person entered therein without having been summoned, was sworn in, and promised to speak the truth:

Witness: Francisco de Villoslada the lad, a citizen of this town. He said he was 22 years old and that in order to unburden his conscience he comes to make known to this Holy Office that last Christmas he and **Francisco Manrique the lad** were in the town plaza sometime between 9 and 10 o'clock at night. They saw about six people come down into the plaza to Lope de Hortubia's house, which they entered and later left. Among the people he saw, this witness recognized **Lope de Cieli** and his stepmother [Ana de Pazencia], the wife of Luis de Cieli.

They saw that Lope de Cieli was carrying a big bundle under his cape; and two of them were carrying it, like they were carrying a corpse; one was at the feet and the other at the head. Francisco Manrique decided to go over and see what it was. He told this witness and Berlandino de Palencia and **Pascual de Villoslada** that it was a white bundle, like an enshrouded child. The Moriscos did not speak to them. It seemed wrong to this witness and to the rest of them because it seemed like a Moorish ceremony or some foolishness.

This is the truth under the oath that he took and he does not say it out of hatred. He was charged to keep it secret. After it had been read to him and he said that it agreed with what he said, he promised to do so. The lord inquisitor signed it because the witness said he did not know how. This happened in my presence: **Pedro Pérez**, notary.

[Signed:] Dr. Arganda

57

AGAINST THE MORISCOS OF DEZA[65]

In the town of Deza on June 31 [*sic*], 1581, the lord Inquisitor **Dr. Arganda** was in the chamber for the morning audience. A man entered without having been summoned, was sworn in, and promised to speak the truth. He said his name was:

---

[64] Compare this account with Docs. 36, 42, 48 and 54–55.
[65] Compare this account with Doc. 68.

Witness: Juan Manrique, an Old Christian farmer and a citizen of Deza. He said that he was about 40 years old and that in order to unburden his conscience he comes to make known to this Holy Office that last year, on the fifteenth of January, this witness was talking to **Martín [Blasco]** the baker (who was a citizen of this town). He was baking bread in the lower oven for the confraternity of Saint Anthony and told him that if the Holy Office were to come to this town before he departed, he would tell them about more than 14 people from the *Corrillo*, referring to the Moriscos who lived there. This witness asked him why, and Martín responded that he knew about them. He told this witness that he was leaving town because the Moriscos had threatened to kill him.

This witness seems to recall Martín saying that **Lope de Deza** *and* **Juan de Deza** had threatened him. But he is sure that Martín told him that Lope de Deza had said that if he did not leave town, they would have to kill him. This witness does not know Martín's last name, but he now lives in Villaroya de la Sierra in Aragon, where he is a baker. That is where he came from originally. He lived in Deza for seven or eight years and is a good and credible man—that is this witness's opinion. If Martín saw something, it must have been when he got up at midnight to heat the ovens, according to what he led this witness to understand.

This is the truth under the oath that he took and he does not say it out of hatred. When it was read to him he said that it was well written. He was charged to keep it secret and he promised to do so. The lord inquisitor signed it because he said he did not know how. This happened in my presence: **Pedro Pérez**, notary.

[Signed:] Dr. Arganda

58

In the town of Deza on July 5, 1581, the lord Inquisitor **Dr. Arganda** was in the afternoon audience. A person entered therein without having been summoned, was sworn in, and promised to speak the truth:

Witness: Hernando de Torres, a native of Medinaceli in service to the Duke of Medinaceli. He said that he was 30 years old and that in order to unburden his conscience he comes to make known to this Holy Office that more than ten years ago he was in the town of Medinaceli. He heard so-and-so Moreno (a cleric who was serving as the Duke's chaplain at that time; he does not know where he lives now) talk about one of his lodgers. This witness cannot remember the man's name now, but he is a blacksmith. Moreno the cleric said, "This Moor, my lodger, he deserves the devil! He hasn't stopped washing himself or doing the *azala* all night long!"[66]

Item: He said that four or five days ago, he was talking with a *convertido*[67] from Deza (whose name he does not know) about a little Indian[68] slave whom this witness owns. The *convertido* told him that **Fray Luis de Estrada** of the Bernardine Order[69] said that members of the Indian nation did not sin by being in their law. And this witness said to him, "Watch out! There's no sense in what you are saying." The Morisco responded, "Sir, it's true that it's poorly said."

AGAINST ISABEL DE LIÑÁN

Item: He said that a month ago when his little slave got sick, this witness gave his hostess **Isabel de Liñán** (**Juan de Hortubia's** wife; both are Moriscos) a chicken to kill. When he told her, "Take this chicken, ma'am, and kill it for that boy," she replied that she did not want to. And when he asked her why not, one of her neighbors who was present (also a Morisca; called Luisa) responded, "Sir, we women don't have much energy. Give it to me, Your Grace, so I can kill it." But this witness did not want to, and instead he wrung the chicken's neck; none of the women did it.

This is the truth under the oath that he took and he does not say it out of hatred. He signed it with his name after it was read to him, and he promised to keep it secret. This happened in my presence: **Pedro Pérez**, notary.

[Signed:] Hernando de Torres

59

AGAINST GERÓNIMO DE MORAGA, A CITIZEN OF ARIZA[70]

In the town of Deza on July 5, 1581, the lord Inquisitor **Dr. Arganda** was in the chamber and afternoon audience. A woman appeared who had been summoned. She was sworn in and promised to speak the truth. She said she was called:

Witness: **Ana Ramírez Ropiñón**, a native of Deza, the wife of **Gerónimo de Moraga** a sandal-maker and citizen of the town of Ariza.

---

[66] The *azala* are a series of daily prayers performed by Muslims.
[67] See footnote 27.
[68] That is, Native American.
[69] That is, the Cistercian Order.
[70] Compare this account with Doc. 45.

She said that she was 20 years old and that she would celebrate her birthday at Christmas.

Asked, she said that she does not know or presume the reason why she was summoned; if she knew she would say so. She said the inquisitor should not hesitate to ask her anything because she will speak candidly about anything that she knows.

Asked if she knows or has heard talk of someone doing or saying something that was or might seem to be an offense against God our Lord or His holy Catholic faith and the evangelical law to which our holy mother Church holds, preaches, and teaches; or against the proper and free use and exercise of the Holy Office.

She said she knows nothing, on her mother's life.

Asked if she knows of anyone who performed some Moorish ceremony or if she presumes someone to have performed one. She said she knows nothing about that.

Asked if this witness knows of anyone who performed a Moorish ceremony while in Deza. She says she knows nothing about that.

Asked if anyone requested that she bring a jug of clean water and whether she then left the house and if her little sister was also made to leave the house.

She replied: the truth is that while she was engaged to Gerónimo de Moraga she made him a new shirt and he arrived in town on Sunday, when it was time for mass. He asked this witness, "Ana, have you made me a shirt?" And this witness told him, "Yes." But it was at the seamstress's house because she could not pay for it. The shirt her fiancé was wearing was filthy because he had been fleeing from the lord of Ariza, where he was a citizen. He asked this witness, "Do you have any water?" And she replied, "What for?" Gerónimo told her, so that he could wash his face and head. She said that she had none but would fetch some. So she went to the fountain for a jug of water and carried it back. Gerónimo used his dirty shirt to wash himself down to his chest in her presence.

He gave this witness three *sueldos* and she went to the seamstress's house. He told her, "Since you're going out, shut the door," so that no one would see his bare chest. She left and came back with the new shirt, and he washed himself in her presence just like she said. At that time, the younger sister about whom she was asked was not at home.

Asked if she found a wet floorboard when she returned. She said, "No." They did not have floorboards in her house.

Asked if it is true that this witness said that it seemed wrong to her that her fiancé asked her for water and then told her to leave the house.

She said that what happened was that she discovered her fiancé naked from the waist up, washing himself while sitting on the bed. So she told him, "Hey, what's that you're doing?! You should go out to the Argadil and wash yourself in a pool there." This witness mentioned this to [**Francisca Borque**], Gonzalo Martínez's widow, and told her what had happened and how it played out and why she got that jug of water: so her fiancé could wash his arms, face, head, and chest with part of his shirt and then dry himself off with the rest. And Gonzalo Martínez's wife told her, "I don't know, Ana. In the time of the Moors, everyone washed themselves from top to bottom."

Asked if Gerónimo her husband has ever told this witness that her relatives had told him that she was wasted on him; and also if, for some reason, she said something to her brother that made him gloomy.

She said that what happened was that while they were engaged, her fiancé told her that her brother must have been upset that she was betrothed to Gerónimo de Moraga, for they had gotten engaged against the wishes of her parents and relatives. This witness told Gonzalo Martínez's wife everything that happened, just as if she were her mother.

Asked, she said that one night when she was praying and commending herself to God, Gerónimo said to this witness, "What are you praying? We already know that you pray. Speak!" And he made her recite all the prayers, which she did. She has taught him the prayers of the Church, which he has learned. This witness drinks wine and eats pork but her husband does not. And when she has pork, she makes herself a stew; her husband never forbids her from eating it.

This is the truth under the oath that she took and she did not sign it because she said that she does not know how. She was charged to keep it secret and she promised to do so.

No further questions were asked nor was she questioned again over the same material because she was pregnant—and because she was a woman who struck one as evil hearted. The lord inquisitor signed it. This happened in my presence: **Pedro Pérez**, notary.

[Signed:] Dr. Arganda

60

AGAINST THE LICENTIATE PÁEZ, PHYSICIAN[71]

In the town of Deza on July 7, 1581, the lord Inquisitor **Dr. Arganda** was in the chamber and morning audience. A person entered having been summoned, was sworn in, and promised to speak the truth:

---

[71] Compare this account with Docs. 40 and 62–63.

Witness: **Miguel Benito**, the town's vicar and commissioner of this Holy Office. He said that he was 61 years old.

Asked, he said that he does not know or presume the reason why he has been summoned to appear.

Asked, he said that he does not know nor has he seen nor heard talk of anyone having done or said any things that were or could be perceived as being contrary to God our Lord and His holy Catholic faith.

Asked if he knows of anyone having said that Jesus Christ our Lord, insofar as he was man, was not the Son of God.

He said that what he knows and what happened is that about seven or eight years ago he was in Deza's church together with **Juanes Valles** (cleric) and the **Licentiate Páez**. Páez was a physician and a native of Atienza,[72] reputedly a descendant of Jews, and a citizen of Deza. They were discussing Christ's divinity and humanity in this witness's presence. Licentiate Páez said that Christ, insofar as he was man, was not the Son of God, but he was saying it *su correctione sancte matris ecclesie*.[73]

This witness and Juanes Valles told him to watch what he was saying. Then they took out a breviary or diurnal and instructed him using the Athanasian Creed. This witness worked his way through it until he came to the verse that reads: *equales patrii secundum divinitatem, minor patrie secundum humanitatem.*[74] And Licentiate Páez said ~~that~~, "Now I believe it!" This witness does not remember if they discussed anything else, but all this was related to the fact that on that same day a friar had preached a sermon about Christ's humanity. And Licentiate Páez was very clever and discrete and he liked to stick his nose into everything. This is all he knows about this business.

Item:[75] He said that two months ago, more or less, **Juan de Ozuel** (an ordained priest from this town) was discussing the removal of a saint's reliquary; the saint was not canonized. Juan de Ozuel claimed that the bodies of many people who are actually in hell are venerated on earth as saints. He claimed this citing the authority who says, *multa corpora santorum venerantur in terris quorum anime cruciantur infernis.*[76] *Bachiller* Ozuel concluded it was possible that the souls of some saints who were prayed to on earth were actually in hell. Then this witness said that

---

[72] About 60 miles southwest of Deza in Castile.
[73] See footnote 16.
[74] Latin: "Equal to the Father according to his divinity, inferior to the Father according to his humanity." Compare with footnote 18.
[75] Compare this account with Docs. 40 and 62.
[76] Latin: "Many saints' bodies are venerated on earth whose souls are in hell."

bachiller Ozuel had claimed it was possible that the Church prayed to some saints whose souls were in hell and that he based his argument on that authority.

This witness and the **Licentiate Miguel Benito** (this witness's nephew) and *bachiller* **Montero** and Juan García (all clerics who were present) said to him, "Watch what you are saying! For the Church couldn't err, and the authority you cited isn't interpreted in the way you said." And then *bachiller* Ozuel was convinced and mended his ways.

Asked, he said of **Beatriz Pérez de Luna** (who was the wife of Beltran de Ocáriz and a citizen of this town) that he performed her wedding and he saw her wearing silks and fine clothes on her person and gold for more than 24 years, until her husband died, which was six years ago. He has heard it said publicly that she is the daughter or granddaughter of **Álvaro de Luna**, a citizen of Almazán whom the Holy Office condemned.

This is the truth under the oath that he took and he does not say it out of hatred. He signed it with his name after it had been read to him and he said that it was well written. He promised to keep it secret. The phrase "This happened in my presence" goes here.

[Signed:] Miguel Benito
[Signed:] **Pedro Pérez Ullivarri**

61

AGAINST JUAN NAVARRO[77]

In the town of Deza on July 8, 1581, the lord Inquisitor **Dr. Arganda** was in the chamber for the morning audience. A man who had been summoned appeared, he was sworn in, and promised to speak the truth. He said he was called:

Witness: Juan de Arenas, a farmer and a citizen of Deza. He said he was 31 years old.

Asked if he knew or presumed the reason why he had been summoned. He said that he suspected why he had been summoned.

He was told to say it. He said that on the Sunday when the Holy Office's edict was read in the town church at the end of the high mass, this witness, Alejos (Pedro Raso's son), and Cristóbal Ruiz (a farmer; all citizens of Deza) left the church. As the three of them came to the road that goes up

---

[77] Compare this account with Docs. 64–66.

to the plaza they discussed the edict.[78] Alejos Raso said that when he and Juan Navarro (a farmer and citizen of Deza) were plowing together, Juan Navarro had been talking about women and claimed that simple fornication was not a sin, nor was having relations with a prostitute. Alejos Raso had challenged him, but Juan Navarro had remained obstinate and said that he would convince him of the truth.

Later on the same Sunday, this witness went to talk with Alejos Raso and told him, "Alejos, take care about what you said Juan Navarro told you today. Reveal it to the lord inquisitor since you heard it; if you don't do it, I'll have to." And Alejos Raso said that he would do it. That is the reason why this witness has been negligent in coming to reveal this—and because he has been harvesting in Aragon until now in order to earn something to eat.

This is the truth under the oath that he took and he does not say it out of hatred. He did not sign it because he said he did not know how. The lord inquisitor signed it. He was charged to keep it secret and, after it had been read to him and he pronounced it well written, he promised to do so. This happened in my presence: **Pedro Pérez**, notary.

[Signed:] Dr. Arganda

62

AGAINST *BACHILLER* OZUEL[79]

In the town of Deza on July 8, 1581, the lord Inquisitor ~~in the~~ **Dr. Arganda** was there [*sic*] entered, having been summoned, and was sworn in:

Witness: Juan García, cleric of Deza, 48 years old.

Asked, he said that he neither knows nor presumes the reason why he was ordered to appear in this Holy Office.

Asked if he knew or had heard it said that some person or persons might have done or said something that might be or seem to be offensive to God our Lord or against His holy Catholic faith and evangelical law. He said that he knew of no such thing.

Asked if he knew or had heard it said that someone might have claimed that the souls of some of the saints to whom the Church prayed were in hell.

---

[78] The Edict of Faith referenced here was read in anticipation of Dr. Arganda's visitation. It enumerated the offenses that fell under the jurisdiction of the Holy Office and obliged everyone to confess any such sins of which they were aware.

[79] Compare this account with Docs. 40, 60, and 63.

He said that one day about a month and a half previously, give or take, Deza's old vicar, his nephew the young vicar, **Juan de Ozuel**, and *bachiller* **Montero** (clerics) were in the town plaza.[80] This witness came late to the conversation in question. He heard nothing more than *bachiller* Ozuel saying that it was possible that some saints existed who had not been canonized and that other saints were secret and known only to God.

This is the truth under the oath that he took and he signed it with his name after it had been read to him. He was charged to keep it secret and he promised to do so. When it was read to him, he pronounced it well written. This happened in my presence: **Pedro Pérez**, notary.

[Signed:] Juan García

63

AGAINST *BACHILLER* OZUEL[81]

In Deza on July 8, 1581, the lord Inquisitor **Dr. Arganda** was in the chamber for the afternoon audience. A person appeared therein having been summoned, was sworn in, and promised to speak the truth:

Witness: The *bachiller* **Bartolome Montero**, one of the town's ordained priests. He said that he was 30 years old.

Asked, he said that he neither knew nor presumed the reason why he had been summoned.

Asked if he knew or has heard it said that someone might have done or said something that might be or appear to be offensive to God our Lord or against His holy Catholic faith and evangelical law or against the right and free exercise of the officers and ministers of the Holy Office of the Inquisition.

He said that what he knows and what happened is that about a month ago, more or less, he, **Miguel Benito** (commissioner of this Holy Office), **Licentiate Miguel Benito** (the town's vicar), *bachiller* **Ozuel**, and lots of other people were in the town plaza, all of them discussing the canonization of saints. *Bachiller* Ozuel, referring to that authority who says *multa corpora santorum venerantur in terris eorum anime cruciantur in infernis*,[82] claimed that it was possible for witnesses to err or make mistakes about a saint's

---

[80] The old vicar is **Miguel Benito** and the young vicar is his nephew, the **Licentiate Miguel Benito**.

[81] Compare this account with Docs. 40, 60, and 62.

[82] See footnote 76.

relics, thinking they belonged to one saint when they actually belonged to another.

And asked, he said that he never heard him say that the Church prayed to any saint who was in hell nor did *bachiller* Ozuel diverge from the quotation to which this witness has referred. He is certain ~~that~~ and knows that nothing else happened because this witness was present the whole time and was engaged in the debate. If anything else had happened, this witness would have heard it.

This is the truth under the oath that he took and, after it had been read to him and he pronounced it well written, he signed it with his name. He promised to keep it secret. The word "that" was struck out. This happened in my presence: **Pedro Pérez**, notary.

[Signed:] *Bachiller* Bartolome Montero

64

AGAINST JUAN NAVARRO[83]

In the town of Deza on July 10, 1581, the lord Inquisitor **Dr. Arganda** was in the chamber for the morning audience. There entered a man who had been summoned. He was sworn in and promised to speak the truth. He said he was called:

Witness: Alejos Raso, an Old Christian and a citizen of Deza. He said that he was 24 years old.

Asked if he knew or presumed the reason why he has been summoned.

He said that he did not know unless it was on account of some words he heard Juan Navarro (son of Rodrigo Navarro, a citizen of Deza) speak when they were plowing together near the Magos ravine after Easter of this year. Among other things, they discussed prostitutes, and Juan Navarro claimed that having carnal relations with them was not a mortal sin, but merely a venial one.[84] He said this two or three times. It seemed to this witness that it was more than just a venial sin, but Juan Navarro remained obstinate that it was not a mortal sin, just a venial one. He maintained his opinion and was obstinate.

---

[83] Compare this account with Docs. 61 and 65–6.

[84] In Roman Catholic theology, a venial sin is a minor sin that does not require sacramental confession to be forgiven, but a mortal sin kills the grace of God in one's soul and requires absolution from a priest.

When this witness saw how obstinate he was, he stopped talking with him about it. But when the Holy Office's letter of excommunication (or anathema) was read,[85] this witness went and told Juan Navarro that he ought to come confess before his lordship what had gone on between them. He told him that if he failed to do so, this witness would come, for he did not want to be excommunicated. He said this to him seven or eight times at his front door, but Juan Navarro simply refused.

This witness and Juan Navarro eventually agreed to go together and ask *bachiller* **Montero** whether they were obliged to come and tell the inquisitor what happened. And the *bachiller* took them to the house of [**Miguel Benito**], the commissioner of the Holy Office, but they were unable to speak with him. Yet, *bachiller* Montero advised Juan Navarro to tell the commissioner.

That same day, this witness parted ways with Juan Navarro in the plaza and then, after a while, he returned. And Juan Navarro came out to this witness on the plaza road. He told him, "Alejos, there's no need to bother yourself with what happened. I already went to the commissioner and discussed it with him. He said there was no need to make a big deal out of it; it was a little thing. Since I didn't say it with malice, I don't need to make it known to the lord inquisitor." And so this witness told him, "I'm pleased that you weren't punished to keep me from being excommunicated."

He just recalled that when Juan Navarro was being obstinate with him, saying that it was not a mortal sin—when he was corrupting this witness by claiming that having carnal knowledge of a prostitute was not a mortal sin—Juan offered a comparison in order to prove his point. This witness rejected it. What he said was that when Jesus Christ was on earth, he had asked Saint Peter where he was going. And Saint Peter had responded that he was going to multiply. And Jesus Christ replied, "Do it quickly and come back."[86]

This is the truth under the oath that he took. He signed it with his name after it had been read to him and he said that it was well written and set down. He was charged to keep it secret. This happened in my presence: **Pedro Pérez**, notary.

[Signed:] Alejos Raso

---

[85] This is a reference to the Edict of Faith read from the pulpit in preparation for the inquisitor's arrival. Failure to denounce someone whom one knew had committed a heretical act—in this case, denying the sinfulness of a wicked action—resulted in excommunication for withholding the information.

[86] There is no obvious passage in the New Testament to which Juan could be referring.

65

AGAINST JUAN NAVARRO[87]

In Deza on July 10, 1581, the lord Inquisitor **Dr. Arganda** was in the chamber for the morning audience. He commanded a person who had been summoned to enter and swear to God our Lord and by his [religious] orders:

Witness: ***Bachiller* Bartolome Montero**, a cleric of Deza. He said he was 30 years old.

Asked, he said that this is what he knows happened: on the same Sunday that the Holy Office's Edict (or Anathema) was read in the town church, Alejos Raso and Juan Navarro (native Dezanos) came to him.[88] Both of them told him that they wanted to know what one would have to do about (or maybe they said that they wanted to denounce) a young man who said that having sex with a prostitute was not a sin. This witness told them to visit the lord inquisitor or ask the commissioner's advice about their obligations in this matter.

Later on the same day, this witness went with them to the house of [**Miguel Benito**], the commissioner of the Holy Office, but he was busy. So they left without speaking to him and this witness told them they ought to come back to see his lordship. Then, later that afternoon, Juan Navarro returned and spoke with this witness. He said that when he and Alejos Raso were plowing a field, he had said that having carnal relations with a prostitute was not a sin. This witness turned to Juan Navarro and told him to go confess it and throw himself on the mercy of the lord inquisitor on account of the words that he had spoken. And he said he would.

A little while after this happened, Juan Navarro returned to this witness and told him that he had remembered that he had not said "having carnal relations with a prostitute" but rather that he had asked which sin was worse: having carnal relations with a married woman or with an unmarried prostitute. This witness responded that he should pay attention to the words of the Edict of Faith and to what this witness had said. A little while later, they ran into each other and Juan Navarro told this witness that he had already gone to the lord inquisitor.

This is the truth under the oath that he took and he does not say it out of hatred. He signed it with his name after it had been read to him and he

---

[87] Compare this account with Docs. 61, 64, and 66.
[88] See footnote 85.

THE VISITATION OF DR. ARGANDA (1581)   101

said that it agreed with what he said. He was charged to keep it secret and he promised to do so. This happened in my presence: **Pedro Pérez**, notary.

[Signed:] *Bachiller* Bartolome Montero

66

AGAINST JUAN NAVARRO[89]

In the town of Deza on July 10, 1581, the lord Inquisitor **Dr. Arganda** was in the chamber for the afternoon audience. He commanded a person to enter, be sworn in, and promise to speak the truth:

Witness: **Miguel Benito**, the town vicar and commissioner of the Holy Office. He said that he was 61 years old.

Asked, he said that when his lordship had come to this town and after the Edict of Faith had been read, Juan Navarro (son of Rodrigo Navarro, a citizen of Deza) came to him. He said that he and Alejos Raso had been plowing a field and discussing prostitutes and that he had claimed that having carnal relations with a prostitute was not a mortal sin. This witness referred him to the lord inquisitor.

Asked if this witness told Juan Navarro that this matter was insignificant and that he did not need to come before the lord inquisitor.

He said that no such thing happened while he was present. He told Juan Navarro to go to the inquisitor before someone else denounced him and to tell the truth. And he told him that if he went himself, his sin would be less serious. This is all he knows about what happened. And when it happened, he gave an account of it to his lordship, the lord inquisitor.

This is the truth under the oath that he took. After it was read to him and he said that it agreed with what he said, he signed it with his name. This happened in my presence: **Pedro Pérez**, notary.

[Signed:] Miguel Benito

67

AGAINST GERÓNIMA DE TRUILLO

In the town of Deza on July 10, 1581, the lord Inquisitor **Dr. Arganda** was in the chamber for the afternoon audience. A woman entered without

---

[89] Compare this account with Docs. 61 and 64–65.

having been summoned, was sworn in, and promised to speak the truth. She said she was named:

Witness: Juana Biziosa, an Old Christian and the wife of Juan Jiménez, a citizen of this town who breeds and keeps pigs. She said that she was more than 40 years old and that in order to unburden her conscience she comes to make known to this Holy Office that in 1578 there was a great famine. There was a Morisca woman, a native of Ariza,[90] whom this witness understands was named Gerónima de Truillo. She is the widow of a Morisco named Álvaro [blank] and the sister of María de Truillo, the wife of **Alejos de Deza** who is living in Ariza. That year, Gerónima was in Deza visiting her sister María, who died.

Oneday after her sister's death, Gerónima came to this witness's house and asked her to bring a load of firewood. It was very late at night but she took it. She called at Alejos de Deza's house but realized that she was at the house of **Luisa [Vizcaina]**, **Francisco de Baptista**'s wife. When she got to Alejos de Deza's house she opened the door and she told this witness to wait for her to bring a light; they did not have one in the house.[91] But, seeing a light in the bedroom where her sister María had been ill and died, this witness asked her, "Isn't there a light in that bedroom?" Gerónima denied that there was, but this witness insisted that there had been a light.

Gerónima stepped out of the house, still insisting that there had been no light. She shut the front door and then explained that she did not want to leave the door open onto the street. After this, Gerónima went for a light, saying there was no light in the bedroom where her sister had died. Suspecting that something was wrong, this witness took note, and when Gerónima returned with the fire, they entered the house together.

This witness followed her in through the entryway of the house. Then Gerónima went to the room where her sister had died. She pushed aside a blanket nailed up in the room's doorway and serving as a partition. And because this witness was suspicious, she drew near and, before the blanket swung back into place, she saw the shape of a person in the room's bed. There were pillows and the head was lying on the pillows—but she could not see exactly what it was.

She suspected that they had disinterred María and put her in the bed in order to take and rebury her in a Moorish graveyard in the town of Ariza. She suspected this because she could see a bench in the bedroom near the head of the bed. On it was a half-*fanega* measure for wheat turned face

---

[90] Ariza is about 30 miles south of Deza in Aragon.
[91] The pronouns in this sentence are particularly confusing. It is frequently unclear who is doing what.

down. And on top of the half-*fanega* measure, a half-*celemín* measure also turned face down. On top of that was a round bowl, one of the big ones out of which Moriscos eat olives, and a jug a little bigger than half an *azumbre*, with which they drink water and carry milk.[92] This witness suspected that the food was there for María, as if she were alive.

Gerónima snuffed the light that was in the bedroom and this witness turned and asked her why she had denied that there was a light, since she had seen it. And Gerónima, who was very upset, responded, "Oh, Juana, you're fooling yourself." Four months later, Gerónima left for Ariza, and three or four days after she left, María's burial plot collapsed in on itself. The deceased woman's son and one of Alejos' nieces (the daughter of a cobbler who lives in Torrijo; this witness does not know the girl's name nor where she is) put more dirt on the grave.

This is the truth under the oath that she took and she does not say it out of hatred. She did not sign it because she said that she did not know how. When it was read to her, she said that it was well written and set down. The lord inquisitor signed it. She was charged to keep it secret and she promised to do so. This happened in my presence: **Pedro Pérez**, notary.

[Signed:] Dr. Arganda

68

AGAINST LOPE DE DEZA AND HIS WIFE, ANA DE ARELLANO, AS WELL AS THE WIVES OF CAVALLERO, ANTÓN DE DEZA, LUIS DE CEBEA THE ELDER, LUIS DE CEBEA THE YOUNGER, CAVALLERO'S SON, AND JUAN MARTÍNEZ[93]

Inside of the house and hermitage of Our Lady of the Sierra, which is in Aragon at the edge of Villaroya de la Sierra on June [*sic*] 13, 1581. The lord Inquisitor **Dr. Arganda** commanded a man to be summoned and to appear before him. When he was present, he was sworn in according to the law and promised to speak the truth. When asked he said he was called:

Witness: **Martín Blasco**, a citizen and native of the town of Villaroya de la Sierra in Aragon. He is a baker and 40 years old.

---

[92] A *fanega* is a measure of volume equivalent to 55.5 litres. A *celemín* is equivalent to one-twelfth of a *fanega*. An *azumbre* is a measure of liquid volume equivalent to a little more than two litres.

[93] Compare this account with Doc. 57.

Asked if he knew or presumed the reason why he has been summoned and commanded to appear. He said that he presumed that it is so he might tell what he knows and what he saw of Deza's Moriscos.

He was told to say and declare what he knows and has seen of Deza's Moriscos and who they are.

He said that he lived in the town of Deza and resided there for about five and a half years, more or less. He worked as the baker at the oven of the *Corrillo*, where the town's *convertidos*[94] do their cooking. During that time, **Lope de Deza**'s wife (who is called **Ana [de Arellano]**) and the wives of Cavallero, **Antón de Deza**,[95] **Luis de Cebea the elder**,[96] and **Luis de Cebea the younger**[97] would normally leave their houses on Thursday nights and bring meat stews and empanadas to the oven to cook them.

One Thursday night, when Cavallero's son brought a stew and an empanada, this witness asked him about the empanada and stew. And Cavallero's son told him that they were going to eat them at night between 11 o'clock and midnight. Juan Martínez's household also brought stews and empanadas on those Thursday nights; one of his boys bought them, the young one but he does not know his name. This witness knows that Juan Martínez's wife and daughter (Antón's wife) sent the food. This witness has seen all of the people he named eat between 11 o'clock and midnight. All of them are Moriscos.

AGAINST OLD LIÑÁN (CALLED LUIS), MEDRANO THE POT MAKER, JUAN DE FADRIQUE HIS BROTHER, AND LUIS DE CEBEA'S SONS

Item: He said that they gather night and day in Old Liñán's[98] house: Medrano the pot maker, his brother Juan de Fadrique,[99] and Luis de Cebea [the elder]'s sons. They shut themselves up and stay there until after midnight. The house is outside of town,[100] so this witness does not have a good sense of those gatherings, and also because they refused to allow this witness or any of the other Old Christians to enter. And this witness knows

---

[94] See footnote 27.
[95] María Fadrique.
[96] **María de Hortubia.**
[97] **Francisca de Baptista.**
[98] **Luis de Liñán.**
[99] Martín Blasco may have been confused here. According to Ana Fadrique in 1608, her father, Juan de Fadrique (aka Juan de San Juan), did not have a brother named Medrano, but rather a brother and sister named Diego and María.
[100] The pottery works just north of town.

and is certain that they cook those empanadas and stews on Thursday nights because Friday is the Moors' holiday and they celebrate it on Fridays.

AGAINST LIÑÁN, LOPE DE DEZA, CAVALLERO, GABRIEL ALIGER

Item: He said that he understands that Old Liñán, Lope de Deza, Cavallero, and **Gabriel de Aliger**—all of whom are Morisco citizens of Deza—fasted for Ramadan last year before Christmas. He saw they were lean and very faint during the day, and they did not work. But they were up and about in their houses all night until midnight.

This is the truth under the oath that he took. And he does not say it out of hatred although it is true that he had some angry words with Lope de Deza about a window that fell from the oven; he left Deza for fear of him. When it was read to him, he said that it was well written and set down. He was charged to keep it secret and promised to do so. The lord inquisitor signed it because he said he did not know how. This happened in my presence: **Pedro Pérez**, notary.

[Signed:] Dr. Arganda

69

AGAINST FRANCISCO ESCUDERO, SHEPHERD[101]

In the town of Deza on July 15, 1581, the lord Inquisitor **Dr. Arganda** was in the chamber for the afternoon audience. A young man who had been summoned entered. He was sworn in and promised to speak the truth. When asked, he said he was called:

Witness: **Miguel Donoso**, son of **Juan Donoso**, a citizen of this town. He said that he was 19 years of age.

Asked, he said that he did not know or presume the reason the reason [*sic*] why they had commanded him to appear.

Asked, he said that what he knows and has seen is that about two and a half months ago this witness was in the mill that they call the Upper Mill.[102] He heard **Francisco Escudero, shepherd** (a citizen of Deza) yell and swear a lot because of the type of wood they brought him. He repeatedly said, "I swear to God." When this witness and **Juana Muñoz** (**Blasco Muñoz**'s daughter) told

---

[101] Compare this account with Docs. 47 and 70.
[102] That is, the Cubo Mill.

him not to curse or swear to God, he responded: he swore to God that he had to swear to Him, even if he were thrown into the devil's house.

When it was read to him, he said that it was well written and that Francisco Escudero is his uncle. He was charged to keep it secret and promised to do so. The lord inquisitor signed it because he said that he did not know how. This happened in my presence: **Pedro Pérez**, notary.

[Signed:] Dr. Arganda

--------------------------------- 70 ---------------------------------

AGAINST FRANCISCO ESCUDERO, SHEPHERD[103]

In the town of Deza on July 15, 1581, the lord Inquisitor **Dr. Arganda** was in the chamber for the afternoon audience. A person entered therein having been summoned, was sworn in, and promised to speak the truth:

Witness: **Juana Muñoz**, daughter of **Blasco Muñoz**, a citizen of Deza. She said that she was 18 years old.

Asked, she said that she does not know or presume the reason why she has been summoned to appear.

Asked, she said that what she knows and what happened is that about three months ago more or less, **Francisco Escudero** (a miller) was in the Upper Mill. He repeatedly swore oaths and said that he swore to God. This witness and [**Miguel Donoso**], **Juan Donoso**'s son, challenged him about it and Escudero said that he had to swear, even if he were in the devil's house.

This is the truth under the oath that she took and she does not say it out of hatred. When it was read to her, she said that it was well written. She was charged to keep it secret and promised to do so. The lord Inquisitor signed it because she said that she did not know how. This happened in my presence: **Pedro Pérez**, notary.

[Signed:] Dr. Arganda

--------------------------------- 71 ---------------------------------

AGAINST GABRIEL, A NATIVE OF TERRER[104]

In the town of Deza on July 15, 1581, the lord Inquisitor **Dr. Arganda** was in the chamber for the afternoon audience. A man who had been

---

[103] Compare this account with Docs. 47 and 69.
[104] Compare this account with Doc. 46.

summoned entered. He was sworn in and promised to speak the truth. He said he was called:

Witness: Francisco Donoso, a miller and a citizen of this town. He said he was 50 years old.

Asked if he knew or presumed the reason why he has been commanded to appear before this Holy Office.

He said that he did not know unless it had to do with what happened last Holy Thursday, when this witness and a lad named Gabriel, a native of Terrer[105] and the servant of a Dezano tile maker went for firewood. (The tile maker is a native of Terrer also, but he does not know his name.) On that Holy Thursday morning, they went for firewood. While they were in the woods, this witness told him they should hurry up so they could get back in time to hear the Passion. Gabriel asked him what sort of thing the Passion was, saying they did not talk about it in Terrer. This witness rebuked him for it, but nothing else happened.

This is the truth under the oath that he took. Neither on that day nor on any other has anything else happened to Gabriel nor to anyone else that he should make known. When read to him, he said that it agreed with what he said and it is not out of hatred. He was charged to keep it secret and promised to do so. The lord inquisitor signed it because he said that he did not know how. This happened in my presence: **Pedro Pérez**, notary.

[Signed:] Dr. Arganda

72

AGAINST ANTÓN DE DEZA[106]

In the town of Deza on July 16, 1581, the lord Inquisitor **Dr. Arganda** was in the chamber for the morning audience. He commanded a man who had been summoned to enter. He was sworn in and promised to tell the truth. When asked, he said that he was called:

Witness: Cristóbal Ruiz, a farmer and a citizen of this town. He said that he was 27 years old.

Asked, he said that he well knows the reason why he has been commanded to appear. It is because a month ago on Las Peñuelas, **Alejos de Deza**[107] (a Morisco) ran into a very old Morisco who was called [blank], a

---

[105] Terrer is about 25 miles southeast of Deza in Aragon.
[106] Compare this account with Doc. 46.

citizen of Terrer.[108] (Las Peñuelas is a street or road leaving Deza, marked with packed earth on both sides.[109]) Alejos knelt down in front of the old Morisco and kissed his hand. The Morisco lifted Alejos de Deza up with his hands. Their encounter seemed wrong to this witness even though they say that Alejos had been a servant to the old Morisco and eaten his bread for a long time. They say that is why he did it.

This is the truth under the oath that he took and he does not say it out of hatred. When it was read to him he said that it was well written. He promised to keep it secret as he was charged to do. The lord inquisitor signed it. This happened in my presence: **Pedro Pérez**, notary.

Focus Questions

Docs. 35–72: What, if anything, has changed in Deza since the inquisitorial visitation of 1569? Was the Edict of Grace successful?

Doc. 35: If Catalina Moraga was an Old Christian, what might this suggest about Islamic dietary practices in Deza?

Doc. 36: How does Gonzalo's account of this event compare to those recorded in Docs. 42, 48, and 54–56?

Docs. 37–38: How does it change the way you read these documents if you know that Francisco de Hortubia was a Morisco?

Docs. 37–38: Compare María's apology with the one Román Ramírez offered to Dr. Arganda (Doc. 74). What are the similarities and differences? Why did the two Moriscos feel it was necessary to offer apologies? Is there evidence of sincerity (or insincerity)?

Doc. 39: Why would Lope risk passing through Aragon in order to save himself an hour of travel time?

Doc. 40: The Latin phrase *su correctione sancte matris eglesie* contains several minor errors. (The correct formulation is: *sub correctione sanctae matris ecclesiae*.) Who do you think made the mistakes: Páez

---

[107] Note the disagreement between this reference and the title assigned to the audience. The confusion in the names of the person whom Cristóbal Ruiz is denouncing probably arises from the fact that Alejos de Deza is the son of **Antón de Deza**. Despite the confusion, Alejos is being denounced here, not his father.

[108] See footnote 105.

[109] Las Peñuelas goes east from the northern edge of town.

(in speaking it originally), Valles (in reciting it to the inquisitor), or Pedro Pérez (in writing it down)? What questions does this raise about the reliability of inquisitorial sources?

Doc. 41: Outside of this testimony, nothing is known about Dr. Diego Martínez Navarro. Based simply on the evidence in this document, how would you describe his life, interests, and personality?

Doc. 42: Why does María situate her denunciation of Isabel with reference to the Edict of Grace?

Doc. 43: What is the significance of the fact that Miguel García, an inquisitorial *familiar*, lives in the Upper Neighborhood?

Doc. 44: What does Juan mean when he says that Gerónimo "sat down on the ground, pretending"?

Doc. 44: What is the significance of the Morisca spitting out the sacramental wine?

Doc. 45: Ana is the daughter of a Morisco father and an Old Christian mother. How does this fact recast the nature of her actions as described by Francisca? (Compare with Doc. 59.)

Doc. 46: Why is the lad's ignorance so troubling? How is it compounded by the fact that he comes from Aragon? (Compare with Doc. 71.)

Doc. 47: What was problematic about the way Francisco was cursing?

Doc. 48: Why is it significant that Gabriel Aliger was serving as one of Deza's aldermen in 1581?

Doc. 49: Why did Antón's exclamation make Juan de Gonzalo so angry? (Compare with Doc. 51.)

Docs. 50–51: What gender element do Morisco burial practices exhibit? Why?

Doc. 52: How does this account of events differ from that of Doc. 49? Which is more likely to be accurate?

Doc. 52: The statement "they ended up leaving together and they drank in a house" is ambiguous. Do you think that Antón and Juan ended up sharing a drink at the local pub? What do you make of Antón's claim that he and Juan were related by marriage and had always been friends?

Doc. 53: How do you explain Isabel's peculiar behavior? Was she really oblivious to the fact that people were observing her?

Docs. 54–56: By comparing these documents, can you create a coherent narrative of what occurred in Deza on Christmas night of 1580?

Docs. 54–56: The young men in the town plaza seem surprisingly unsympathetic about the death of a child. How do you explain their reactions and behavior?

Doc. 57: Why would the Moriscos have threatened Martín?

Doc. 58: How does Hernando's comment about Fray Luis de Estrada's words compare with those in Docs. 13 and 21?

Doc. 59: Why does Ana's pregnancy matter to the inquisitors? And why do you think that they doubted her sincerity?

Doc. 60: Why does Ozuel rely upon a quotation from Saint Augustine to argue his point? What argument do Montero and García make against Ozuel? Is it compelling? (Compare with Docs. 40 and 62–63.)

Doc. 61: Juan de Arena's testimony is the first of four against Juan Navarro (Docs. 61 and 64–66). The inquisitor summoned all four witnesses to appear. So how did he know to summon them? What does this suggest about how information was being exchanged behind the scenes?

Docs. 62–63: Where did this theological debate take place? Would the debate have been such a concern if it happened privately rather than publicly? What local controversy sparked the debate? (Compare with Docs. 40 and 60.)

Docs. 64–66: Is the Inquisition more concerned about Juan Navarro's sexual relations with prostitutes, his *beliefs* about sexual relations with prostitutes, or what he *says* he believes about sexual relations with prostitutes? Why?

Docs. 64–66: Why does it matter that Juan Navarro was "obstinate" in his opinion? Why is Navarro reluctant to go to the inquisitor or even the commissioner to sort the mess out? (Compare with Doc. 61.)

Doc. 67: How does food figure into Morisco burial practices? (Compare with Doc. 49.)

Doc. 68: Was Martín Blasco's testimony worth a trip to Villaroya de la Sierra? (Compare with Doc. 57.)

Docs. 69–70: No record exists of Francisco Escudero's case ever having developed into a full trial in spite of the fact that multiple witnesses confirmed his blasphemy. Why didn't the Inquisition pursue the case? (Compare with Doc. 47.)

Doc. 71: How does this account of Francisco's interaction with Gabriel differ from the one given in Doc. 46?

Doc. 72: What does the behavior of Alejos toward the Aragonese Morisco here and in Doc. 46 suggest about the old man? Why might he have been so revered?

4

The Examinations of Román Ramírez the Younger and Angela de Miranda (1581)[1]

Beginning in late June of 1581, as part of his visitation to Deza, Dr. Arganda *summoned and examined the Moriscos who had taken the Edict of Grace a decade earlier and been reconciled to the Church. His purpose was to assess whether, in the intervening years, they had carried out the punishments and penances that had been imposed upon them. Virtually everyone that he interviewed was found to have been derelict in some way or another. According to the terms of their reconciliations, the Holy Office could have tried the Moriscos as relapsed heretics; instead, he merely reprimanded and fined them.*

One of the obligations that had been placed upon all of the reconciled Moriscos was to confess their sins sacramentally to a priest three times each year—at Easter, Pentecost, and Christmas. (Other Christians had to confess only once a year, before they communed at Easter.) Confessors were supposed to provide the Moriscos with a signed receipt when they confessed so that they could demonstrate their fulfillment of this requirement. Virtually all of the Moriscos failed to complete all of the required confessions, or at least they proved unable to provide the inquisitor with proof that they had complied. Below are the records of Arganda's examinations of Román Ramírez the younger and his first wife, Angela de Miranda.

---

[1] ADC, legajo 707, expediente 625.

73

AGAINST ROMÁN RAMÍREZ, CITIZEN OF DEZA, AND HIS WIFE ANGELA DE MIRANDA, 1581

In the town of Deza on July 4, 1581, the lord Inquisitor **Dr. Arganda** was in the chamber for the morning audience. He commanded the entrance of a person who had been summoned, sworn an oath, and promised to tell the truth:

~ **Román Ramírez the younger**, Morisco, a citizen of the said town. He said he was 48 years of age.

~ Asked if he knew **Román de Deza**, a citizen of this town.

~ He said, yes, he knew him, that he is a relative of this confessant. Dr. Camargo[2] in the town of Soria convicted Román de Deza of horse smuggling. On the feast of Saint Michael in 1576 he sent word to this town to have him arrested along with Juan de Hidalgo, a citizen of Molina.[3] But instead of arresting Román de Deza, they arrested this confessant and took him under heavy guard as a prisoner to the town of Molina, where he was held for 15 months, until Christmas of 1577. On Christmas Eve some of the prisoners broke out of Molina's jail, and he left with them. He sorted matters out with Camargo and about two years ago they arrested the aforementioned Román ~~Ramí~~ de Deza.

Before they arrested this confessant, he had been in Madrid for the feast of Saint Martin in 1575 and he was there until the end of April of the following year because this confessant returned to this town on the first of May. For the period of the eight years preceding 1575, he worked for **Gerónimo de Salamanca**, [*inserted:* six years] at Court and in the dry ports that he had leased and on the customs tariff. He would spend 16 or 18 months away from Deza at a time. And during those six years he did not reside in the town of Deza for 15 days at a time.

This is the truth under the oath that he took and he signed it with his name, having had it read to him. And he agreed that it was what he said. "Ramí" was crossed out and "six years" was inserted. This happened in my presence: **Pedro Pérez**, notary.

[Signed:] Román Ramírez

---

[2] Dr. Camargo was a judicial official with jurisdiction over matters related to dry ports and presumably would have known Ramírez, who was a port guard, personally.
[3] This location is unclear. Perhaps Molina de Aragón, about 50 miles south of Deza in the Kingdom of Aragón.

In Deza on July 6, 1581, the lord Inquisitor Dr. Arganda was in the chamber for the morning audience. He ordered the aforementioned Román Ramírez to enter therein. He formally swore and promised to tell the truth.

Asked, he verified that when he was summoned he appeared in this chamber before his lordship. Under oath, he declared that he had complied with the terms mandated by his sentence of reconciliation during the time of grace and every year he has confessed all three holy days. He had confessed with the **Prior [Juanes] Valles**—as was confirmed by the receipts that his wife presented to his lordship—except for one Easter when he confessed with [**Juanes de**] **Altopica** (cleric). Being shown the receipts, Ramírez acknowledged that they were the very ones he had presented for his defence. (They are initialled by me, Pedro Pérez, notary. I bear witness that all of the aforementioned occurred in this way one day this past June.)

CHARGE

~ And the lord Inquisitor, having inspected both the confessions made by Román Ramírez and the receipts, said that he was charging and charged him with having perjured himself before this Holy Office and with having failed to confess on each of the holy days as commanded and with having presented a counterfeit receipt to the lord Inquisitor from Juanes Valles (cleric). That it is a counterfeit is clearly deduced by comparing his statements with the receipt, which claims that Ramírez confessed with Valles at the same time he was imprisoned by Dr. Camargo as well as while he was serving Gerónimo de Salamanca at Court and elsewhere. Before that, he had been in Madrid from the feast of Saint Martin in 1575 until April 1576.

Román Ramírez was ordered to confess the truth or dispute the charge within the next three days, whichever he considers appropriate. The inquisitor warned that at the end of the stated time period, justice would have preferment.

~ Román Ramírez said that while he was imprisoned in the town of Molina, he occasionally traveled to Deza and confessed with the Prior Juanes Valles, except for one Pentecost when he did not confess. And the Prior Valles assigned him penance for that. Because he was in Madrid one Christmas, he traveled to Deza early in April. He confessed upon his arrival and, likewise, the Prior Valles assigned penance to him because he was late confessing. This is all he has to unburden himself of and he does not have anything else to say in his defense or to dispute. He asks and requests that his lordship treat him mercifully. Then he said that he was concluding and concluded his defense and he was renouncing and renounced the time period that he had been given. This happened in my presence: Pedro Pérez, notary.

JUDICIAL DECREE

~ In Deza on July 16, 1581, after the lord Inquisitor Dr. Arganda viewed the confessions and the charge described above, he said that he was commanding and commanded Román Ramírez the younger, who was present, to continue confessing the three holy days each and every year, just as his sentence of Reconciliation commanded him to do, and that he abide by everything else in his sentence. And for each of his confessions he must acquire receipts and maintain possession of them. He warned that if he does the contrary, he will be proceeded against with all rigor. And regarding the present guilt, Dr. Arganda is sentencing and has sentenced him to pay six thousand *maravedís* to cover the Holy Office's extraordinary expenses. Thus he warned and sentenced him and he signed it with his name. The aforementioned Román Ramírez, being notified, said that he was consenting and consented. Witness: **Miguel Benito** (commissioner) and Luis Abad (cleric) and me, Pedro Pérez, notary.

[Signed:] Dr. Arganda

RATIFICATION OF ROMÁN RAMÍREZ
AGAINST JUANES VALLES

~ In the town of Deza on July 16, 1581, while the lord Inquisitor Dr. Arganda was in the chamber for the morning audience, he commanded Román Ramírez the younger, citizen of Deza to enter therein. In the presence of honest and religious persons—Miguel Benito (the vicar of Deza and commissioner of this Holy Office) and the *bachiller* **Bartolome Montero** (an ordained priest)—he took the oath and promised to speak the truth.

Asked if he remember having made a statement in this Holy Office against someone and about something.

~ He said that other than what he has said in his confessions regarding his description of the sacramental confessions that he is obliged to make annually on the holy days, he does not recall having made a statement about anything.

~ He was told that he was being made to understand that the prosecutor of this Holy Office is introducing him as a witness against the *bachiller* **Ruiz**[4] (cleric of this town). This pertains to the statements he made in his confessions, which they will read to him, so let him be attentive.

---

[4] This is clearly a transcription error and should refer to the Prior Juanes Valles.

If anything in them should be removed, altered, added to, or emended it will be done. As for that which he has spoken true, let him ratify it without fear that what he now says will lead to any prejudice against him.

~ And his confession, apparently made in this Holy Office on the fourth day of this present month of July, was read to him according to what is contained in them. After stating that he heard and understood it, he said that it was well written and set down and nothing in it needed to be removed, altered, added to, or emended. It was being ratified and was ratified. If necessary, he would return to state and repeat his testimony against Juanes Valles, not out of hatred or any fear but rather because it is the truth, under the oath that he has taken.[5] He promised to keep it secret. This happened in my presence: Pedro Pérez, notary.

74

Although not mentioned in the official record, Román Ramírez the younger apparently lost his temper during one of his appearances before Dr. Arganda. Afterward, he wrote the inquisitor a note of apology. Although Ramírez wrote it on the same day as his final audience, the note seems to have been delivered to Arganda as he was traveling west toward Almazán and Arcos de Jalón.

On July 16, 1581, which was given to him after 15 days when they were on the road in Almazán or Arcos.[6]

Most illustrious and reverend Lord,

Román Ramírez [the younger], a citizen of this town of Deza. With the respect that I owe, I kiss your reverend and Christian hands. I beg you that if I have been at all rude or impolite with your lordship that you pardon me. For I might have acted out of some slight anger or with insufficient understanding, like a weak man.

Allow me to seek your blessing and may you give me your grace. For I consider everything that your lordship did to be good; I understand that nothing but piety and mercy can be born from so Christian a breast as that of your lordship's, which I understand is eager with all mercy. I beg for mercy, that your lordship might be pleased with the penance that you have given to me.

---

[5] Dr. Arganda was concerned enough to record statements from several of Valles's Morisco confessants about the priest's willingness to manufacture receipts for them, but so far as can be determined the Holy Office never attempted to pursue the case against Valles.

[6] These lines are written in a different hand from the rest of the letter. It appears to be a note written by the inquisitor or his secretary indicating when the letter was received.

Grant me time in order to complete it in the way that your lordship has commanded me. For I will be unable to do it as I should, as I want, and as I could (with Jesus Christ's favor), unless you give me time. In this, may your lordship serve God and show great mercy to me and to my children.

75

~ In the town of Deza on July 6, 1581, the lord Inquisitor **Dr. Arganda** was in the chamber for the morning audience. He commanded a woman to enter therein. She was summoned and sworn in and promised to speak the truth. She said she was called:

~ **Angela de Miranda**, the wife of **Román Ramírez [the younger]**, a citizen of Deza. She said that she was 30 years of age, more or less.

~ Asked, she said that she took the Edict of Grace that was granted to this town's New Converts in 1571 and she was reconciled by it.

~ Asked, she said that she has complied with the terms of her sentence. She has confessed all three holy days each and every year since then, as she was commanded. She always confessed with the **Prior Juanes Valles** (cleric) except on one holy day when she confessed with **Altopica** (cleric). She has presented receipts to his lordship for this.

~ The lord Inquisitor said that he was charging and charged her with having presented the receipt from the said Juanes Valles (cleric). Consequently, she failed to confess all of the holy days that the receipts claim.[7] He was commanding and commanded her to unburden herself. Within three days, let her speak and plead her case as seems appropriate to her. He warned that once the said time period expired, justice would have preferment.

~ She said that she does not have anything else to say or plead nor does she have anything of which to unburden herself. She begged his lordship that, if she had offended in some way, she be granted penance with mercy. She did not want any time at all, and she was concluding and concluded her defense definitively. This happened in my presence: **Pedro Pérez**, notary.

JUDICIAL DECREE
~ In the town of Deza on July 13, 1581, the lord Inquisitor Dr. Arganda having viewed the confession of Angela de Miranda (wife of Román Ramírez

---

[7] A word appears to be missing from the transcript, making the charge unclear. But since the confessions of both husband and wife were confirmed on the same receipts, Arganda is presumably claiming that Angela de Miranda, like her husband, provided a counterfeit receipt.

[the younger]), who was present, and having charged her, said that he was commanding and commanded that she keep and comply with the terms of her sentence of reconciliation. She must confess all three of the holy days each and every year of her life, acquire receipts after completing them, and keep the receipts until they are requested of her. She was warned that if she does otherwise, she will be proceeded against with all rigor. And regarding the present guilt, he is condemning and condemns her to pay one thousand *maravedís* for the Holy Office's extraordinary expenses. Thus, he decreed and commanded and signed it with his name. When Angela de Miranda was notified, she said that she was consenting and consented. Witnesses: **Miguel Benito**, commissioner of the Holy Office, and Luis Abad, cleric. And me, Pedro Pérez, notary.

[Signed:] Dr. Arganda

76

[INITIALED:] P[EDRO] P[ÉREZ]

Dr. Arganda confiscated the confessional receipts of Román Ramírez the younger and Angela de Miranda. Neither receipt gives the appearance of being a forgery. They were probably both written by the priests whose signature is on them. Arganda's notary, Pedro Pérez, initialed both receipts.

I, **Juanes Valles**, benefice holder in this town of Deza and a citizen of it, declare that **Román Ramírez the younger** and **Angela de Miranda** his wife (citizens of this town of Deza) are confessed. They have confessed with me all of the times that have been commanded by the lord inquisitors since the year 1571 until today's date in 1581. Made in Deza on June 6, 1581.

And I say that I did not confess them on the Christmas of 1572. And for the truth of it, I sign it with my name.

[Signed:] Juanes Valles

[INITIALED:] P[EDRO] P[ÉREZ]

I, **Juanes de Altopica**, priest and confessor appointed by the very reverend and very magnificent lord, the lord provisor[8] of Sigüenza, my lord. I testify

---

[8] The provisor was the chief judge in the episcopal court.

that Román Ramírez the younger and Angela de Miranda his wife have confessed with me at Pozuel today, Sunday, the day of lord Saint Thomas of 1572.

And I signed it with my name because they were commanded to do it by the reverend lord inquisitors of the diocese of Cuenca and Sigüenza and their district and because it is true that they confessed with me. Done on December 21, 1572.

[Signed:] Altopica

Focus Questions

Docs. 73–76: To what extent were Román and Angela at fault for not fulfilling the terms of their reconciliation in the 1571 Edict of Grace? To what extent was the sloppiness of local priests or the actions of other individuals to blame?

Doc. 73: Why did the inquisitors ask Román Ramírez if he knew Román de Deza? Were they setting him up?

Doc. 73: How did Román attempt to explain the discrepancy with his confessional receipts? Do you find his explanations convincing?

Doc. 73: Why was the inquisitor so lenient toward Román in the Judicial Decree?

Doc. 74: What aspects of Román's personality does this letter reveal or emphasize? What might have caused him to lose his temper? Why doesn't the record of his examination mention that he lost his temper?

Doc. 75: Why was Angela's examination so much more perfunctory than her husband's?

Doc. 76: Why did Pedro Pérez initial the confessional receipts?

Doc. 76: Why did Juanes Valles draw up the receipt as he did rather than giving Román and Angela a new receipt after every confession?

5

The Sentence of Román Ramírez
the Younger (1599–1600)[1]

In 1595, Román Ramírez the younger, who had become well known around
the region as a master storyteller, thanks to a prodigious memory that
allowed him to recite virtually any chivalric tale his audience requested, was
invited to the city of Soria by a local judge to entertain a prominent visitor to
his home. Unfortunately and inadvertently, Ramírez was drawn into a local
feud and denounced to the Holy Office. The charge, unexpectedly, was that
he had made a pact with a devil, which explained his unnatural memory.
Ironically, that same year he was serving his second term as town magistrate.

Although he was briefly taken into custody, Ramírez was allowed to
return to Deza—perhaps the Duke of Medinaceli interceded once again.
The Morisco paid a huge bond of 2,000 ducats to the local warden and was
granted "the town as his jail." He remained active in Deza for the next four
years, married a second time, and had two more children. But in 1599,
the inquisitors at Cuenca transferred him to the secret jails. In a series of
examinations, Ramírez confessed first to Islamic activities and, eventually,
to having made a pact with a devil named Liarde.

By the fall of 1599, Ramírez's health had taken a turn for the worse. He
was transferred to a local hospital but continued to decline. In early November, he requested a priest to hear his confession and died on December 8,
1599. His body was buried in unconsecrated ground and his trial continued.
Early the next year, he was found guilty. His bones were exhumed and, along
with an effigy of the deceased, were transported to Zodocover Plaza in Toledo
for an auto-da-fe that was attended by some of the most important figures at
the Spanish court, including the king and queen.

Below is the formal declaration of Ramírez's guilt and his sentence, a version of which was publicly read at the auto-da-fe in 1600.

---

[1] ADC, legajo 343, expediente 4876, folios 235r–260r.

77

Román Ramírez [the younger], Morisco [handed over to the secular authorities] in effigy and bones.

~ Seen by us, the apostolic Inquisitors, together with the ordinary.

A judicial process and criminal trial that has been and is pending before us and in this Holy Office, between the prosecuting attorney on the one hand and the Accused on the other: Román Ramírez, Morisco, citizen, and native of the town of Deza in the diocese of Sigüenza, his effigy being present.

With respect to and regarding Román Ramírez, the aforesaid prosecuting attorney provided us with an account in his previously presented Accusation stating that Román Ramírez was a baptized Christian and, as such, had used and enjoyed the graces and privileges that faithful and Catholic Christians do and should enjoy.

In particular, having confessed of his own free and spontaneous will, he enjoyed the Edict of Grace that was granted and conceded to the Moriscos of Deza in the year one thousand five hundred and seventy. He confessed that when he was 26 years old, having been instructed and persuaded by certain persons of his caste and generation, he had fasted 20 days of the month of Ramadan. He neither ate nor drank during the day until the stars appeared at night. He did this in observance of the sect of Mohammed and the law of the Moors, for he believed that he could be saved by doing it and he considered it to be good and better than the law of the Christians.

Having asked for penance with mercy, he was reconciled and received back into the association and union of our holy mother Church, which imposed certain spiritual penances upon him. And he formally abjured the errors to which reference has been made as they pertained to the decrees of his first trial.

These errors were presented and it was requested that they be collected together with the present material.

~ Subsequently, like a person who had demonstrated himself to have falsely and feignedly converted to our holy Catholic faith and who had made the abovementioned confessions out of pretense and deception, solely in order to enjoy the Edict of Grace, like an impenitent backslider wickedly taking advantage of the mercy shown to him, he continued to live, and had lived, in the said sect of Mohammed, in which his ancestors lived and remained; he performed and repeated their rites and ceremonies.

For many years he fasted for the month of Ramadan, just as he had previously. He performed the *guadoc* and *zala*, washing his entire body and dressing himself in clean clothes.[2] He prayed the surahs and prayers of that sect, turning his head toward the *qibla*[3] (which is in the direction of the rising sun), raising and lowering his head, humbling himself, bowing to the ground at that time called *alaqibir*[4] (which means God is great), and extending the palms of his hands upward. He also arose early in the day to perform the *zahor*.[5] And after finishing his fast, he had kept and celebrated the festival of Ramadan for three days—he neither worked nor performed manual labor during that time, especially on the first day. Instead, he dressed himself in clean clothes and performed the *guadoc* and *zala* along with many other rites and ceremonies of the said sect.

~ Adding offense to offense and guilt to guilt for wicked effects and ends, for many years and much time hence, he had made and did make an express accord and pact with the devil. He adored him and promised to be his and to give him his soul if the devil would favor him and provide help and counsel when he needed it or when he asked for it.

And thus he had asked the devil, and the devil enabled him to know and see many hidden and secret illnesses and to cure many people of them. By using herbs, burning incense, and employing superstitious charms the Accused caused people to believe and think that he was very well read and learned in the stories of holy Scripture and the books of chivalry and also that he had a remarkable memory. Yet, all the while, he knew neither how to read nor write. As an occupation and for his job, he had taken to reading such stories and books from memory to audiences. He did so with such precision that it was as if he had them before him and was reading from them, but he did this by the industry and art of the devil and by these means he heaped up and gained great wealth and fortune.

And when asked how he came by such a memory, he had responded that a close associate, a very great herbalist who kept a familiar spirit, gave him a potion for that purpose.[6]

---

[2] The *guadoc* is the ritual washing done by Muslims in preparation for prayers (*azala* or, as here, *zala*).

[3] The direction a Muslim should face when reciting prayers.

[4] That is, *Allahu akbar*, a phrase known as the *Takbir*, used in the formal Muslim call to prayer as well as at the beginning of the prayers themselves.

[5] A predawn meal eaten by Muslims during Ramadan.

[6] The "close associate" referred to here is Ramírez's maternal grandfather, Juan de Luna.

Furthermore, this close associate had performed the incantation of *bon y varón*[7] in order to travel a distance of 15 leagues to the city of Zaragoza.[8] This had caused a horse to appear, which they both mounted, and they were quickly deposited in the city. Removing the horse's bridle, they left it at the city gates. After finishing their business, they returned to that same place, cast the bridle on the horse, mounted it, and were returned to their starting place in a mere moment.

~ And in continuation of his sins: a certain woman from the town of Deza had commended herself to the devils, and one night she was made to disappear around bedtime. This prompted her husband to ask for aid from the Accused, who told him not to worry, for his wife would not be lost. He gave the man a letter and told him to go to a specific place amongst some vines, make a circle, and stand in the middle of it. And when he heard a group of people pass by, although he saw no one, he was to ask, "Where is the King going?" And if they responded, "That way," then let him fling the letter toward them. And when he did this, they came back and restored his wife to him, but the man never saw who had taken her or how it was done.

~ And like a person who had interacted constantly with the devil, he knew about and mentioned closely guarded secrets and things that had occurred in far off lands. He could not have been aware of such things at the time that he revealed and spoke of them, except by means of the said demonic accord and pact.

Specifically, one day when he was on the road, he had left word at his house that a certain stranger would be coming to look for him so that he could go cure his daughter, who was possessed. He told them to let him know when the man arrived. And that is exactly what happened. Based on this as well as what later happened (while he was curing the said woman) it became clear that it was the Accused himself who had cursed and bewitched her. For on her wedding night, he had made her blood flow, which caused her great nausea and anguish. Subsequently, she was greatly dismayed and felt a deep hatred for her parents and husband, whom she did not want to see and with whom she refused to sleep.

---

[7] The meaning behind the incantation's title is obscure. The nineteenth-century Englishman George Henry Borrow proposed that it referred to a root used by gypsies and named after Satan, the "good baron" (or *buen barón*). Borrow, *The Zincali: An Account of the Gypsies of Spain* (London, 1888), 187. However, the story also carries overtones of the Isra, a journey taken by Mohammed from Mecca to Jerusalem on the back of a heavenly steed in a single night.

[8] A league is traditionally defined as the distance a person can walk in one hour—about four miles.

A cleric who believed the woman was possessed had attempted to cast the devils out of her. For 18 days, he conjured at them with exorcisms and prayers from the ecclesiastical manual. Finally, a devil had appeared to him and said that 101 demons were dwelling in that body, but he was the only one there at present. Using the exorcisms, the cleric had forced the devil to say where the others had gone, and he had admitted and declared that they had gone to the town of Deza to visit the Accused, Román Ramírez, and to receive his commands. The devil said they would abandon the woman's body only when he gave them permission to do so.

That day she was tormented more fiercely than ever and sunk into a stupor. The priest commanded the devil, "Stop tormenting her! Allow her to live with her husband!" and demanded the return of a jewel that the devil had taken from her. He responded that Román Ramírez had commanded him to torment her and said that *he* had the jewel.

Because of the devil's words, the girl's parents summoned the Accused to cure her. As soon as he entered the house in which they lived, the girl began to behave very strangely. She said she knew he had arrived and also knew why Román Ramírez was coming. When she saw him, she fainted and fell into a stupor. Her mouth became contorted and she went three days without eating, drinking, or being able to do anything of substance.

The Accused enveloped her with a thick cloud of incense—sandalwood, juniper oil, and other things—which returned her to her senses. Addressing the devil inside of the woman, he said, "Leave her! Leave her! Go! Go! Get out unless you want me to give you more of the incense!" But when the devil refused to respond to him, he made everyone leave the room. And thinking that no one could hear him, he complained to the devil, saying, "Why won't you answer me? My grandfather's devil showed more humility. What have I done that you won't speak to me? Isn't it enough that I've served you and given myself over to you for such a long time?" And he told the devil to make sure that the woman was sound asleep so that she did not overhear their conversation.

When he became aware that another devil had entered the room, he had said, "Welcome. How goes it over there? How are my son, wife, and grandson?" To this, the devil responded that his son had been gravely ill but that he was better now and out of danger. And he said that his wife had been indisposed but that she was recovering. His grandson, however, was very ill and in danger of dying. The Accused told the first devil that it was in his debt and that he had served it. So, he would be obliged if the devil would abandon the woman's body for at least 15 days and leave her in good health. This way they would pay him well for his work and then he could pay his debt, for he needed 200 *reales* to pay the rent on his garden. Otherwise, he would fall far short and his reputation would be badly hurt. Then, later, the devil could return and possess the woman again and do whatever it wanted. The devil had agreed to comply.

The Accused wanted the Great Turk[9] to go to war against the Christians, so, like a great enemy of our holy Catholic faith, he had asked the devil to cause men and a great Armada to attack the King our lord. In order to satisfy this desire, the devil responded that the Great Turk was arming his men to invade Spain. Later, the Accused learned that the devil had revealed their conversation and made it public. So, he had threatened it—like a man who had authority over it—declaring that he would bind it and make sure it paid attention to him the next time.

~ And like a treacherous man who focuses only on his own interests and benefit, he threatened the parents of the woman when they did not pay him well for the cure that he had performed, saying that they would soon realize their need. Then he bewitched the woman's husband and commanded the devils to enter his body and torment him. Just so, they tormented him one whole day with a thousand figments of his imagination and with despair.

And when asked to cure the man, Román Ramírez came to see him and said, "Buddy, you've defended yourself well against the attacks you've suffered from the devil." Then he enveloped him with the same incense he used previously and departed, disappointed about how little he had been paid.

The said cleric, conjuring on the said man, discovered that three demons named Satan, Beelzebub, and Barabbas had possessed him. He cast them out and expelled them from him. As a sign of their obedience, he forced them to give a silver *cuartillo*,[10] a single aiguillette,[11] and a pin from a ribbon.

~ Later, the woman's parents realized she had not been healed of her malady but rather was worse off than before. They summoned Román Ramírez and sent him some money, promising him more if he would leave the woman cured. He sent them some more incense, gave orders to the messenger, and wrote down a magical formula for them to recite. He told the messenger that when he arrived at the house, he would find her condition improved, she would be dancing with her friends. (And that is exactly what happened.)

But the woman still did not want to sleep with her husband. For this reason, the messenger gave the incense to the husband for him to use along

---

[9] That is, the sultan of the Ottoman Empire.

[10] A small coin valued at one quarter of a *real*.

[11] Aiguillettes were decorative tips, usually made of silver or gold overlaying the tips of cords or ribbons and normally worn in pairs.

with the magical formula. It read as follows: "Devils, get out of her, for Román commands it. And if you don't, I'll have to call and send for him. Then he'll come throw you out, since that's what he promised me." When this conjuration was performed, the woman let out a very loud yell, and she has remained healthy ever since then and has made a life with her husband.

~ Moreover, the Accused has done, said, held, and believed many other errors, sins, and heresies against our holy Catholic faith and has known of many other people who committed them. Like an aider and abettor of heretics, he has kept silent about them and concealed them, refusing to accuse them during the course of his trial. And although he was warned many times to speak and declare the whole truth, he refused to do so, and, instead, like a wicked Christian, he perjured himself.

It was requested of us that we accept his account as true insofar as it suffices for our final sentence, that we might declare his intention to be well proved, that Román Ramírez committed the sins of which he was accused, and that he was and is an apostate, impenitent, and relapsed Mohammedan heretic as well as an aider and abettor of heretics. As a consequence, he has fallen and incurred the sentence of greater excommunication. He is bound by this as well as by the other laws, pragmatics, and instructions established by the Holy Office. Furthermore, we order him to be handed over and we hand him over to the secular justice and arm, declaring his goods confiscated and the property of the chamber and treasury of the King our lord. Let everything be done fully, in compliance with justice. I swear to the said Accusation.

~ In our first audiences with Román Ramírez, he gave his name and said he was a Morisco, descended from Moors, a gardener and herbalist, a citizen and native of the town of Deza from the duchy of Medinaceli, and 60 years old. He said that he believed he had been arrested and brought to the secret jails of the Holy Office on account of his many enemies and because, as an herbalist, he had performed many great and famous cures. Specifically, it had been publicly said that he had cured a woman from Tajahuerce[12] by commanding the devil and by using witchcraft and incenses.

He said that what really happened in that case was the following: When he was summoned to cure her, he discovered her unconscious and in a stupor, so he incensed her, which somewhat brought her to her senses. When he discovered that her illness had progressed very far and that curing her of it would be extremely arduous and difficult, he returned to his house but left an unguent with the woman's parents to use as incense whenever

---

[12] About 25 miles north of Deza in Castile.

she fainted. He also advised them to have her recite the gospels frequently and to take her to visit two shrines dedicated to Our Lady for a pair of novenas.[13]

He said that he never knew or believed she was possessed, nor did he know any cure or medicine that would drive demons from human bodies, nor had he ever used or possessed a familiar spirit.[14] He was well aware that if he had one, he would be arrested. He had not used witchcraft or superstitions or commanded a devil to perform either the incensing or any other cure, but rather used herbs. He knew a great deal about herbs and about their virtues for his grandfather had been a physician and herbalist and had taught him.

He described many of the cures that he had performed using herbs as well as the manner and form that he had used to cure them. And he said that the common people say that he has a familiar because they have seen him recite various books of chivalry, which he had memorized, but they did not know his secret and mystery. What happened was that when he was a youth, his mother gave him a certain potion, which produced in him a remarkable memory. And although he did not know how to read or write—except to sign his name—when he heard books read to him, he retained in his memory the names of all those places, the knights errant, and the substance of the adventures that were contained in each chapter. Later, he recounted them, adding whatever details seemed appropriate in order to better adorn the stories. When he saw how this practice pleased his audience and the interest and profit it produced, he used and practiced it all the more on a daily basis.

~ When he was warned to scour his conscience and to speak the truth about every offense that he had committed against God our Lord and His holy Catholic faith, he replied that he wanted to do so. He confessed that when he was a lad of 14 years, a certain Morisco instructed him and he fasted four or five days for the month of Ramadan. He neither ate nor drank during the whole day—from star to star. He arose very early and performed the *zahor* and he kept the festival of Ramadan. He ended his fast by abstaining from work on the last day and dressing in clean clothes. And he had believed in one single true god.

In his heart he always held fast to the faith and error of the sect of Mohammed, but he stopped performing its fasts and ceremonies for 11 or

---

[13] A novena is an act of religious devotion repeated for a period of nine days. It typically involves a series of set prayers and is performed in the hope of obtaining special intercessory grace.

[14] A familiar (or familiar spirit) was popularly believed to be a personal demon or supernatural entity that assisted witches and folk healers.

12 years because he had no one to tell him when the moon of Ramadan had risen. Later he went to the Kingdom of Aragon and resumed performing the said fasts in the company of other Moriscos.

He continued performing them in the town of Deza until he took advantage of the Edict of Grace in the year one thousand five hundred and seventy [*sic*]. At that point he truly desired and wanted to convert to our holy Catholic faith and he went more than 20 years without performing any Moorish ceremonies. Yet in his heart he was always inclined to be a Moor, and he vacillated within himself over which was the better law, that of the Moors or of the Christians, and in which he would be saved.

Then, about seven or eight years ago, a Turkish slave persuaded him and he resumed believing in and observing the sect of Mohammed. He fasted the month of Ramadan and performed the *guadoc*, washing his entire body with water. He performed the *zala*, dressing himself in clean clothes and turning his face at midday and raising and lowering his head with the palms of his hands extended before him. He humbled himself to the ground at the time called *alaqibir*,[15] reciting the surah that reads, *ynanta yneca Alcauçara* façebique *lica vira guanaha enaja ynecha hua gualautar,* which means: "God is merciful and compassionate, and he will have mercy on my soul for I do not act out of arrogance, and, Lord, receive from your servant this small service."[16]

When this was done and after reciting that surah, he held and believed that he had gained as many pardons as if he had traveled to Mohammed's grave in Mecca and that he would be saved by these ceremonies. He had performed them knowing and understanding that they were contrary to our holy Catholic faith and evangelical law and that which our holy mother Church of Rome holds, preaches, and teaches.

He also recited another surah of the same sect that goes: *Alfan du liley. Alamina, guayeca nazahin edina çirata. Aleygayre, guahadobi en debli.*[17] He said that no one in all of Turkey knows what it means, except that it is the first surah of the Qur'an. And when the true Allah was asked by some of his servants about the meaning of those words, he responded that he could

---

[15] See footnote 4.

[16] This is clearly meant to refer to a chapter (or surah) from the Qur'an, but (whether as a result of scribal error or Ramírez's pronunciation) it has not been possible to identify it.

[17] This appears to be a corrupt version of the *Surat al-Fatiha* ("The Opening"), which is the first surah Muslims recite in the daily cycle of prayers. A translation reads: "All praise is due to Allah, Lord of the worlds—the Entirely Merciful, the Especially Merciful, Sovereign of the Day of Recompense. It is you we worship and you we ask for help. Guide us to the straight path—the path of those upon whom you have bestowed favor, not of those who have evoked your anger or of those who are astray."

not say, but that whoever recites them would gain as many pardons as there were stars in the heavens. And whoever knew this surah knew everything in the world that he needed to know; no one could serve God without it.

When he finished praying the surah, he had said *yemauleo, yemauleo* seven times—these words meant that Allah responded to his servants' prayers, saying, "He is true and is my servant. I am the honorable one and the noble one, and on my honor and nobility I will give you paradise."

And he had been very determined to go to Constantinople[18] to become a Moor but had given up the idea on account of having a wife and children.

~ When he responded to this Accusation, the Accused claimed to be a baptized and confirmed Christian. He said that after enjoying the Edict of Grace, being reconciled, and abjuring his errors, he committed the sins and heresies that he has confessed, thereby becoming an impenitent backslider. He made reference to his confessions, asking God for pardon and us for penance with mercy.

With regard to the charge that he had made a pact with the devil, the Accused asserted that the truth of what happened is that when he was about ten or twelve years old, his grandfather had been near death. He told and commanded the Accused that if the need arose after his death, then between 11 and 12 o'clock at night he should call upon a devil called Liarde, with whom he had made a pact and whose friend he was. This devil would come to him and answer him whatever he asked.

The first time that he called on him, the devil had responded, saying: "What do you want? Do you think that *I* have to serve *you* in the same way I did your grandfather? You don't have his skill. May you cure no one! Rather, stay put so they don't take you to the Inquisition like they did him."

He asked the devil who he was and what he had to do for him and if he had a body. He responded to him, "You have a lot to learn, kid. We spirits don't have bodies. And don't ask me anything that'll cause anyone harm, for I'm under orders not to speak about such matters." Then, because it was nearly 12 o'clock he departed, leaving the Accused very sad.

He called on the devil again and asked him to tell him about some money or show him where a treasure was hidden. To this, the devil responded that he could not do anyone any good nor be of any use to him. All he could do was provide the Accused with information about certain herbs.

So, he had not performed any more cures with the devil's help until four or five years later, when he was asked to go to the city of Calatayud[19]

[18] Constantinople (or Istanbul) was the heart of the Muslim Ottoman Empire and is located in modern-day Turkey.
[19] About 30 miles southeast of Deza in Aragon.

to heal a gentleman. Then, once again, he summoned the devil in order to consult with him about the illness and how to cure the gentleman. He responded that the gentleman had been bewitched by means of herbs that had been given to him and that he could cure him by giving him a drink of scorzonera water[20] mixed with the juice of quince seeds, pimpernel, and presicaria[21] herb. These would drive out many of the worms in his body and then he would be well, which is exactly what happened when he used that medicine to cure him.

Ever since then he had become increasingly famous and performed many cures. On some of them he consulted with that devil. And once, after they quarreled because the devil had failed to tell the Accused that he was wanted by Royal justice (on account of certain things for which he was arrested and jailed), he had sent the devil off. The Accused said: May God neither save his soul nor have mercy on him if he made any sort of pact or alliance with the said devil at any time or promised him anything, showed him any reverence, or used him for anything else except what he has said and declared.

We commanded that the Accused [inserted: *be given*] a copy of the Accusation, and a copy was given to him as was an attorney to advise him in his suit. The Accused denied everything else in the Accusation. With the agreement and opinion of the attorney, the trial was concluded and record of it received.

While the prosecutor's witnesses of request were in the process of being ratified and before they were publicized, Román Ramírez died. Having contracted an illness, he passed from this present life. All of the people who, by law, should have been called and summoned to defend the memory and reputation of the Accused were called and summoned; they were assigned appropriate times and places to do so. Since no one appeared or came forward to defend his memory, we provided a defender who resumed the suit.

The testimony of 20 witnesses against the Accused and his sins were publicized in the suit. The defender responded to them, alleging certain excuses. The suit was concluded definitively. We examined all of this. Anything requiring additional consideration and examination beyond our full accord and deliberation received the examination of learned persons of good conscience.

---

[20] The scorzonera (or black salsify) is a perennial plant that is cultivated in Spain as a root vegetable. The root is typically boiled and peeled before serving. Presumably, "scorzonera water" was the water left after the root had been boiled.

[21] A flowering plant of the knotweed family; often called smartweeds.

~ Xρ[ist]i nomine invocato²² ~

We find that with regard to the acts and merits of the said trial that the said prosecutor proved his Accusation and complaint well and completely, just as it was expedient for him to prove. We consider and pronounce that his intentions were well proved. Wherefore, we ought to declare and we do declare Román Ramírez to have been and to be an apostate Mohammedan heretic, an aider and abettor of heretics, an impenitent backslider, one who falsely and feignedly confessed and who, on that account, has fallen into and incurred a sentence of greater excommunication and was bound to it, as well as to the confiscation and loss of all his goods—since the day and time that he began to commit the said sins. We apply these to the chamber and treasury of the King our lord and to his receiver in his name, the declaration of which is reserved to us.

We should [inserted: con]demn and we do [inserted: con]demn the memory and reputation of Román Ramírez, commanding, as we do command that on the day in which a public auto-da-fe is celebrated, an effigy representing him be taken to the gallows with a *coroza*²³ of condemnation and a *sanbenito* with the markings of condemnation²⁴ on one side and on the other a sign bearing the name of Román Ramírez. After this our sentence has been publicly read, let both the effigy and his bones be handed over to the secular justice and arm in order that they might be publicly burned in abhorrence of such great and grievous sins.

Any monument (if there be one set over his grave) or coat of arms (if any be set or painted anywhere) is to be taken down and blotted out in order that no memory of Román Ramírez remain on the face of the earth, save this our sentence of execution, which we command to be carried out by it. And so that it might remain more firmly in the memories of the living, we command that the said *sanbenito* or a similar one with the same markings and sign of condemnation be displayed in a public place in the parish church of the town of Deza, where he was a parishioner. Let it remain there in perpetuity.

Furthermore, we pronounce and declare that the sons and daughters of Román Ramírez and his grandchildren through the male line be deprived of any and all public dignities, benefices, offices—whether ecclesiastical or secular—or any honors that they might hold or possess. And they cannot and are incapable of holding other honors or of going on horseback,

---

²² Latin: "Invoking the name of Christ."

²³ A tall painted hat made of paper, similar to the popular image of the witch's hat.

²⁴ The *sanbenitos* of those who would be relaxed to the secular arm featured flames and pictures of devils driving the condemned heretics into the fires of hell.

bearing arms, wearing silk, camlet,[25] or fine cloth, gold, silver, precious pearls, and corals. Nor may they exercise or use anything else prohibited to the children and descendents of such delinquents by common law and the pragmatics of these Kingdoms and the instructions of the Holy Office.

And, having thus pronounced our final judgment, in these documents and by them we pronounce, declare, and command it.

[Signed:] Licentiate don Pedro Girón
Licentiate don Gaspar de Quiroga
Licentiate don Francisco Manuel
Dr. Gabriel Suáres de Toledo

[The remainder of the document is written in a different hand.]

~ The said sentence was given and pronounced by the apostolic lords Inquisitor of the city and Kingdom of Toledo and the ordinary. They signed their names to it in the presence and by special commission of the most illustrious and reverend lord cardinal **don Fernando Niño de Guevarra**, the apostolic inquisitor general for his majesty's Kingdoms and estates.

A public auto-da-fe was celebrated in Toledo's Zodocover Plaza on Sunday the fifth day of the month of March in the year one thousand six hundred before the Licentiate Sotocamero, the Holy Office's prosecutor, and in the presence of Román Ramírez's effigy and of his bones, which were contained in a box. Both the bones and the effigy were handed over to the secular justice and arm according to the sentence.

All of this was attended by their majesties King don Philip the Third and Queen doña Margaret his wife, our lords (may God keep them many years), as well as by the lord Duke of Lerma and don Rodrigo de Silva and don Álvaro de Zúñiga, alderman of Toledo, and many other persons, both ecclesiastical and secular, from this city and from outside of it.

In my presence: [Signed:] Jusepe Pantoja, scribe.

Focus Questions

Why is it significant that Román was both a crypto-Muslim *and* a sorcerer in league with the devil? What would that conjunction of roles suggest and how might it have affected the thinking of King Philip III, who was in the audience at the auto-da-fe?

---

[25] A valuable fabric that often interwove silk with goat's hair, wool, or cotton.

Why was Román's sentence here so much harsher than in 1571 or 1581?

What do you make of Román's explanation of his memory? Why did he explain it in this way?

The inquisitorial scribe wrote about Román that "in his heart he was always inclined to be a Moor, and he vacillated within himself over which was the better law, that of the Moors or of the Christians, and in which he would be saved." To what extent does this statement capture Román's religious journey?

If the Holy Office was so eager to blot out the memory of Román Ramírez from "the face of the earth," why did they order his *sanbenito* to be displayed in Deza's parish church?

6

Letters Home from the Royal Jails of Cuenca (1611)[1]

Early in the seventeenth century, many of Deza's Moriscos—often the children and grandchildren of those who experienced the visitations of 1569 and 1581—were arrested by the Holy Office and transported to Cuenca as part of a final inquisitorial onslaught. They found themselves undergoing trials even as King Philip III of Spain moved forward with the expulsion of the Moriscos. After the conclusion of their trials, the Moriscos from Deza who had been reconciled to the Church were transferred from the secret jails of the Inquisition to Cuenca's royal jails. While there, they secretly wrote and dispatched several caches of letters to friends and relatives back home. One of these was intercepted by inquisitorial agents in March 1611. Nine of the letters are translated here.

78

Letter 1: A note from **Miguel Ramírez** *(the son of* **Román Ramírez** *the younger), included in a letter from* **Francisco el Romo** *to* **Francisco de Arcos** *written in Francisco el Romo's hand but signed by Ramírez. March 4, 1611.*

Miguel Ramírez commends himself to you greatly and may you take this note as his, for he is not able to write you. I did not write you that he left the Holy Office on February 24—they set him free from the debt of heresy— and that the prosecuting attorney could not prove anything against him. And so, he didn't take the penitential habit and isn't wearing it.[2] But on the

---

[1] ADC, legajo 813, expedientes 6676 and 6677.
[2] That is, Ramírez was not obliged to wear a *sanbenito*.

basis of whatever reasons are motivating them and because of the common suspicion of all, they condemned him to four years in the galleys.

In everything, he is commended to you and begs you for his sake that you remember him and everyone. And look to his wife and daughters at every opportunity.

And with that, may our Lord keep you as he can. Tell how you are and what's going on there.

[Signed:] Miguel Ramírez

———————————————— **79** ————————————————

Letter 2: From María la Jarquina *to* Francisca de Ropiñón *(her sister), written by* Francisco el Romo. *March 11, 1611.*

Sister of my soul,
The present letter will inform you how my son and I are doing in this city outside the jails of the Holy Office. I was released with irremissible habit[3] and my son, [**Luis de Hortubia**], was released with five years in the galleys, God be praised, which is the thing that most touches my soul. I left sick and very weak and needy (and I still am) and very poor, trusting only in the mercy of God and in your help.

Even though your troubles are great, you have liberty, and may God give it to you and preserve it by his hand as he is able so that you can watch over me and those poor orphans,[4] whom I commend to you, for such is my need.

And since I'm in a foreign land, I dare to cause you grief, so I beseech you for the love of God that you remember me if you can. Out of your poverty, attend to my own, favoring me with something to help and sustain me until God provides something else from his own hand. For such is my need that I am daring to give you an account and am confident you won't fail me. I say no more. He writes there to the neighborhood.[5]

---

[3] That is, she was ordered to wear a *sanbenito* for the rest of her life, although in practice most people who received this sentence received permission to remove their *sanbenito* after a few years.

[4] The orphans are María's granddaughters, María (b. 1601) and Ana (b. 1603).

[5] Francisco el Romo's handwriting is particularly difficult to read at this point. The meaning of the passage is unclear.

Don't stop attending to our need since it is a matter of such importance. May God our Lord repay you from his divine hand.

Give my greetings to Gerónimo de Liñán and María de Hortubia[6] and to **Juan de Hortubia**, your sons, and to Luis de Liñán[7] and to his wife and children and Luis de Cieli[8] and **Juan de Cieli**,[9] and Isabel de Cieli and to Diego Martínez her husband with all the rest and to María Adrian my cousin and to everyone in general. And let us know of your health and the state of your affairs. We very much want to know what is going on there. I send two pieces of silk fabric and twelve little needles for those poor orphans, for I have nothing else.

From Cuenca on March 11, 1611. Very certain about what you will command.

Your sister,
María la Jarquina[10]

Francisco el Romo commends himself to you and to everyone in general.

---

8 o

Letter 3: From Luis de Cebea the youngest *to María de Hortubia, his wife. March 11, 1611.*

To María de Hortubia,[11] my wife, in Deza.
In days past, I wrote to you twice. I sent the first letter with the fellow from Arcos and the other with Juan Miguel, and I haven't had a response to either. In both, I charged you to look out for me and gave you an account of what's happening here and of our need.

I don't know why you would care so little as to not have written, knowing your obligation to write to me, your husband, and to give me an account of your health and of my daughters'. One letter from me should

---

6 This is a different María de Hortubia from the one included in the Cast of Characters.
7 This is a different Luis de Liñán from the one included in the Cast of Characters.
8 This is a different Luis de Cieli from the one included in the Cast of Characters.
9 If this is the same Juan de Cieli who appears in the Cast of Characters, then María was unaware of the fact that he had died in 1607, not long before her arrest.
10 María's name here does not appear to be her signature, but rather to have been written by Francisco el Romo, who transcribed the letter.
11 This is a different María de Hortubia from the one included in the Cast of Characters.

have sufficed so that, considering when you received it, you might have left for this city to obtain my remedy and liberty as you ought to do (for you are my wife) and to obey my command as if God commanded it.

It may be that, because of your carelessness, although you want to see me you won't be able to because I will have been taken to the galleys, which I lament—to go without seeing you or my daughters. After God, there's nothing that I want more.

I wrote to my lady[12] and to your mother[13] in particular—I've held her and hold her in the place of my own mother—and am worried because she, in whom I had confidence after God to be my remedy and liberty, has not written to me. Well, whatever the carelessness up to this point, from here on out let there be none. Speed is now necessary because we are waiting night and day for them to transport us to the galleys. So, let one of my brothers immediately set out for this city. I understand that by then my father[14] will be released by the Inquisition, and it would be appropriate for my brother to be here in order to seek and attend to our remedy and liberty.

We have written to Deza, to all those just lords of the neighborhood,[15] regarding what is advisable for our liberty and the manner and means by which they might obtain it so that those lords might perceive what is most advisable for our liberty. For we are informed by our attorney that if there be persons who act on our behalf before the Supreme Council of the Inquisition, then we will have liberty. So, it's appropriate for you to obey those lords of the neighborhood if they issue an order, and if necessary for you to go to Madrid together with the rest.

Make the effort and come seek my liberty. I'm asking you to do it even if you have to visit the king our lord and beg for me as alms, since he shows mercy and releases prisoners during this holy time.[16] And let there be no carelessness. Even if you know that you will have to sell yourself and my daughters for it, God giving me health and liberty, I will get you out of hock and sale.[17]

I discussed your health and the health of your mother and your (and my) daughters with the carrier of this letter.[18] We discussed whether you received the letters from the last trip and what those lords of the neighborhood

---

[12] That is, his mother, **Francisca de Baptista**.

[13] His mother-in-law is **Isabel de Liñán**.

[14] A reference to **Luis de Cebea the younger**, who would die as a relapsed heretic in an auto-da-fe two months later.

[15] It is unclear to whom this phrase referred. Perhaps he meant the Moriscos from the Upper Neighborhood who sat on the town council.

[16] Luis de Cebea wrote the letter during the season of Lent in the Church calendar.

[17] Luis de Cebea may have been using hyperbole at this point.

[18] **Fabian de Roble**.

ordered regarding them. I don't have more to say, except may our Lord keep you and receive me with contentment and liberty for his holy service.

From Cuenca, on March 11, 1611.

[Signed:] Luis de Cebea

To my uncle and cousins and in-laws, relatives, and kin: I kiss your hands. If you go to Madrid, then let me know where you go by means of the postal substation so that we can correspond. Give the letter carrier three *reales* for his work because I don't have them. And advise me if you received the few small items that I sent with the fellow from Arcos.

I say, don't come to this city unless you're bringing some aid. If not, let God handle it. The carrier who bears this letter is a person of confidence, and you can give him and send with him anything you want to get to us. He will bring a good note.

81

Letter 4: From Juan de Cebea *to* Francisca de Baptista, *his mother. March 11, 1611.*

To Francisca de Baptista, my mother
In the town of Deza
By this letter Your Grace[19] will know how, thanks be to God our Lord, I have been released from the jails of the Holy Inquisition with a sentence of three years in the galleys, and my brother Francisco remains in this city wearing the habit.[20]

We are waiting daily for my father to be released, confident in God that he will get out quickly. It's appropriate, then, for one of my brothers to come so that, when my father is released, someone is around who can pursue our liberty. And maybe it's also appropriate, since the necessity is so great—for we're on the verge of becoming servile and enslaved—for Your Grace, as my mother and lady, to go to court, if necessary, and take advantage of this holy time when our lord the King performs acts of mercy and redemption and releases prisoners from the jails and galleys.

For the love of God, Your Grace, secure our ransom. Pay close attention to the fact that we're crippled and have other infirmities that make us

---

[19] That is, **Francisca de Baptista**.
[20] That is, he is wearing a *sanbenito*.

useless for the galleys. For our lawyer informs us that if we have someone who pursues our liberty before the Supreme Council of the Inquisition, we will have it.

And, Your Grace, if they[21] manage to stay there in that town, let us know what's happening so that we who are here will know where we need to turn. Because when we were in front of these lords [inquisitors], we agreed to comply with His Majesty's expulsion decree. Don't dawdle, for the love of God, for we are daily expecting them to transport us to the galleys; they've already announced it to us.

For this purpose, the bearer goes about deliberately,[22] seeing that in Deza they have so dawdled that no one has come to find out what or how we are doing. Thus, our need is so great that we are eating what we get from begging and relying on what my aunt **María [la Jarquina]** earns spinning on her wheel. She shares part of her own sustenance in order to give it to my brother **Luis [de Cebea the youngest]** and me. We can't repay her for her good work. May God repay her as he can and may God give us liberty so that we might show gratitude for it.

May my uncle and my cousins and in-laws regard this letter as having been written to them. Inform me of everyone's health, for I'd like to know that they are well. May God keep them and allow me to see them with liberty.

Your Grace's humble son, Juan de Cebea (who would rather be the bearer than the writer), to Your Grace. Well, God wants his will to be done in heaven as it is on earth.[23] Written in Cuenca on March 11, 1611.

[Signed:] Juan de Cebea

Miguel Ramírez was released on February 24 and he left my father well.[24] The two of them have been together the whole 35 months, and Ramírez left him fat and very healthy. Commend me greatly to my aunt María

---

[21] It is unclear to whom Juan de Cebea is referring here, but he probably has in mind Deza's Moriscos, hoping that they will somehow escape the royal expulsion.

[22] The meaning of this phrase is obscure, but is perhaps meant to contrast the letter bearer's purposefulness with the dawdling of the Moriscos in Deza.

[23] Interestingly, here Juan de Cebea misquotes the Lord's Prayer, reversing the order of earth and heaven. The correct version can be found in Matthew 6:9–13.

[24] That is, Ramírez was released from the inquisitorial jails and transferred to the royal jails, where Juan de Cebea was located.

de Deza and to Francisco Ramírez,[25] my brother-in-law. Miguel is very unwell in one arm; hopefully it won't amount to anything. Let them continue sending him money, for he needs it and such a good brother deserves much.

——————————————— **82** ———————————————

Letter 5: From **Juan de Hortubia the soldier,** *the son of* **Íñigo de Hortubia,** *to his father-in-law Diego de Fadrique the elder and brother-in-law Diego de Fadrique the younger. March 12, 1611.*

I'm concerned that I haven't seen a response to the letter I wrote you via the messenger from Arcos. I want very much to know of your health and about my in-laws. Your niece[26] and I are healthy, glory to God our Lord, and long to see all of you who are from the neighborhood. We wrote everything in the previous letter and you will see what it contains.

For my part I earnestly beg you that you, for your part, look to our aid if there's a way. You have my assurance that if I need to repay something, I will (if God gives me liberty) and I will give thanks as is right. If it's our luck that there's no solution, do me the courtesy of making sure to send me letters of favor from doña Paula and Francisco Fernández for Bartolome del Águila[27] so that he might show me favor at the port in every way that he can.

I can't think of anything else, so I won't say more, except may God our Lord give you health as he can. Give my uncles and in-laws my greetings on behalf of my wife.

From Cuenca, March 12, 1611.

[Signed:] Juan de Hortubia, soldier

---

[25] Miguel Ramírez's brother. Francisco is married to María de Cebea, Juan's sister.

[26] It is not clear why he refers to the Fadriques' "niece" (*sobrina*). Presumably, Juan means his wife, Ana de Fadrique, who was reconciled on November 7, 1610.

[27] Francisco Fernández-Alcarea was a hidalgo in Dez and briefly the town's warden. He was married to doña Paula. Bartolome del Águila probably refers to the man who served during this period as governor and warden of the Port of Santa María, where Juan and his companions expected to be pressed into service. As it happens, the Port of Santa María was one of the lands controlled by the duke of Medinaceli.

83

Letter 6: From Juan de Hortubia the Soldier *to his uncles, Lope and Luis de Hortubia.*[28] *March 12, 1611. This letter is written in a very different (and much more practiced) hand than the previous one.*

Fathers,

You already know what happened to me and the need I have in this royal jail—naked and barely healthy (thank God), ailing in some of my limbs, and lacking any other support beside God's, unless it's your own.

I'm confident that you will attend to my needs as you've always done, and now you must do it all the more extensively since the situation is so urgent. Secretary Poveda[29] has reported and informed me that if we have someone in Madrid who acts on behalf of my business (and that of the others), it will be easy to commute the galleys to another penance that would serve their lordships. So, amongst your merciful selves and my in-laws, each one of them for their part and all of them together, commit this business to them as if it were their own, since it is. A letter urging haste (because its absence could cause great harm) is being sent, in all of our names, to the neighborhood and everyone else, so that they might be diligent, dutiful, and courageous.

So, tell me more about what's going on and about everyone's health. If my liberty costs some money, don't hold back on that account. So long as God gives me health, I can make good on it and pay it back, for I've only been condemned to have a quarter of my goods confiscated.

Give my greetings to my aunt María and her children, to my aunt Guiomar and her husband and children, to my aunt Cecilia and her husband and children, and likewise to all of my relatives and kin along with everyone generally. With that, may our Lord fulfill my desire by keeping you safe and healthy.

From Cuenca and this royal jail on March 12, 1611.

[Signed:] Juan de Hortubia

---

[28] This is a different Luis de Hortubia than the one included in the Cast of Characters.

[29] Alonso de Poreda held the office of Notary of the Secret at the tribunal of the Holy Office in Cuenca.

84

Letter 7: From Leonor de Hortubia *to Guiomar Carillo, with a note from* Lope Guerrero the younger, *Leonor's son-in-law. March 12, 1611. Both signatures at the end of the letter appear to be written in the same hand, but both are initialed. This suggests that a third party wrote the letter but that both Leonor and Lope made their marks.*

Guiomar Carillo,[30]
This letter is to inform you that—glory to God, our Lord has been served—we are in this need and travail and are unable to help ourselves. May God, who is able, help us.

I find myself worn out with work, since I can't return to my native land with my sister and relatives.[31] So, seeing my ruin and need, that I am helpless and without shelter (for my son-in-law who would work on my behalf is in such straits that he can't, since he lacks liberty) and considering that you have always shown me good will, I'm daring to plead and to beg all of you in that town: consider it worthwhile to care for me, for I am exiled from my town. For the love of God, if it's possible, act quickly. Get me out of this city, for I'm in torment. If you won't do it for me, then do it for the love of God. I beg it of you, for in the end I am your blood and you are obliged since my brothers can't help me in their native land.

This fellow who's traveling to Deza can inform me of your decision to help me when he returns. I don't have anything else to write except may God our Lord keep you as he is able. Give my greetings to your children and to Diego de Almotazán and to your whole family. I beg everyone to attend to my aid and need, just as I am confident you will do.

From Cuenca and this jail cell, March 12, 1611.

My son-in-law, Lope, earnestly commends himself and, on his behalf, entrusts this business to you.

[Signed:] Leonor de Hortubia [initialed]
Lope Guerrero the younger [initialed]

---

[30] This is probably Leonor's cousin, the daughter of Francisco Carillo and her maternal aunt, María Almotazán.
[31] According to the terms of her reconciliation, Leonor was exiled from Deza for four years.

85

Letter 8: From Luis de Cebea the youngest *to* Isabel de Liñán, *his mother-in-law. March 13, 1611.*

To my mother, Isabel de Liñán, in the town of Deza, may God keep her.

[Initialed with the mark of Luis de Cebea the youngest]

Deza
Mother,
I earnestly beg you to take care of your granddaughters, my daughters. I'm fully confident that you will look after them as your own until the end. And I beg you to obtain my remedy, if there be any way to do so, even if it means going to Madrid—either you or my wife. If you attend to the Queen for alms this Holy Week, she will grant me liberty.
　　Confident in everything you will do, may our Lord give you health as he can.
From Cuenca, March 13, 1611.
[Signed:] Your son-in-law, Luis de Cebea

We beg you that you provide well for this letter's carrier, for we are greatly obliged to his mother. She often feeds all of us and is a very worthy person. Lest there be any carelessness in this, give news of it to everyone so that they follow suit.

86

Letter 9: From Miguel Ramírez *to* María de Almotazán, *his wife. March 13, 1611.*

To María Almotazán, my wife in Deza, may God keep her.
Deza
Sister,
After I wrote to you,[32] your uncle Mateo [de Almotazán] told me that your father[33] and mine (for that's how I think of him) had died as has my

---

[32] The previous letter from Miguel to María is lost.
[33] That is, Pedro de Almotazán (c.1538–1611).

good uncle Francisco de Miranda.[34] May God our Lord keep them in his holy glory, as he is able. God our Lord is very merciful for taking them out of the world.

I don't have anything more to say except give my greeting to my cousin Ana de Deza and my cousin Ana de Miranda and your aunt Ana de Mancebo. I beg you on my behalf, for the love of God, if they can, let them do me some favor, for my need is so great that I can't exaggerate it. And the same to María de Deza, my mother-in-law, and to your ~~aunt~~ cousin and mine, María Ramírez.

Commend me to everyone generally and may they remember me.

On March 13, 1611.

Your husband,

[Signed:] Miguel Ramírez

Focus Questions

What concerns are most apparent in these letters? How much do they tell us about the actual religious beliefs of Deza's Moriscos? How about their attitudes toward the Inquisition or the monarchy?

How would you describe the emotional state of the letter writers? Were they, for example, despairing, hopeful, angry, or sad?

How would you describe the physical state of the letter writers? In what conditions were they living? And how were they surviving from day to day?

What indications are there in these letters that the Moriscos were trying to execute a scheme to secure their freedom?

---

[34] This is the son of the **Francisco de Miranda** mentioned in **Licentiate Reynoso's** 1569 visitation. Like his father, this Francisco also became a painter.

7

Efforts to Evade the Galleys (1611)[1]

As their letters home suggest, several of the Moriscos had been sentenced to work the oars of the king's galleys. Because of the danger involved and the poor conditions, this was a sentence that frequently resulted in death. Once transferred from the inquisitorial prison to Cuenca's royal jails, the condemned men began concocting plans to avoid galley service. In their letters, for instance, they urged friends and relatives back home to pursue their release by any means necessary. Yet they also took matters into their own hands.

Details about the negotiations in which the men engaged are murky, but one of the schemes they pursued was to convince the authorities that some of them, at least, were physically unfit to serve in the galleys. To that end, 12 Moriscos composed the following letter to King Philip III, explaining their plight. The immediate result was a physical examination in Cuenca.

87

Letter from the Moriscos to King Philip III
A letter from the royal jails of Cuenca, written by 12 Moriscos—11 from Deza and 1 from Tarancón—to King Philip III, requesting the commutation of their sentences. No date, but probably before January 22, 1611.

Lord,
Francisco el Romo and **Rodrigo Fajardo**, **Juan Mancebo** and **Román el Romo**, ~~Luis de Hortubia~~ [*inserted:* **Miguel Ramírez**] and **Juan Corazón**, **Lope Guerrero** and **Luis de Cebea the youngest** and **Juan de Cebea**,

---

[1] ADC, libro 227, folios 163r, 165r-167r, and 227r-228r; libro 240, folios 15v-16r and 26v-27r.

Juan de Hortubia [the Soldier] and **Pedro Zamorano**, New Christians, citizens of the town of Deza (except for Rodrigo Fajardo, who is a citizen of the town of Tarancón and comes from the Kingdom of Granada²), and prisoners in the royal jail of this city of Cuenca by order of the inquisitors.

We declare that we have been condemned to His Majesty's galleys. We wear the penitential habit³ and, on account of being so long in prison, we are ill, broken, crippled in arms and hands; we suffer discharges of blood and other secret infirmities, are [sick?]⁴ and poor of heart. Consequently, we can hardly be of use serving His Majesty in the said galleys, and many of us are old and have wives and children. We beg and beseech Your Highness to order the doctors and surgeons to truthfully confirm our infirmities and, once we have been seen and examined, command that our penance be commuted from the galleys to something else that Your Highness considers to be of service to God our Lord. We are prepared to comply with great humility, no matter how burdensome it might be and we implore this of the Holy Office.

Moreover, we beseech Your Highness to order your provision given so that the ordinary justice⁵ does not transport us to the said galleys until we have been examined by Your Highness, lest Your Majesty pay for us to eat rather than us begging for alms.

[Signed:] Francisco el Romo
Román el Romo

88

Medical Examination of the Moriscos
In response to the proceeding letter, the Suprema, *the royal council responsible for inquisitorial affairs, ordered a medical examination of the Moriscos. The* Suprema's *letter (which no longer exists) was dated January 22, 1611, but the inquisitors at Cuenca did not acknowledge receipt of it until April 11. Two days later, they ordered the examination of the Moriscos by medical professionals in order to determine their fitness for galley service. The inquisitorial*

---

² Tarancón is 50 miles west of Cuenca. Fajardo is a Morisco who hailed from southern Spain but was relocated by the government after the War of the Alpujarras that erupted in the late 1560s.
³ That is, they are wearing *sanbenitos*.
⁴ The page is torn here.
⁵ That is, the secular authorities.

secretary Diego de Peñalver officially recorded the results of the examinations in the following account.

~ In the city of Cuenca on April 13, 1611, the lord Inquisitor **Licentiate don Diego de Quiroga** was in his afternoon audience, which he attended alone on account of the illness of the lord Inquisitor **Dr. Claudio de la Cueva.** He acted in compliance with the command of the lords of His Majesty's Council of the Holy General Inquisition in their letter dated January 22 and received on April 11 of the aforementioned year, ordering that **Rodrigo Fajardo, Román el Romo, Francisco el Romo, Juan Mancebo, Miguel Ramírez, Juan Corazón, Lope Guerrero, Luis de Cebea [the younger], Juan de Cebea, Juan de Hortubia [the Soldier]**, and **Pedro Zamorano** (Moriscos condemned to the galleys by this Holy Office) be brought from the royal jail of this city. They entered the chamber, each one of them under his own strength.

The aforesaid lord Inquisitor ordered Dr. Diego Fernández (physician) and Diego de Morales (surgeon of this Holy Office) to examine the said Moriscos and assess their ailments and whether any of them have impediments prohibiting them from serving in the galleys. He charged them to be conscientious, warning them that they had to declare their opinion and assessment under oath. They said that they would comply with it. Of this I, the secretary, bear witness, and the lord Inquisitor initialed it.

[Initialed by Diego de Quiroga]

This happened in my presence. [Signed:] Diego de Peñalver

~ And then, continuing on this same day, month, and year, while the said lord Inquisitor was in the said afternoon audience, he commanded the said Dr. Diego Fernández, physician, and Diego de Morales, surgeon, to enter therein. Together and individually they swore that they would truthfully declare what they knew and understood about the Moriscos regarding the impediments that they claimed prohibited them from serving in the galleys, as declared below. Having been sworn in, they said the following:

~ That they have examined Rodrigo Fajardo, Morisco, who complains of a urinary ailment and of an abundance of blood from hemorrhoids and of a crippled hand. While it is true that he has a malady in his urinary tract, the witnesses believe that the blood produced by the hemorrhoids are a kind of medicine for the ~~ordi~~ [*inserted:* ur]inary malady because the humors that normally attend to the urine are being diverted along this other direction and are soothing the urinary elements and tracts so that the pain in them is less severe than it might be. And with regard to the damaged hand, although he has some shriveled cords and hardened tendons and muscles, it appears to them that over time and in the summer heat they will soften up and extend. So, the fingers and hand should cut a fair figure and be able to grasp anything. Thus, it appears to them that he is not legitimately impeded from serving His Majesty in the galleys.

~ And likewise they have examined Román el Romo, who as a result of having fallen, has a hernia of the *omentum*[6] on his ~~flesh~~ [*inserted:* scrotum], or sack, into which some of the gut always extends. Moreover, it does not impede him from any necessary actions. Thus it appears to them that he does not have a legitimate impediment to leave off serving His Majesty in the galleys.

~ And likewise they examined Miguel Ramírez, who said that he suffered from a heart malady and that he had a swollen hand. With regard to the heart malady, they were unable to find anything having to do with it nor any evidence indicating that he had one. While his left hand was swollen as he said, it was not at all crippled, and the swelling is of little consideration. As it happens, it seemed to them that he could reduce the swelling with simple remedies and, even if none of them were performed, given his natural robustness, his own natural heat will overcome and reduce the said swelling. For this reason he seemed to them not to have a just impediment for leaving off serving His Majesty in the galleys.

~ And likewise they examined Lope Guerrero the younger, who suffers from an intestinal hernia, but it seems to them that the hurt is not so great that as a result of this infirmity he cannot serve His Majesty in the galleys.

~ And likewise they examined Juan de Hortubia the soldier, who complained of a numb hand. But they did not find any notable hurt or disability in it whereby he would be unable comfortably to serve His Majesty in the galleys. With seasonal heat, exercise, and working the hand, the numbness will easily be overcome; besides there is no clear evidence that he is actually experiencing numbness.

~ And likewise they examined Juan Corazón, who has an intestinal hernia that does not appear to be particularly serious. Since he is young, it has seemed to them that he is not legitimately impeded from leaving off serving His Majesty at the oar.

~ And likewise they examined Luis de Cebea the youngest, who claimed to have a crippled and numb left hand and to be ruptured. With regard to the hand, it is not crippled in any fashion and the numbness is not constant. When it is absent, it is not an impediment for that very reason. And with regard to the rupture, or hernia, no evidence was found, so he does not have just cause or impediment to leave off serving His Majesty in the galleys.

---

[6] The examiners used the Latin term that refers to the membrane surrounding the abdominal organs.

~And likewise they have examined Francisco el Romo, sandal-maker, who said he had a heart malady and asthma. With regard to the heart malady there was no evidence of it nor was credence given to him because it is a common complaint. And with regard to the asthma, at present, his chest is somewhat tight and he also has a cough, but this could derive from some catarrh, of which there are many in this city at present. And it was not clear to them that it was a pre-existing, deep-rooted, and habitual asthma. So, as far as they can determine at present, it does not appear to be a just impediment to leave off serving in the galleys of His Majesty.

~ And likewise they have examined Juan de Cebea, who currently has a bit of a fever and in days past has had some fevers on account of which the said Dr. Fernández has examined him in this city's royal jail. He has bled and purged him and he is consequently already much improved. There is every hope, by Dr. Fernández's judgment, of his recovering and of being free of fevers and very suitable to serve His Majesty in the galleys.

~ And likewise they examined Pedro Zamorano, Juan Mancebo, and **Luis de Hortubia *el jarquino*[7]** and none of them demonstrated any impediment to leave off serving His Majesty in the galleys at the oars as has been declared above, nor any other infirmity or lesion whereby they can be excused from it. In no way are Rodrigo Fajardo, Román el Romo, Miguel Ramírez, Lope el Guerrero, Juan de Hortubia [the Soldier], Juan Corazón, Luis de Cebea, Francisco el Romo, Juan de Cebea, Pedro Zamorano, Juan Mancebo, or Luis de Hortubia *el jarquino* legitimately impeded in such a way as to be excused from service to His Majesty in the galleys at the oar. They stated and declared this under oath, and they signed their names to it. The words "flesh" and "ordi" are crossed out; "scrotum" is inserted.

[Signed:] Dr. Fernández Diego de Morales

This happened in my presence. [Signed:] Diego de Peñalver

89

Letter from the Inquisitors at Cuenca to the Suprema *(April 16)*
The following is Cuenca's letter to the Suprema *describing their assessment of the Moriscos' health based on the medical examinations recorded in the previous document.*

---

[7] Luis de Hortubia *el jarquino*'s name was struck off of the original letter to King Philip III and replaced by Miguel Ramírez's. He was also not named at the beginning of this document among the Moriscos to be examined by Fernández and Morales.

~

~ Your lordships' letter dated January 22 was received in this Holy Office on the eleventh of the present month along with copies of the three petitions given by **Rodrigo Fajardo, Román el Romo, Francisco el Romo, Juan Corazón, Juan Mancebo, Miguel Ramírez, Lope Guerrero, Luis de Cebea, Juan de Cebea, Juan de Hortubia [the Soldier]**, and **Pedro Zamorano** (Moriscos) reconciled and condemned to the galleys. In them the Moriscos requested that, because they were ill and unable to serve therein, their sentence be commuted to some other punishment. Carrying out your lordship's command that we inform you of our opinion, what we can say is that all of the said Moriscos left the secret jails healthy and without serious injury and they remain so now.

For even greater justification, Dr. Diego Fernández and Diego de Morales, surgeon of this Holy Office, have visited them and they declared under oath that none of the Moriscos have either a legitimate infirmity or an impediment whereby they can or should be excused from serving in the galleys at the oars.

These are a crafty people who have always managed, with lies and fabrications, to hide their sins. And now, they are doing it again in order to be excused from the punishment that they have so justly earned. Based on other schemes and cunning acts that the same individuals perpetrated involving a bundle of letters that has come into our possession—we do not go into detail in this letter to avoid long-windedness—as well as the false account that they have made to your lordship, it seems to us that there is no reason to commute the said punishment from the galleys as they claim. It seems to us that they do not deserve to be shown any grace whatsoever.

May God keep your lordship, etc.

From this Holy Office and Castile from Cuenca on April 16, 1611.

The **Licentiate Quiroga**. The lord Inquisitor is in attendance alone.

90

Letter from the Inquisitors at Cuenca to the Suprema *(October 13)*
After their examinations, the Moriscos were sent to the galleys. When they arrived at the Port of Santa María, the place of embarkation, however, some of them were deemed physically unfit and refused a place at the oars. Below is the pertinent portion of a letter sent by the incredulous inquisitors at Cuenca to the members of the Suprema *describing this turn of events.*

~

~ Concerning those condemned to the galleys by this Holy Office: they refused to receive four of the Moriscos onto the galleys, saying that they are useless.[8] Considering the reliable report given by the person who took them to the port of embarkation as well as the extraordinary formalities that these Moriscos have undertaken in order to free themselves from the galleys before they departed from here, there is a very great presumption that they have undertaken negotiations to avoid being received onto the galleys. For the physician and surgeon of the Office examined them and declared under oath that the Moriscos had no impediment excusing them from service in the galleys at the oars. We informed your lordship of this by letter on April 16 as well as by letter on June 18 of this year. And, having seen them, your lordship responded in a letter dated April 22 that our opinion was good, that the said Moriscos should go to the galleys.

~ The said Moriscos are: **Román el Romo**, a native and citizen of the town of Deza, against whom a multitude of witnesses testified that he was a Moor. Not having desired to confess everything until he was put to the question under torture, he finally confessed to 23 years of apostasy and to having falsely converted. He was condemned to the habit and perpetual and irremissible incarceration with reconciliation and confiscation of goods and to serve the first five years on the galleys. He currently is age 42.

~ **Juan Mancebo**, Morisco, a native and citizen of the town of Deza, 40 years of age. A multitude of witnesses testified that he was a Moor but he denied it. When he began to confess, he left much out and retracted his confessions. After the conclusion of his case, he again confessed to apostasy with belief and pertinacity. His case received a sentence of reconciliation with the habit, perpetual incarceration, and confiscation of goods, with the first five years of his incarceration to be served in the galleys. Both of these were in the roster of cases for the year 1610.

~ **Miguel Ramírez**, Morisco, citizen and native of the town of Deza, age 39 years. Three witnesses testified that he was a Moor and had, by that point, followed the sect of Mohammed for six or eight years. Two witnesses confirmed that he had conspired with other Moriscos (who were also under arrest) to deny all this. It was discovered, through various witnesses, that at the death of one of his brothers, Miguel Ramírez was found reciting the prayers of the sect of Mohammed and that he congregated with other Moriscos and went to court to negotiate a settlement so that

---

[8] Three of the Moriscos were from Deza. The fourth was **Íñigo de Moraga** from Arcos de Jalón.

the Moriscos of Deza would not henceforth be sent to prison. Both in his audiences and under torture he denied that he communicated with other Moriscos while he was in the jails. He was sentenced to abjure under grave suspicion and to four years in the galleys along with the confiscation of a fourth part of his goods. This is the son of **Román Ramírez [the younger]**, Morisco, who was relaxed in effigy having died in the jails. He is just as fine a Moor as his father was.

------------------------------ **91** ------------------------------

Statement of Compliance from the Inquisitors at Cuenca
Despite the exasperated letter sent by the inquisitors in Cuenca, on October 29, 1611, the Suprema *ordered the release of the four Moriscos who had been deemed unfit for the galleys. Now the Moriscos were ordered to comply with the royal expulsion decree. Here, in early November, Cuenca provides a sulky response to the* Suprema's *order.*

~ In the city of Cuenca on November 3, 1611, the lords Inquisitor **Licentiate don Diego de Quiroga** and **Dr. don Juan de la Torre** were in their morning audience. By means of a letter dated the thirteenth of last month, they have communicated to the lords of His Majesty's Council of the Holy General Inquisition their opinion in the matter concerning the release of **Íñigo de Moraga**, **Miguel Ramírez**, **Román el Romo**, and **Juan Mancebo** (Moriscos) whom His Majesty's galleys have refused to accept on account of their uselessness. This refusal appears in two testimonies originally exhibited in this Holy Office by Pedro Rodríguez Catalan, the person who transported the aforementioned galley slaves as well as the ones who remained on the galleys.

The inquisitors have also received a letter from the aforementioned lords of the Council dated the twenty-ninth of last month by which they commanded (as seems to the lords Inquisitor) that the said Moriscos be released so that they might go and comply with His Majesty's expulsion decree and depart from these Kingdoms. So, to that end, the inquisitors declared that as far as it concerns this Holy Office, they were commanding and commanded that the said Íñigo de Moraga, Miguel Ramírez, Román el Romo, and Juan Mancebo be released from their prison. And let notice be given of it to the prisoners and to the city's royal representative or his chief magistrate. And let a sufficient number of copies be made of the said testimonies so that they remain with these orders, then return the originals to the aforementioned Pedro Rodríguez Catalan. And they initialed it.

[Initials]

~ This happened in my presence [Signed:] Luis Conde de Zamora

---

92

The Fulfillment of the Suprema*'s Order*

Most of the Moriscos who remained in Deza were exiled from their homes in early July 1611. It is very likely that they were transported to Muslim North Africa, but no hard evidence has yet come to light. As recorded in the document below, the Suprema*'s order to release the four remaining Moriscos was carried out on November 3, 1611. Even if the men had wanted to return home, they would have found little comfort in doing so. This final document represents one of the last pieces of evidence about the fate of any of the members of the town's Morisco community.*

~ In the city of Cuenca on November 3, 1611, I, Agustín Cano de Aguilera, notary and caretaker of the Holy Office of the Inquisition, personally gave notice to **Íñigo de Moraga**, **Miguel Ramírez**, **Román el Romo**, and **Juan Mancebo** (Moriscos) that the lords Inquisitor commanded that they be released in order to comply with the expulsion decrees of His Majesty and that they depart from these Kingdoms. Being witnesses: Julian Pérez, Bautista Gabaldón, Juan Herraez, all citizens of the said city, of which I testify. In my presence:

[Signed:] Agustín Cano de Aguilera, notary

~ On the same day, month, and year as above, I went to the houses of Dr. Pedro Carranza, chief magistrate of the said city, and informed him and delivered a certificate from the secretary Luis Conde about how the lords Inquisitor had commanded the release of Íñigo de Moraga, Miguel Ramírez, Román el Romo, Juan Mancebo (Moriscos) so that they might comply with His Majesty's expulsion decrees and depart from these Kingdoms as well as the above mentioned testimony and decree from the lords Inquisitor to the chief magistrate so that it might be done as commanded therein.

In the presence of don Antonio Agustín de Cuellar, he said he was prepared to comply. Concerning which I testify and make my mark ~

That it is such   It is true testimony

[Signed:] Agustín Cano de Aguilera, notary

Focus Questions

Docs. 87–92: Why did the Moriscos appeal to the king when the Inquisition had already condemned them to serve on the royal galleys? What does this suggest about the interests of the king and the Holy Office? Were they always fully aligned?

Docs. 87–92: What reason did the Moriscos have to hope that the king would accept their petition?

Doc. 88: What sequence of events must have led to the involvement of the *Suprema* in this case?

Doc. 90: In addition to the Moriscos' poor physical health, what else might have contributed to some of them being refused a seat at the oars? Why were some Moriscos accepted and others refused? Was this merely a fortunate turn of events for Juan Mancebo, Román el Romo, Miguel Ramírez, and Íñigo de Moraga? Or was something more going on behind the scenes?

Doc. 91: How do you imagine the inquisitors at Cuenca felt when they learned that, despite their efforts, the *Suprema* ordered the four Moriscos to be released? What does this suggest about the relationship between the various levels of inquisitorial bureaucracy?

Appendices
Appendix I: Glossary of Terms

alaqibir: That is, *Allahu akbar*, a phrase known as the *Takbir*, used in the formal Muslim call to prayer as well as at the beginning of the prayers themselves.

alcaide: A warden or castellan. In Deza, he was the chief local representative of the duke.

alfaquí: An Islamic instructor, from the Arabic *al-faqīh*.

Aljamiado: A literary convention used by Moriscos whereby phonetically Spanish words were written in a stylized Arabic script.

Anniversary Mass: A mass commemorating the anniversary of a specific event such as a death.

Athanasian Creed: An important early Christian creedal statement that helped to formulate the doctrines of the Trinity and of Christ's dual natures.

auto-da-fe: An "Act of Faith." A public ceremony in which the Spanish Inquisition displayed those convicted of error. Those who had been reconciled to the Church were punished in accordance with the terms of their reconciliation. Obstinate or relapsed heretics were "relaxed" (i.e., handed over) to secular authorities for execution by burning at the stake.

azala: Islamic prayers. A corrupted version of the classical Arabic word *ṣalāh*.

azumbre: A measure of liquid volume equivalent to about 2 litres.

banns: A public announcement of a couple's intent to marry. The Council of Trent stated: "Before a marriage is contracted, the proper parish priest of the contracting parties shall three times announce publicly in the Church, during the solemnization of mass, on three continuous festival days, between whom marriage is to be celebrated; after which publication of banns, if there be no lawful impediment opposed, the marriage shall be proceeded with in the face of the church."

bachiller: A title indicating the receipt of a university degree.

beata: A lay holy woman in Spain.

breviary: A liturgical book containing the canonical hours used in the Roman Catholic Church to organize public worship on a day-by-day basis. The breviary was revised in 1568, in the wake of the Council of Trent. Most of the Spanish Church quickly adopted the updated version.

Bull of Crusade: *See Crusade, Bull of.*

celemín: A measure used in agriculture equivalent to one-twelfth of a *fanega*.

cleric: A member of the clergy, that is, one who has been set apart for religious ministry.

comisario: *See commissioner.*

commissioner: An inquisitorial officer. In the case of Deza, the commissioner was one of the town's priests who functioned as the local representative of the Holy Office. He received denunciations and corresponded with the inquisitors at the Tribunal of Cuenca.

confesso/a: A synonym for Judeoconverso.

converso/a: Usually refers to a Judeoconverso, but the term can have a broader meaning and in Deza was sometimes used to refer to a Morisco.

convertido/a: One of the terms used by Dezanos to refer to the town's Moriscos.

coroza: A tall, cone-shaped, painted hat made of paper. Corozas were worn at autos-da-fe by those whom the Holy Office condemned.

Corredero: A large multi-purpose ring—used for bull fights, among other things—located on the eastern edge of town in the Morisco quarter, the Upper Neighborhood. By extension, the term also referred to the street that led to the *Corredero* proper.

Corrillo: A Spanish word translated by John Minsheu in 1623 as "a company standing round." The *Corrillo* was a small plaza in Deza's Upper Neighborhood, populated largely by Moriscos. By extension, the term also referred to the street entering and leaving the *Corrillo* proper.

Council of the Supreme and General Inquisition: *See* Suprema.

Council of Trent: *See Trent, Council of.*

Crusade, Bull of: A cheap indulgence granted for only two *reales* that was taken by millions of Spaniards every year. Those who took the Bull of Crusade received a printed broadside known as a *buleta* that explained the benefits they received. These included a plenary remission of sins, permission to consume dairy during Lent, and the privilege to choose one's confessor (rather than being limited to the parish priest). Furthermore, the bull granted that confessor the authority to absolve his penitent of virtually any sin, even those that would otherwise have required the approval of the bishop.

diurnal: A liturgical book in the Roman Catholic tradition containing the liturgical hours for the daily offices.

don/doña: An honorific title typically reserved for members of the nobility.

Edict of Faith: A catalogue of heretical beliefs and practices that were read from the pulpit after Sunday mass in preparation for an inquisitorial visitation. All members of the parish were to be in attendance for the reading and all hearers had a given span of time—usually 30 or 40 days—to reveal any incidence of heresy. Edicts of Faith preceded the arrival in Deza of Licentiate Reynoso in 1569 and Dr. Arganda in 1581.

Edict of Grace: An opportunity granted by the Spanish Inquisition that allowed individuals who knew about or who had themselves committed heretical activities to confess them and receive mercy. Edicts of Grace lasted a specific term, and those who failed to confess were threatened with the full rigor of inquisitorial justice.

Eucharist: A Christian sacrament instituted by Jesus Christ at the Last Supper and involving the distribution of bread and wine to the members of the Church. Early modern Roman Catholic theologians understood that the bread and wine were miraculously transformed into the physical body and blood of Christ. Also known as the Sacrament of the Altar or the Most Holy Sacrament.

familiar: A lay representative of the Inquisition. Deza had several, and they worked alongside the local commissioner, helping with denunciations and acting as go-betweens with the tribunal in Cuenca. They had to prove purity of blood and, while they received no pay for their work, the office gave them a degree of prestige, authority, and various privileges.

fanega: A measure for volume used in Spain, usually for grains. Equivalent to 55.5 litres.

gentry: The members of the lower nobility.

guadoc: The ritual ablutions performed by a Muslim before saying prayers (*azala*).

heretic: Formally, one who chooses religious error over truth. More practically for early modern Spain, someone who refused to believe what the Church claimed was true, especially in the wake of efforts to correct the mistaken belief.

hidalgo: A member of the lower nobility in Spanish society. Technically, only Old Christians could be *hidalgos*, but in practice there were many exceptions to the rule. In Deza from the mid-sixteenth century, a small but influential group of *hidalgos* was asserting its influence, especially in local political affairs, by taking a more active role in the town council. *Hidalgos* were granted the honorific titles don and doña.

Holy Office: The Inquisition.

humilladero: A place of devotion, adorned with a raised cross or religious image, usually placed along the roads going into or out of Spanish towns.

indulgence: Granted by the pope and used to remit the temporal punishment owed for sins.

jubilee: A particularly abundant indulgence, which the pope usually granted only every 25 or 50 years.

Judaizer: A baptized Jew who returned to or continued to practice Judaism.

Judeoconverso: A Jewish convert to Christianity.

licentiate: A title that indicates either university education beyond the baccalaureate level or formal licensing for a profession (such as physician).

maravedí: A small silver coin used in Spain worth 1/34 of a *real* and 1/374 of a ducat (or *escudo*).

Moor: A pejorative term for a Muslim that was used in early modern Spain.

Morisco/a: A Spanish Muslim (or one of his or her descendants) who had been baptized, often under pressure, and become a member of the Christian Church. In the Kingdom of Castile, all Muslims were ordered to accept baptism or depart the realm in 1502. In the Kingdom of Aragon the same end was accomplished by 1526.

mosén: An honorific title used mostly in the Kingdom of Aragon. It could be roughly translated as "master" but was very flexible and was sometimes used for *hidalgos*, members of the clergy, or even an authority on a specific subject, such as a physician.

mudéjar: A practicing Muslim living in Spain under the dominion of a Christian monarch.

novena: An act of religious devotion repeated for a period of nine days. It typically involves a series of set prayers and is performed in the hope of obtaining special intercessory grace.

omentum: A Latin term designating the membrane that surrounds the abdominal organs.

Qur'an: The holy book of Islam, consisting of a series of 114 chapters (or surahs), which Muslims believe were revealed through the Prophet Mohammed in Arabic and represent the final direct revelation of God to humankind.

Ramadan: The name of one of the lunar months in the Islamic calendar. During the month of Ramadan, Muslims are obliged to fast from sunrise to sunset.

real: A unit of silver currency in Spain worth 34 *maravedís* or one-eleventh of a ducat (or *escudo*).

relaxed: The technical term used when the Holy Office handed over a condemned heretic to the civil authorities in order to execute the terms of their judgment, especially in the case of those condemned to be burned at the stake.

reliquary: A container holding a relic, that is, an object or body part associated with a deceased saint.

sacrament: An outward sign of an inward grace. The early modern Roman Catholic Church recognized seven sacraments: Baptism, Confirmation, Penance, Eucharist, Marriage, Holy Orders, and the Anointing of the Sick.

sanbenito: Probably from the Spanish *saco bendito* (holy sack). The penitential garb, or habit, worn by those who had been reconciled to the Church by the Holy Office of the Inquisition. Some wore the *sanbenito* for a designated number of years, after which it was hung up in their parish church. Others were condemned to wear it for the remainder of their lives.

Suprema: The Council of the Supreme and General Inquisition. The royal council of five or six members that had oversight of the numerous inquisitorial tribunals in Spain, among them the Tribunal of Cuenca, which exercised jurisdiction over Deza. The *Suprema* was founded in 1483 and headed by an inquisitor general, who was himself a royal appointee. Between 1566 and 1572, the Inquisitor General was the Bishop of Sigüenza, Deza's own bishop.

surah: The 114 chapters of the Qur'an that Muslims believe were revealed to the Prophet Mohammed by God.

taqiyya: The Muslim art of dissimulation. *Taqiyya* afforded Spanish Muslims whose lives or livelihoods were threatened the flexibility to conform outwardly to Christianity while guarding their true convictions in their hearts.

Trent, Council of: An important ecclesiastical council that met in three sessions (with long breaks in between) from 1545 to 1563. The council was summoned to respond to the challenge of Protestantism, address abuses within the Church, and consider the possibility of a crusade to Jerusalem. Its *Canons and Decrees* were formative in directing the course of the Roman Catholic Church for centuries.

vecino/a: Citizen.

Vespers: The liturgical service of worship conducted in the evening.

visitador: The representative of a bishop (hence, episcopal *visitador*), who traveled to the parishes in a diocese in order to determine whether or not they were complying with the procedural norms established by episcopal decree or at diocesan synods.

zahor: A pre-dawn meal eaten by Muslims during Ramadan.

zala: *See* azala.

Appendix II: Discussion Questions

1. What insights do these documents provide about the judicial process used by the Spanish Inquisition? What were the limits of its power? How successful do you think it was in getting to the truth? How was it different from and similar to modern judicial systems?
2. Most of the primary source material in this collection was mediated through representatives of the Spanish Inquisition. They heard the testimonies and recorded them; they interpreted the information they received; and they held onto the documents in their own archives. How does this complicate how we might use inquisitorial sources to help us learn about the past? Can we rely upon them as evidence? If so, how? If not, how *should* historians engage with inquisitorial sources?
3. Describe the relationship between Deza and the wider world. To what extent did Dezanos know about the world outside of town? Did it interest them as a source of wonder and opportunity or was it frightening and worrisome? Were Dezanos isolated or cosmopolitan?
4. How was Deza changing in the later sixteenth century? To what extent were those changes part of a broader transformation occurring at the same time elsewhere in Europe and the world?
5. How did local community or peer pressure encourage Dezanos either to denounce their neighbors to or protect them from the Holy Office? What other motivations might play into a decision to appear before the inquisitor and offer a denunciation?
6. Why do dietary practices figure prominently in so many of the accusations? Why were they taken to be an indicator of inward religious belief?
7. Why did marriages, burials, and other life events frequently become points of contention and subjects of denunciation?
8. What do these documents suggest about how well Dezanos understood Roman Catholic Christianity? Do the documents offer

a fair representation of the level of religious knowledge in town? Why or why not?

9. The Spanish Inquisition clearly believed that many of Deza's Moriscos were secret Muslims. Do you agree with them? What specific evidence would you use to make your case? If you think there were secret Muslims in Deza, were all of the town's Moriscos equally informed about Islam or equally devout in adhering to that religion? Finally, what did it look like to be a devout Muslim in Deza during this period?

10. How did the opinions, expectations, and prejudices of the Old Christians, perhaps especially authority figures (including the inquisitors themselves), affect the judicial proceedings against the town's Moriscos? Did outsiders treat Judeoconversos and Moriscos differently than they did Old Christians? Were Moriscos from outside of town treated differently than those born in Deza?

11. What role did Aragon and the Aragonese play in the life of Deza? To whom were Aragonese Moriscos a concern and why?

12. What role does prejudice play in Deza's early modern history? Upon what basis were prejudicial judgments made? How does the prejudice exhibited in these documents compare to what exists today?

13. In Document 26, the witness claims that a scribe advised Luis de Liñán that when someone was arrested by the Holy Office the best course of action was for him simply to confess to anything of which he was accused. To what extent did Deza's Moriscos follow this advice? Would they have been more successful if they had followed it more diligently? Or less rigidly?

14. How did the various levels of inquisitorial bureaucracy interact with one another at the local level (i.e., in Deza itself), the regional level (i.e., at Cuenca), and at the level of central authority (i.e., the *Suprema*)? How did the authority of the king and other powerful people further complicate this dynamic?

Bibliography

PRIMARY SOURCES (ARCHIVAL)
Archivo Diocesano de Cuenca, Sección Inquisición (ADC)
    Legajo 120, expediente 1626.
    Legajo 249, expediente 3352.
    Legajo 343, expediente 4876.
    Legajo 361, expediente 5131.
    Legajo 370, expediente 5232.
    Legajo 377, expediente 5342.
    Legajo 707, expediente 625.
    Legajo 759, expediente 712.
    Legajo 813, expediente 6676.
    Legajo 813, expediente 6677.
    Legajo 820, expediente 7992.
    Libro 227.
    Libro 240.
    Libro 317 (Record of Licentiate Reynoso's inquisitorial visitation).
    Libro 318 (Record of Dr. Arganda's inquisitorial visitation).

Archivo Histórico Municipal de Deza
    Caja 282, documento 6 (Libro de Cuentas de Propios, 1595–98).
    Legajo 16a, documento 7.

Archivo de la Real Chancillería de Valladolid, Registro de Ejecutorias, legajo 1999, expediente 90.
Archivo Diocesano de Osma-Soria, Libro Sacramental de la Villa de Deza, 1605–46.

PRIMARY SOURCES (PRINTED)
de los Apóstoles, Francisca. *The Inquisition of Francisca: A Sixteenth-Century Visionary on Trial.* Edited and translated by Gillian Alghren. Chicago:

University of Chicago Press, 2005. http://dx.doi.org/10.7208/
chicago/9780226142258.001.0001.

Cowans, Jon, ed. *Early Modern Spain: A Documentary History*. Philadelphia:
University of Pennsylvania Press, 2003.

Danvila y Collado, Manuel, ed. *Actas de las Cortes de Castilla*. 61 vols.
Madrid, 1877–2004.

Henningsen, Gustav, ed. *The Salazar Documents: Inquisitor Alonso de Salazar
Frías and Others on the Basque Witch Persecution*. Leiden: Brill, 2004.

Homza, Lu Ann, ed. *Spanish Inquisition, 1478–1614: An Anthology of Sources*.
Indianapolis: Hackett, 2006.

Kagan, Richard L., and Abigail Dyer, eds. *Inquisitorial Inquiries: Brief Lives of
Secret Jews and Other Heretics*. Baltimore: Johns Hopkins University Press,
2004.

de León, Luis. *La perfecta casada*. Edited by Elizabeth Wallace. Chicago:
University of Chicago Press, 1903.

Núñez Muley, Francisco. *A Memorandum for the President of the Royal
Audiencia and Chancery Court of the City and Kingdom of Granada*. Edited
and translated by Vincent Barletta. Chicago: University of Chicago Press,
2007. http://dx.doi.org/10.7208/chicago/9780226547282.001.0001.

Records of the Spanish Inquisition, Translated from the Original Manuscripts.
Boston: Samuel G. Goodrich, 1828.

del Rio, Martín. *Investigations into Magic*. Edited and translated by P.G.
Maxwell-Stuart. Manchester: Manchester University Press, 2000.

de Valencia, Pedro. *Tratado acerca de los Moriscos de España*. Edited by
Joaquín Gil Sanjuán. Málaga: Editorial Algazara, 1997.

SECONDARY SOURCES

Alcalde, Alejandre Vicente. *Deza: Entre Castilla y Aragón*. 2 vols. Calatayud:
Diputación Provincial de Soria, 2009.

Amelang, James S. *Parallel Histories: Muslims and Jews in Inquisitorial Spain*.
Baton Rouge: Louisiana State University Press, 2013.

Anes, Gonzalo. "The Agrarian 'Depression' in Castile in the Seventeenth
Century." In *The Castilian Crisis of the Seventeenth Century*, edited by
I.A.A. Thompson and Bartolomé Yun Casalilla, 60–76. Cambridge:
Cambridge University Press, 1994.

Arnold, John H. "The Historian as Inquisitor: The Ethics of Interrogating
Subaltern Voices." *Rethinking History* 2, no. 3 (1998): 379–86. http://
dx.doi.org/10.1080/13642529809408974.

Baer, Yitzhak. *A History of Jews in Christian Spain*, 2 vols. Philadelphia: Jewish
Publication Society, 1961–66.

Bethencourt, Francisco. *The Inquisition: A Global History.* Cambridge: Cambridge University Press, 2009.

Borrow, George Henry. *The Zincali: An Account of the Gypsies of Spain.* London, 1888.

de Bunes Ibarra, Miguel Ángel. "The Expulsion of the Moriscos in the Context of Philip III's Mediterranean Policy." In *The Expulsion of the Moriscos from Spain: A Mediterranean Diaspora,* edited by Mercedes García-Arenal and Gerard Wiegers, 37–59. Leiden: Brill, 2014. http://dx.doi.org/10.1163/9789004279353_004.

Casey, James. *Early Modern Spain: A Social History.* London: Routledge, 1999. http://dx.doi.org/10.4324/9780203255148.

Christian, William A., Jr. *Local Religion in Sixteenth-Century Spain.* Princeton, NJ: Princeton University Press, 1989.

Clouse, Michele L. *Medicine, Government, and Public Health in Philip II's Spain.* Aldershot, UK: Ashgate, 2011.

Coleman, David. *Creating Christian Granada: Society and Religious Culture in an Old World Frontier City, 1492–1600.* Ithaca, NY: Cornell University Press, 2003.

Dadson, Trevor. *Tolerance and Coexistence in Early Modern Spain: The Moriscos of the Campo de Calatrava.* Woodbridge, UK: Tamesis, 2014.

Del Col, Andrea, ed. *Domenico Scandella Known as Mennochio: His Trial before the Inquisition (1583–1599).* Translated by John A. Tedeschi and Anne Tedeschi. Binghamton, NY: MRTS, 1996.

Edwards, John. *Religion and Society in Spain, c. 1492.* Aldershot, UK: Ashgate, 1996.

———. *The Spanish Inquisition.* Stroud: Tempus, 1999.

Ehlers, Benjamin. *Between Christians and Moriscos: Juan de Ribera and Religious Reform in Valencia, 1568–1614.* Baltimore: Johns Hopkins University Press, 2006.

Elliott, J.H. *Imperial Spain, 1469–1716.* New York: St Martin's Press, 1964.

Fernández Nieva, Julio. "Don Diego Gómez de Lamadrid, Inqisidor apostólico en Cuenca (1566–1578) y Obispo de Badajoz (1578–1601)." *Revista de Estudios Extremenos* 36 (1980): 68–107.

Friedman, Ellen G. *Spanish Captives in North Africa in the Early Modern Age.* Madison: University of Wisconsin Press, 1986.

Galván Rodríguez, Eduardo. *El secreto en la Inquisición Española.* Las Palmas de Gran Canaria: Universidad de las Palmas de la Gran Canaria, 2001.

García-Arenal, Mercedes. *Inquisición y Moriscos: Los procesos del Tribunal de Cuenca.* Madrid: Siglo XXI, 1978.

García-Arenal, Mercedes, and Gerard Wiegers, eds. *The Expulsion of the Moriscos from Spain: A Mediterranean Diaspora.* Leiden: Brill, 2014.

García Pedraza, Amalia. *Actitudes ante la muerte en la Granada del siglo XVI. Los Moriscos que quisieron salvarse.* Granada: Universidad de Granada, 2002.

Giles, Mary E., ed. *Women in the Inquisition: Spain and the New World.* Baltimore: Johns Hopkins University Press, 1998.

Ginzburg, Carlo. *The Cheese and the Worms: The Cosmos of a Sixteenth Century Miller.* Baltimore: Johns Hopkins University Press, 1980.

———. "The Inquisitor as Anthropologist." In *Clues, Myths, and the Historical Method,* edited by Carlo Ginzburg, 156–64. Baltimore: Johns Hopkins University Press, 1989.

———. *Night Battles: Witchcraft and Agrarian Cults in the Sixteenth and Seventeenth Centuries.* New York: Penguin, 1983.

Green-Mercado, M.T. "The Mahdī in Valencia: Messianism, Apocalypticism and Morisco Rebellions in Late Sixteenth-Century Spain." *Medieval Encounters* 19, no. 1-2 (2013): 193–220. http://dx.doi.org/10.1163/15700674-12342129.

Haliczer, Stephen. *Inquisition and Society in the Kingdom of Valencia.* Berkeley: University of California, 1990.

Hamilton, Earl. *American Treasure and the Price Revolution in Spain, 1501–1650.* New York: Octagon, 1965.

Harvey, L.P. *Muslims in Spain, 1500–1614.* Chicago: University of Chicago Press, 2005. http://dx.doi.org/10.7208/chicago/9780226319650.001.0001.

———. "Oral Composition and the Performance of Novels of Chivalry in Spain." In *Oral Literature: Seven Essays,* edited by Joseph J. Duggan, 84–100. Edinburgh: Scottish Academic Press, 1975.

Hegyi, O. "Literary Motifs and Historical Reality in Ruiz de Alarcón's *Quien mal anda en mal acaba.*" *Renaissance and Reformation* 18 (1982): 249–63.

Hering Torres, Max-Sebastián, María Elena Martínez, and David Nirenberg, eds. *Race and Blood in the Iberian World.* Munster: Lit Verlag, 2012.

Hess, Andrew C. *The Forgotten Frontier: A History of the Sixteenth-Century Ibero-African Frontier.* Chicago: University of Chicago Press, 1978. http://dx.doi.org/10.7208/chicago/9780226330303.001.0001.

———. "The Moriscos: An Ottoman Fifth Column in Sixteenth-Century Spain." *American Historical Review* 74, no. 1 (1968): 1–55. http://dx.doi.org/10.2307/1857627.

Hsia, R. Po-Chia. *The World of Catholic Renewal, 1540–1770.* 2nd ed. Cambridge: Cambridge University Press, 2005.

Ingram, Kevin, ed. *The Conversos and Moriscos in Late Medieval Spain and Beyond.* 23 vols. 2009–15. Leiden: Brill. http://dx.doi.org/10.1163/9789004228603.

Kagan, Richard L. *Lucrecia's Dreams: Politics and Prophecy in Sixteenth-Century Spain.* Berkeley: University of California Press, 1990.

Kamen, Henry. *Spain, 1469–1714: A Society of Conflict*. London: Routledge, 2014.

———. *The Spanish Inquisition: A Historical Revision*. 4th ed. New Haven, CT: Yale University Press, 2014.

Knutsen, Gunnar. *Servants of Satan and Masters of Demons: The Spanish Inquisition's Trial for Superstition, Valencia and Barcelona, 1478–1700*. Turnhout: Brepols, 2009.

Lea, Henry C. *A History of the Inquisition in Spain*, 4 vols. New York: MacMillan, 1906–7.

Levine Melammed, Renée. "Judeo-conversas and Moriscas in Sixteenth-Century Spain: A Study of Parallels." *Jewish History* 24, no. 2 (2010): 155–68. http://dx.doi.org/10.1007/s10835-010-9106-y.

Lindberg, Carter. *The European Reformations*. 2nd ed. Oxford: Wiley-Blackwell, 2010.

Lomax, David. *The Reconquest of Spain*. London: Longman, 1978.

MacCulloch, Diarmaid. *The Reformation*. New York: Viking, 2003.

Monter, William. *Frontiers of Heresy: The Spanish Inquisition from the Basque Lands to Sicily*. Cambridge: Cambridge University Press, 2003.

Munro, John H. "Money, Prices, Wages, and 'Profit Inflation' in Spain, the Southern Netherlands, and England during the Price Revolution Era: ca. 1520-ca. 1650." *História e Economica* 4 (2008): 13–71.

Nalle, Sarah T. *God in La Mancha: Religious Reform and the People of Cuenca*. Berkeley: University of California Press, 1992.

———. *Mad for God: Bartolomé Sánchez, the Secret Messiah of Cardenete*. Charlottesville: University of Virginia Press, 2001.

Nirenberg, David. *Communities of Violence: Persecution of Minorities in the Middle Ages*. Princeton, NJ: Princeton University Press, 1996.

O'Banion, Patrick J. "'They will know our hearts': Practicing the Art of Dissimulation on the Islamic Periphery." *Journal of Early Modern History* 20, no. 2 (2016): 193–217. http://dx.doi.org/10.1163/15700658-12342497.

O'Callaghan, Joseph F. *Reconquest and Crusade in Medieval Spain*. Philadelphia: University of Pennsylvania Press, 2003. http://dx.doi.org/10.9783/9780812203066.

Payne, Stanley G. *Spanish Catholicism*. Madison: University of Wisconsin Press, 1981.

Pike, Ruth. *Linajudos and Conversos in Seville: Greed and Prejudice in Sixteenth- and Seventeenth-Century Spain*. New York: Peter Lang, 2000.

Rawlings, Helen. *Church, Religion and Society in Early Modern Spain*. New York: Palgrave, 2002.

———. *The Spanish Inquisition*. Malden, MA: Blackwell, 2006. http://dx.doi.org/10.1002/9780470773314.

Reilly, Bernard. *The Contest of Christian and Muslim Spain, 1031–1157*. Cambridge: Blackwell, 1992.

Rosa-Rodriguez, Maria del Mar. "Simulation and Dissimulation: Religious Hybridity in a *Morisco Fatwa*." *Medieval Encounters* 16, no. 1 (2010): 143–80. http://dx.doi.org/10.1163/138078510X12535199002758.

Ruiz, Teofilo F. *Spanish Society, 1400–1600*. London: Routledge, 2014.

Schwartz, Stuart. *All Can Be Saved: Religious Tolerance and Salvation in the Early Modern Atlantic World*. New Haven, CT: Yale University Press, 2008.

Starr-Lebeau, Gretchen. *In the Shadow of the Virgin: Inquisitors, Friars, and Conversos in Guadalupe, Spain*. Princeton, NJ: Princeton University Press, 2003.

Stewart, Devin. "Dissimulation in Sunni Islam and Morisco *Taqiyya*." *al-Qantara* 34, no. 2 (2013): 439–90. http://dx.doi.org/10.3989/alqantara.2013.016.

Sánchez, Serafín de Tapia. *La comunidad Morisca de Ávila*. Salamanca: Gráficas Varona, 1990.

Tausiet, María. *Urban Magic in Early Modern Spain: Abracadabra Omnipotens*. New York: Palgrave, 2013.

Tracy, James D. *Europe's Reformations, 1450–1650*. 2nd ed. Lanham, MD: Rowman & Littlefield, 2006.

Tueller, James. *Good and Faithful Christians: Moriscos and Catholicism in Early Modern Spain*. New Orleans: University Press of the South, 2002.

Vives, Jaime Vicens. *An Economic History of Spain*. Princeton, NJ: Princeton University Press, 1969. http://dx.doi.org/10.1515/9781400879564.

Vilches, Elvira. *New World Gold: Cultural Anxiety and Monetary Disorder in Early Modern Spain*. Chicago: University of Chicago Press, 2010. http://dx.doi.org/10.7208/chicago/9780226856193.001.0001.

Index of Topics

Each entry is keyed to the document number.

Index

Maps and illustrations indicated by page numbers in italics

Printed in the USA
CPSIA information can be obtained
at www.ICGtesting.com
JSHW021733280724
67099JS00003B/7

9 781442 635135